Startup (

C000141374

Startup Compass serves as a valuable handbook for assisting aspirational and first-time entrepreneurs transform their ideas into reality while also helping them in navigating complexity. As a unique book on enterprise innovation; it will help catalyse Indians to innovate in India and innovate for the world.

—Amitabh Kant, CEO, NITI Aayog

IIM Ahmedabad began the How to Start a Startup lecture series to make entrepreneurship more widely understood. *Startup Compass* sifts through those sessions to unearth the problems that bedevil entrepreneurs. Should they focus on financial value, or devote time to opportunities in tune with their own motivations? Should they continue with control as they grow, or should they exit? A very insightful book.

—Errol D'Souza, Director, IIM Ahmedabad

Startup Compass

How Iconic Entrepreneurs Got It Right

Ujwal Kalra
Shobhit Shubhankar

HarperCollins *Publishers* India

First published in India by HarperCollins *Publishers* in 2022
4th Floor, Tower A, Building No. 10, Phase II, DLF Cyber City,
Gurugram, Haryana – 122002
www.harpercollins.co.in

2 4 6 8 10 9 7 5 3 1

Copyright © Ujwal Kalra and Shobhit Shubhankar 2022

P-ISBN: 978-93-5422-549-9
E-ISBN: 978-93-5422-550-5

The views and opinions expressed in this book are the authors' own
and the facts are as reported by them, and the publishers are not in
any way liable for the same.

Ujwal Kalra and Shobhit Shubhankar assert the moral right
to be identified as the authors of this work.

All rights reserved. No part of this publication may be reproduced,
stored in a retrieval system, or transmitted, in any form or by any means,
electronic, mechanical, photocopying, recording or otherwise,
without the prior permission of the publishers.

Typeset in 11/15.2 Sabon LT Std at
Manipal Technologies Limited, Manipal

Printed and bound at
Thomson Press (India) Ltd

MIX
Paper
FSC FSC® C010615

This book is produced from independently certified FSC® paper
to ensure responsible forest management.

To our parents, and to our alma mater, IIM Ahmedabad

Contents

Foreword

FIRST THINGS FIRST. I am a firm believer in diversity. However, for the sake of brevity, I have used 'he' to mean both genders in this piece.

Much water has flowed down the Ganges since the late sixties when I joined the Indian Institute of Management Ahmedabad (IIMA) as the chief systems programmer at the new computer centre there. My father, a high school teacher, had fed his children, day after day, the staple diet of Nehruvian Socialism. As youngsters, we had become staunch believers in socialism. For us, our government was the solution to every one of India's problems. The general belief in India at that time was that poverty was a virtue, and leftism was the fashion in vogue. At the IIMA computer centre, the young socialistic minds had unanimously decided that our first priority outside the office was to coach the computer centre peon to succeed in the written test to become a clerk in the State Bank of India.

IIMA, with its strong umbilical cord to Harvard Business School, was supposed to be a bastion of capitalism in India. In reality, it was not entirely so. Even amongst the deep-thinking minds of the faculty and the impressionable minds of the bright and curious students, there were a few outliers dedicated to socialism. A few of these deep-thinking and top-ranking students from the MBA batch of 1971 joined the Planning Commission! For the rest of the brilliant youngsters swooned over by capitalism, getting a management trainee job at a multinational company like Hindustan Lever or Citibank or the coveted position of a Tata Administrative Services Trainee in the Tata group was considered 'making it.'

So, when I left IIMA to work for a French software company in Paris in the early seventies, I was a confirmed leftist. But what I saw in Paris—the sumptuous markets, well-maintained roads, a modern airport and an extensive metro system, high-speed (TGV) trains, green parks, prosperous living standards, the wealth, health, education, nutrition and shelter of its citizens— confused me. My entire edifice of leftist beliefs seemed to be crumbling. I was stubborn and not the one to give up easily. I wanted to get to the bottom of this puzzle. I met several bright youngsters from the left, the right and the centre at Sorbonne. I attended several conferences during weekends organized by the ideologues of these different philosophies. I spent quite a few evenings listening to passionate discussions over coffee at cafes in Latin quarter located in the 5th arrondissement of Paris. Seeking enlightenment on this complex issue, I even met Georges Marchais, the then head of the French Communist Party. I travelled extensively to various European cities to confirm if all Western European nations which had rejected leftism were indeed prosperous, its citizens had jobs with good income and the quality of life was much better than what it was in my country. I found it to be so. I read many books on capitalism, socialism and communism. The final nail on the coffin was my being incarcerated for 120 hours unjustly by the Bulgarian police on false charges of conspiracy against the People's Republic of Bulgaria with a well-informed Bulgarian girl as my co-conspirator. The gendarmes said they were releasing me and banishing me to the distant Istanbul on a freight train, since I was from a friendly country called India! If these communist countries treated friends like this, I wondered what they would do to their enemies! I introspected deeply during the twenty-one-hour journey, hungry and thirsty, alone in the guard's compartment of a departing freight train for Istanbul. I had already spent a hungry and thirsty eighty-four hours of incarceration. This brought the much-needed clarity to my mind about the ills of leftism. I was transformed from a confused leftist to a determined compassionate capitalist. I defined a compassionate capitalist as a capitalist in mind and a socialist at heart!

My deep introspection during the journey from Nis in Serbia (then Yugoslavia) to Istanbul in Turkey resulted in the following conclusions, which have remained steadfast even today. They are:

1. The only way a poor country like India can solve the problem of poverty is through creation of productive jobs with good income.
2. The only people who can lead the creation of such jobs are entrepreneurs. They use the power of an idea, hard work, sacrifice, innovation and deferred gratification to create jobs for youngsters and wealth for investors.
3. It is not the responsibility of the government to create these jobs. But it is the responsibility of the government to create

an environment that eliminates any and every friction to the success of these entrepreneurs. It is also the responsibility of the government to create a fair, transparent, well-thought-out and stable policy regime to regulate the entrepreneurs and their companies, and to provide a level-playing field for all market players.

I came back to India and, pretty soon, I set out on an experiment in entrepreneurship in Pune in 1976. The company, Softronics, was to develop software for commercial applications. Within six months of starting Softronics, I realized three major mistakes, two from my side, and one from the government's side.

The first of my mistakes was not conducting a test marketing exercise to assess the potential market for software services in India. I discovered that there was hardly any domestic market for software services. Very few computers were used by corporations in India at that time. These computers were based on obsolete technology from IBM (International Business Machines) and ICL (International Computers Limited). The process for importing computers had been made very tortuous and torturous by the bureaucrats in New Delhi to protect ECIL (Electronics Corporation of India Limited), a Government of India enterprise, that made TDC 312 and TDC 316 machines. Both these models were poor and amateurish imitations of PDP 8 and PDP 11, the highly popular and successful minicomputers produced by Ken Olsen in his company, Digital Equipment Corporation, in the US. I realized that any sensible Indian entrepreneur in software development area had to look at the export market in the US where corporations were using information technology to gain competitive advantage in the market.

The second mistake I committed was that I did not communicate clearly the value that Softronics brought to the table in business terms. Those days, most people who managed these outdated computers in India were highly technical people who hardly understood business. The lesson I learnt was that an entrepreneur should communicate the business value of his product or service to solve the customer's business problems in customer's words in simple sentences and not in complex or compound sentences.

I also observed an important lesson for my country, as narrated by my Hindi-speaking friends in Pune. They used to say, '*Jis desh mein sarkar vyapari ho jati hai, us desh mein log bhikari ho jate hein*' (In a country, when the government becomes a businessman, its citizens become paupers).

These lessons resulted in founding Infosys in 1981. Infosys, a software services company, was to be dedicated to serving the software development needs of the burgeoning US corporate market.

The environment in India during the eighties was strongly anti-business even for export-oriented companies. But the export market for software services in the US was expanding fast. India had a plentiful supply of reasonably competent unemployed engineers. Fortunately, economic reforms were unleashed in 1991 by Dr Manmohan Singh, Sri P. Chidambaram and Sri Montek Singh Ahluwalia, under the leadership of the then prime minister, Sri Narasimha Rao. These reforms brought five fundamental changes for businesses in our country. The government introduced current account convertibility necessary for any business, in general, and for a startup in the area of export of software services, in particular, to succeed; that made travel abroad easier. Second, Delhi abolished most licensing. Instead, the government introduced fiscal barriers to discourage imports rather than banning them. Third, it abolished the office of the controller of capital issues. This office, located in Delhi, had little or no understanding of capital markets. This decision allowed entrepreneurs to decide on the price for the initial public offer (IPO) based on the advice of the investment bankers, the way it happens in the US. Fourth, companies were allowed to open up sales offices outside India and to hire consultants in quality and branding. Fifth, the government reintroduced 100 per cent ownership for foreign companies in technology areas. These MNCs who had been thrown out by the bizarre policies of George Fernandes in 1977 started coming back to India. This policy did not impact competition for customers of the Indian software services companies because the Indian companies focused on the export market in the US. However, it created huge competition for talent. Such competition made Indian startups much stronger, and they introduced lots of innovative ideas to attract, enable, empower, and retain the best and the brightest talent. Finally, by then, access to telephone and data communications had already become a little bit easier.

Thanks to Sri Narasimha Rao and Dr Manmohan Singh, India moved from the Hindu rate of growth of 2 per cent of GDP to a respectable 5 per cent to 9 per cent, and emerged as an economically attractive nation in the world for foreign investors. Spurred by the spectacular success of the non-resident Indians in Silicon Valley and Route 128 in Boston, several young men and women started thinking about becoming entrepreneurs in India. Entrepreneurship appeared as a viable option on the radar screens of the students graduating out of our higher educational system, including the IIMs. The tide was slowly turning in favour of entrepreneurship. Some parents started accepting entrepreneurship as a career option for their sons and sons-in-law!

Today, entrepreneurship is considered macho and sexy. Time has arrived for India to become a nation of entrepreneurs

like the US, China and Israel are. This book is timely. It is a
collection of heart-warming and, in some cases, gut-wrenching
tales of some of the brightest youngsters of the country. CIIE.
CO at IIMA deserves the thanks and gratitude of the entire
community of wannabe entrepreneurs, not just in India but
in the entire world. This book, authored by two illustrious
graduates of IIMA—Ujwal Kalra and Shobhit Shubhankar—is
full of practical wisdom. Most of the entrepreneurs covered in
the book are also from IIMA. The book covers the entire gamut
of knowledge—the dos and don'ts, the tricks to use and the
tricks to avoid in the journey of an entrepreneur. The topics
covered include planning a startup, developing an idea, forming
a team, building a product, raising funding and, importantly,
moving from an entrepreneurial mindset to a managerial
mindset as you scale up your company.

It is clear from the case studies that the entrepreneurs
chronicled here are a bunch of visionary, aspirational, bright,
daring, hard-working and sacrificing leaders. Every one of them
had a noble purpose larger than just founding his company. Every
story paints a vivid picture of the joys, the disappointments,
the triumphs, the failures, daring and sacrifices of these path-
breaking entrepreneurs. There was a lot that I learnt from their
experiences. It will be sacrilegious to summarize the riveting
narration of the two brilliant authors and the experience of the
fifteen impressive entrepreneurs. It must be read carefully, and
the lessons imbibed. I will just add a few lessons that I learnt
from my own entrepreneurial journey.

The entrepreneurial phase is about thinking of an idea that
just did not exist before or that has a sustainable competitive
advantage over the existing ideas in the market. It is about
founding the company, operating with very little financial
resources, getting the first customer, and demonstrating passion,

daring, sacrifice, imagination, determination, austerity, hard work and speed in every task. I am not sure if any entrepreneur can graduate to the managerial phase without a strong and steady financial contribution from this entrepreneurial phase. In fact, hardly 10 per cent of the startups graduate from the entrepreneurial phase to the managerial phase.

The managerial phase is generally about bringing managerial talent from the market and leveraging technology to install systems and processes to scale up customers, employees, investors, production, quality, productivity, physical and technological facilities, training, research and development. It is also about ensuring what I call PSPD—predictability of revenues, sustainability of those predictions, profitability of the achieved revenues and de-risking of various risk parameters. I shall stick to the lessons that we learnt during the entrepreneurial phase of the company rather than the managerial phase of the company.

The first and the most important lesson that we, as a team, learnt was the importance of articulating our values and practising them. Values form the backbone of an entrepreneur's determination. The first and the most important tenet of our value system was putting the interest of the company ahead of our personal interest in every decision the founding team took. There were many tough and unpleasant decisions that we took. A few of my founder–colleagues did not agree with some of those decisions. But they accepted those decisions sportingly and executed them with full commitment since they knew that those tough decisions were taken only to make Infosys stronger and there was no other motive behind it.

The second lesson I learnt as an entrepreneur was that failures are a part of an entrepreneurial journey. I realized that a failure would be beneficial if you quickly analysed the reasons why you failed, learnt the lesson and did not commit the same mistake again. I am talking of my failure in Softronics. I had learnt that the absence of the market was what led to that failure. I decided to focus on export market in my next venture.

The third lesson I learnt was that an entrepreneur had to constantly scan for signs that his or her venture was likely to encounter a structural problem and that the company was likely to fall into an irretrievable situation. This is the time for the entrepreneur to tone down his passion about the idea, keep emotions aside and quickly bring the venture to a decent closure. Softronics had no domestic market and there was no way I could recover from it quickly. So, I closed it in nine months.

The fourth lesson I learnt was that luck plays a very important role in the entrepreneurial journey. There were so many friends and classmates who were much smarter than I was. Their teams had better credentials than we had. They had better ideas than we had. But God chose us to smile on. There were so many critical situations and deals when it could have gone either way. Somehow, God helped us take the right decision in those situations. Let there be no doubt that values, smartness, hard work, sacrifice, daring, discipline and teamwork are all necessary attributes to maximize the probability of success in entrepreneurship. But they are not sufficient. You need luck and God's grace. 'Fortune favours the prepared mind' was how Louis Pasteur put it. Faith in God gives you hope in situations when no logic seems to show a way forward. Faith in God also teaches us humility.

The fifth lesson we learnt was that market competition was the best management school, as my friend, Sri Rahul Bajaj, has often said. Market competition taught us how to attract and retain good customers and employees, and how to enhance the trust of our investors. In every area of our operation, we benchmarked ourselves with the best practices in the world, and created some 'next' practices as my friend, Late C K Prahalad, often said. We benefitted immensely from it.

The sixth lesson I learnt was that leadership by example, walking the talk, and practising the precept were what made a leader trustworthy in the eyes of his team members. This is a time-invariant and context-invariant lesson that Mahatma Gandhi taught us. This is the most powerful instrument that a leader has to encourage his colleagues to adhere to the company's values. For example, during the initial years of Infosys, I realized that we needed to be austere with our overheads. So, at Infosys, I took just 10 per cent of my compensation that I earned at Patni Computer Systems Private Limited (PCS). However, from the day one, I wanted to keep the confidence and enthusiasm of my younger colleagues high. So, I gave them 20 per cent higher salary than what they earned at PCS. We travelled economy class even on international flights till we reached a revenue of US$ 1 billion. I travel by economy even today on domestic flights. I would be in the office at 6.20 a.m. every morning till I retired in 2011. That sent an indelible message to youngsters about reaching office on time. We kept the ratio of the salaries of the executive directors to the lowest salary in the company to about forty from the founding day of 7 July 1981 till 10 October 2014 when we, the founders, retired from the company. During the period of market downturn, the Infosys leaders took the biggest percentage cuts in salary increases. These percentages were reduced as we moved down the corporate hierarchy.

The seventh lesson I learnt was that sustaining the enthusiasm and confidence of a team of the seven founding professionals over a period of thirty years was extremely difficult, if not impossible. I instituted several unwritten rules right from the first day. The most important was that we would put the interest of the company ahead of our personal interest and that we would practise total fairness, transparency and accountability in every transaction. The sentence 'In God we trust; everybody else brings data to the table' has become popular in business circles in the world today. I also decided that none of us would discuss with our spouses whatever differences of opinion we have had amongst ourselves on an issue in the office. I followed it strictly. The reason was very simple. Our spouses may look at the issue in isolation and it had the potential to destroy the camaraderie amongst them.

The eighth lesson we learnt was from observing our cohorts in the field. We learnt that there should be one and only one leader in any company at any time. No company can be run by committees. We learnt that a leader has to lead by example in values; must work the hardest; must make the biggest sacrifices; must welcome ideas and opinions from competent and expert colleagues before taking any decision; must consider those ideas in his decision; and the buck must stop at his table for every major decision. Thirteen companies were started between 1979 and 1982 by technical professionals who also came together like us. Only one company, Infosys, has reached where it has amongst these thirteen companies. According to my management expert friends, one of the reasons is that these companies did not have a single, undisputed leader who earned the complete loyalty and the trust of every member of the founding team.

The ninth and the final lesson we learnt was that competence and a sound value system are the essential ingredients of a successful knowledge company. That is how the phrase 'Powered by intellect; driven by values' became the tagline of the company.

We have committed our share of mistakes. After all, we are human. We learnt from our mistakes. But there was no occasion when any of us put our personal interest ahead of the interest of the company. We fully accepted deferred gratification, made all the necessary sacrifices and showed abundant patience. These sacrifices and this mindset of deferred gratification have made every one of the six remaining members of the founding team billionaires. I am very proud of the team. The seventh one, Mr Ashok Arora, left us in 1989 to settle down in the US. I wish him the best.

I can go on and on and my foreword would end up as a book! But the glory of the book belongs to the two authors and the fifteen wonderful individuals who have brought so many learnings to the Indian entrepreneurial scene. I thank CIIE. CO, the two authors, and the fifteen impressive individuals for the opportunity to write this foreword. My congratulations to them on this book.

Narayana Murthy

Introduction

HOME TO THE SECOND largest population in the world, increasingly digitally connected, India is a land brimming with possibilities. In a country long averse to risk-taking, the entrepreneur, as the creator of wealth and value, is now rightly feted.

Backed by CIIE.CO at IIM Ahmedabad, the *How to Start a Startup* lecture series as well as extensive subsequent interviews were started with the aim of imparting practical knowledge on starting a company, scaling it and succeeding at being an entrepreneur. In a series of lectures by those who had 'been there, done that', the series sought to traverse the journey of starting up—the lectures told of paths trodden by successful entrepreneurs, the paths they wished they had not taken, and the highs and the lows that entrepreneurship entails. Above all, the lectures were meant to kindle both inspiration and self-belief; *if they could do it, so can we.*

This book seeks to bring together learnings and insights from the lecture series as well as extensive subsequent interviews in an easily comprehensible format. It is a compendium of the experiences of some of the most illustrious members of the startup ecosystem in India, a how-to manual, a ready-reckoner and a collection of inspirational tales to dip into when the going gets tough. While the book mainly draws upon the experiences of entrepreneurs in India in scope and sweep, it also goes beyond; we have sought to distil ideas from some of the foremost entrepreneurial minds worldwide.

The book is divided into ten chapters, each covering a stage in a startup's journey. While it is ideal to read them in the arranged sequence, each is self-contained and may be read on its own.

The first chapter, 'Before the Startup', is all of this: a bird's-eye view of the road ahead; a list of the survival-kit items to be packed; a manual on how to give oneself tactical first aid as one jumps headlong into the bush and gets nicked and slashed; and the initial pitfalls leap over. In short, it has the signposts to help an aspiring entrepreneur to avoid starting on the path blindfolded. It paints no rosy picture and tells it as it is.

The next two chapters—'The Idea' and 'The Team'—address the core of the early stage of the startup journey. Not every idea holds a startup within it, though some do. The second chapter addresses ways of ideation, and offers frameworks to verify initial hypotheses. Once a promising idea has been identified, it is up to the founding team to make a product which can be offered through a startup. Perhaps more startups fail or fall apart because of dysfunctional teams than for any other single reason. The chapter offers counsel on how to build a great team and avoid early pitfalls. The following two chapters—'The Product' and 'The Launch'—are joined at the hip. During this stage, the team must iteratively build upon the idea to create a minimum viable product, test it in the market, draw lessons and rapidly refine it. 'The Product' illustrates the process of iteratively building a minimum viable product, while 'The Launch' covers an initial entry into the market.

Once a startup achieves a certain viability, it often becomes imperative to raise capital to fund the next stage of the journey. 'Raising Money' offers insights into how to attract the right kind of investors. 'Scaling Up' and 'Setting Up for Success' are the seventh and eighth chapters respectively. These cover the journey of an early-stage startup achieving scale, as it transforms into a full-fledged organization. 'Building a Behemoth' addresses organizational complexity, preserving a culture of innovation, and continuing to expand. 'The Exit', the final chapter, is the final stage of a startup, and deals with the processes of public offerings and acquisitions.

Over ten chapters, the book covers the ten stages in the journey of a startup through the journeys of several of the most inspirational entrepreneurs in India and beyond. These are stories of grit and ambition, of vision being transformed into tangible reality, of dreamers, of pioneers, of steely-eyed achievers. These are their stories, and these are the insights they have to offer, for those who may follow after.

Entrepreneurs' Profiles

Abhiraj Bhal, Urban Company

Abhiraj Bhal holds B.Tech. in electrical engineering from IIT Kanpur and MBA from IIM Ahmedabad. He worked at the Boston Consulting Group, advising Fortune 500 companies across India, Germany and Southeast Asia, before he quit to begin his entrepreneurial journey. Abhiraj is the co-founder and CEO of Urban Company, a fulfilment-led marketplace for home services. An avid tennis and squash player, Abhiraj has won numerous awards, such as the Fortune 40 Under 40 (2017), the Forbes 30 Under 30 (2017), and The Entrepreneur Award at NTLF 2020 Global Leadership Awards. He is on the NASSCOM Internet Council, and the Domestic Workers Sector Skill Council of the Government of India.

Anand Daniel, Accel Partners

Anand Daniel, a partner at Accel, joined the company in 2010. He has been investing in technology startups since 2006, initially with Intel Capital in Silicon Valley and later with Flybridge Capital Partners in Boston. Prior to that, he spent several years in key engineering and management positions at Intel Corporation. At Accel, Anand focuses on investments in consumer technology, online marketplaces and healthcare technology. He has led investments in Swiggy, BlackBuck, Bounce, TaxiForSure and other early-stage companies. Anand holds an MBA from MIT, an MS in electrical engineering from Purdue and a BE in computer science from the University of Madras.

Anu Hariharan, Y Combinator Continuity Fund

Anu Hariharan is Managing Director and Partner at Y Combinator's Continuity Fund, where she has worked with leading companies across the globe including Brex, Convoy, Faire, Groww, Gusto, Monzo. Previously, Anu was an investment partner at Andreessen Horowitz, where she worked actively with the management teams of portfolio companies, including Airbnb, Instacart, Medium, OfferUp and Udacity. Prior to this, Anu worked at Boston Consulting Group and Qualcomm. Anu holds a BE from NIT Karnataka, MS in electrical engineering from Virginia Tech and an MBA from Wharton.

Deep Kalra, MakeMyTrip

The pioneer of online travel in India, Deep Kalra founded MakeMyTrip in April 2000. Drawing on his experience from his years at GE Capital, AMF Bowling Inc. and ABN AMRO Bank, he made MakeMyTrip a Nasdaq-listed online travel company. He has won numerous awards, such as KPMG's most powerful digital influencer in India and Indian Digital Media Awards Person of the Year, among others. Outside of MakeMyTrip, he serves as an independent director of IndiaMart.com, chairs the NASSCOM Internet Working Group and is CII's Tourism sub-committee member. He is also a founder member of Ashoka University. Deep holds a bachelor's degree in economics from St. Stephen's College and an MBA from IIM Ahmedabad.

Falguni Nayar, Nykaa

A graduate of IIM Ahmedabad, Falguni joined A.F. Ferguson & Co., a consulting company, right out of the college. Post that, Falguni joined Kotak Mahindra Bank. In over eighteen years, she helmed several businesses and was the managing director of Kotak Mahindra Investment Bank and director at Kotak Securities. After reaching the echelons of the corporate world, Falguni followed her passion to set up Nykaa. India's wealthiest female billionaire, Falguni took Nykaa public in 2021. Falguni has won many accolades, including Woman Ahead award at the Economic Times Startup Awards 2017, Businesswoman of the Year at the Economic Times Awards for Corporate Excellence 2019, Asia's Power Businesswomen 2019 by Forbes Asia and Vogue India Businessperson of the Year 2019.

Girish Mathrubootham, Freshworks

Girish Mathrubootham founded Freshworks in 2010 after spending a considerable number of years in the SaaS space.

He has been building helpdesk systems since 2004. Girish is a product-management veteran and has worked as the VP-product management for a SaaS provider when the entrepreneurship bug bit him. Freshworks is a truly global company with most of its clientele outside India. It has won the Economic Times Startup of the Year in 2016 and the Business Standard Startup of the Year in 2017. Girish is part of the Product Council for NASSCOM. He is an active angel investor.

Kunal Shah, FreeCharge, CRED

Kunal Shah is the founder of FreeCharge and CRED. He dropped out of Narsee Monjee Institute of Management Studies in 2010 to start FreeCharge, a pioneer in digital payments in India, that was acquired by Snapdeal for US$450 million. He founded CRED in 2018, with a mission to bring the benefits of high-trust communities to creditworthy individuals, brands and institutions. Kunal has been an advisor to the board of Bennett Coleman & Co. Ltd, the chairman of the Internet and Mobile Association of Indian and an advisor to Y Combinator and Sequoia Capital India. He is an active angel investor who has made investments in and mentors companies from RazorPay to Go-Jek, Innov8 and Zilingo, among others.

Raghunandan G, TaxiForSure

Raghunandan G, an IIM Ahmedabad and NIT Surathkal alumnus, transformed India's commute with his startup TaxiForSure (TFS). Prior to starting TFS, he worked as a consultant at Feedback Ventures and also worked at Texas Instruments before pursuing his MBA. A marathon runner, an ardent reader, and a human encyclopaedia, Raghunandan is a man of many talents. He was recognized as one of the 40 Under 40 business leaders of India in 2014 by Fortune India and received the IIMA Young Alumni Achiever Award. Since TaxiForSure's acquisition by Ola in 2015, Raghu has been working as an angel investor. He has embarked upon the second innings with his startup, Zolve.

Rajan Anandan, Sequoia Capital

As part of the leadership team at Sequoia India, Rajan Anandan focuses on developing Surge, a rapid scale-up programme for startups in India and Southeast Asia. Prior to Sequoia, as head of Google India and Southeast Asia, Rajan played a key role in expanding the regions' internet ecosystem while accelerating Google's innovation and growth units. Rajan also led Microsoft and Dell in India and was earlier a partner at McKinsey & Company in Chicago. He is also a prolific angel investor who has backed many successful startups at very early stages. Rajan is a graduate of MIT and Stanford University.

Ritesh Agarwal, OYO

A college dropout at the age of seventeen, Ritesh founded Oravel in 2012, which morphed into OYO in 2013. OYO has revolutionized the budget-hotel category worldwide and is one of the biggest unicorns from India. The prodigy is the sole Indian recipient of the Thiel fellowship and Business World Young Entrepreneur Award, and has featured in Forbes 30 Under 30 in the consumer tech space. Ritesh is one of the youngest self-made billionaires in the world.

Sachin Bansal, Flipkart, Navi

Sachin Bansal is the CEO of Navi and former chairman and co-founder of Flipkart, India's leading e-commerce marketplace, acquired by Walmart in 2018. Under Sachin, Flipkart pioneered innovations that have redefined India's e-commerce ecosystem, such as cash on delivery, replacement guarantees on products, UPI payments and owned logistics network, among others. An Indian software engineer and internet entrepreneur, Sachin graduated from IIT Delhi with a computer science degree in 2005. He was among the 40 Under 40 by Fortune Magazine in 2012, Entrepreneur of the Year by Economic Times in 2013 and among TIME's Most Influential People of 2016.

Sanjeev Bikhchandani, Info Edge

The pioneer of India's internet space, Sanjeev Bikhchandani is the man behind InfoEdge, which owns portals for job search (Naukri, Naukrigulf), matrimony (Jeevansathi), real estate (99acres) and education (Shiksha). It also owns stakes in Zomato and Policybazaar. Sanjeev is an alumnus of St. Stephen's College, University of Delhi, post which he pursued his MBA from IIM Ahmedabad. Before starting InfoEdge in 1990, he worked at GlaxoSmithKline. Outside of InfoEdge, he is the co-founder of Ashoka University. In January 2020, Sanjeev was awarded the Padma Shri.

Sahil Barua, Delhivery

Sahil is the CEO and co-founder of Delhivery, and is responsible for setting the company's overall strategic direction; he also works closely with the engineering and product teams. Sahil began his career as a strategy consultant at Bain and Company, working across the London and New Delhi offices. At Bain, he worked on growth strategy, M&A, and performance improvement across the private equity, telecommunications, healthcare and consumer products spaces. Sahil is a gold medallist from IIM Bangalore and has a B.Tech. degree in mechanical engineering from the National Institute of Technology, Surathkal.

Tarun Mehta, Ather Energy

Tarun Mehta is a graduate from IIT Madras with a dual degree in engineering design. He has been associated with over a dozen prototypes and has six co-patents (pending) to his name. He moved out of his job at Ashok Leyland in 2012 and started Ather Energy to revolutionize the Indian transport space through its electric and internet-enabled products. Tarun is recipient of numerous accolades including being featured in the Forbes 30 Under 30 Asia, Fortune 40 Under 40 and The Economic Times 40 Under Forty lists.

Yashish Dahiya, Policybazaar

Yashish is the co-founder and group CEO of Policybazaar.com. Since 2008, Yashish has grown Policybazaar to become a key influencer in consumer decisions around insurance. He believes death, disease and disability products are the future of the insurance industry, as India strives towards social security. He is an avid sportsperson and has worked in the past as managing director of Ebookers Plc and consultant with Bain & Company in their London office. Yashish received his education from IIT Delhi, IIM Ahmedabad and INSEAD.

1

Before the Startup

As you set out for Ithaka
hope your road is a long one,
full of adventure, full of discovery.

—C.P. Cavafy, 'Ithaka'

FOR EVERY STARTUP THAT succeeds, there are countless others that fail. The reality of starting up is often a lot messier than might seem from mainstream narratives. Linear progressions and neat resolutions are rare. Far more often, entrepreneurship is a long and winding path, with the end uncertain and out of sight.

While every entrepreneurial journey is unique, there are broad markers that each one shares with the others, stemming from the very nature of startups. The quality of the terrain, the vagaries of weather, a certain turn in the road perhaps. Before you embark, it would serve you well to understand what the journey might entail.

1

As you set out for Ithaka

In a career spanning over three decades, Sanjeev Bikhchandani has donned many hats. A graduate of St. Stephen's, he started his career in advertising before going on to study business at IIM Ahmedabad. Upon graduation, he joined HMM, now GlaxoSmithKline Consumer Healthcare, as a product executive for Horlicks. He left within a couple of years, his heart firmly set on being an entrepreneur. He started and ran a series of businesses before eventually hitting upon the idea for Naukri. com. Today, Naukri.com is the largest job portal in the country. Its parent company, InfoEdge, a publicly listed company, also runs online businesses in other sectors: 99acres.com in real estate, Jeevansaathi.com in online matrimony and Shiksha. com in education. Sanjeev is one of the most respected voices in the Indian startup ecosystem, widely sought out for counsel. In building pioneering companies himself, as well as over many years of investing in and mentoring startups, he has had a ringside view of the Indian startup ecosystem. He also intimately understands what it takes to start and build a company.

Sanjeev notes that for a prospective entrepreneur looking to start up, it is crucial to first understand the 'why', the reason they are looking to become an entrepreneur. 'The "why" needs to be very strong because it is what will drive you to continue even when you have to make personal sacrifices such as in terms of your salary compensation or material benefits,' he says. 'You have to be committed, and able to go on. It is a way of life that you are choosing.'

When Sanjeev left a coveted job at HMM, a large and widely respected multinational company, it was a highly unconventional choice. 'In 1990, when I quit my job, failure was not forgiven. Failure was not tolerated, or celebrated the way it is today,' he says. 'If you actually quit your job in a large multinational to become an entrepreneur, and after three-four years of doing that you came back, you had lost your career. You would always be on the slow track, because you will be regarded as a failure. The experience was not valued.' Moreover, in the 1990s, there was limited venture capital that could help meet a startup's expenses including paying salaries. When Sanjeev chose to become an entrepreneur, he was forced to forego a salary.

What allowed him to first take the step and then continue on the path was that he was firmly convinced he wanted to be an entrepreneur. It was an aspiration that Sanjeev had harboured from an early age. Even by the time he was finishing high school, he knew he wanted to start his own business eventually. It was this calling that became his 'why'. It was simply enough for him to work on his own idea in his own company. 'I just loved the independence and the freedom to create,' he says.

In fact, when he started, he did not foresee his startup becoming a multibillion dollar enterprise. 'The truth is, I was very happy to run a small company. I didn't really have an ambition to build a large company. It just so happened that it became a large company.'

If you are looking to become an entrepreneur, it is critical to understand what your underlying motivation is, what is driving you to start a company: Is it a burning desire to set up your own enterprise? Is it a problem that you see that you're trying to solve, and the excitement of finding solutions to the problem? Is it a larger sense of purpose? Understanding what drives you at your core becomes increasingly important as you go on; it is what allows you to continue on your path over a long period of time.

Great things take time

Startups take time to build. A promising startup idea might take several years to develop into a sustainable business, and even then, there is no certainty that it will not fail. In the case that the startup shows some promise, it will almost certainly take up a significant portion of your working life. You must be prepared to play the long game.

MakeMyTrip founder Deep Kalra says that when he is talking to younger entrepreneurs, or when his colleagues quit to start up and ask him for advice, he tells them just one thing, and it has remained constant for a long time: 'Don't look in the rear-view mirror for four to five years. When you decide to start a company, you must be prepared to stay on the path for a meaningful period of time, not giving way to doubt and distraction as you go about building.'

A graduate of St. Stephen's College, Delhi University, and IIM Ahmedabad, Deep worked in banking before leaving to engage in his first entrepreneurial pursuit. He had set up a company to sell bowling alleys in India to tap into the expected boom in family entertainment. When that failed, he went back to corporate life.[1]

Deep's eyes opened to the possibilities of the internet when he sold his wife's car online, making 15,000 rupees more than if he had sold it offline, while avoiding a brokerage fee. Then, while booking a holiday to Thailand, he discovered that the hotel was $15 a night cheaper online than the neighbourhood travel agent's quote. This was a revelation for him. He was convinced that the internet would change the way we lead our lives.

Deep launched MakeMyTrip in October 2000, aiming to cut out the middleman from the business of travel. Having set up

---

[1]   Subroto Bagchi, 'Deep Kalra: Making His Own Trip', *Forbes*, 23 March 2010, https://www.forbesindia.com/interview/zen-garden/deep-kalra-making-his-own-trip/11462/1

an office in the dusty industrial neighbourhood of Okhla in New Delhi, he focused on selling tickets and hotel rooms to immigrant Indians travelling back from the US, outdoing mom-and-pop rivals by offering customer support through Web chats and a call centre.

His idea found a taker in eVentures India, a short-lived venture capital firm backed by NewsCorp and Softbank. Its $2 million infusion, coming at the head of the dot-com boom, offered instant validation; the term sheet was scribbled on a paper napkin at the Crossroads Mall in Mumbai.[2] However, the dot-com bubble burst soon after. For the next five years, venture capital would not touch online startups.

On the heels of the dot-com bust came 9/11 and the SARS outbreak, both of which severely impacted air travel. Deep soon had to let go of most of his employees, cutting the team down from forty to twelve. He went without pay himself, and moved operations to a tiny mezzanine in Okhla. 'From 2001 to 2003, we went through a trial by fire. The only thing that kept us going at that time was just some kind of innate faith and confidence that we were on to something,' Deep says.

Things finally started looking up by the mid-2000s. Indian Railways launched online reservations, making Indians comfortable with internet transactions, and the country was in the midst of a low-cost airline boom. Having raised a fresh round of funding from SAIF Partners (now Elevation Capital), MakeMyTrip finally commenced its India sales in 2005. It eventually listed on Nasdaq in 2010, raising $70 million in its initial public offering, with a $450 million valuation.

---

2   Saritha Rai, 'The Bumpy Ride for Deep Kalra's MakeMyTrip Web Operation', *Forbes*, April 2013, https://www.forbes.com/sites/forbesasia/2013/04/03/the-bumpy-ride-for-deep-kalras-makemytrip-web-operation/?sh=3fda8a9df89c.

It took Deep ten years from setting up his office to finally listing his company. MakeMyTrip has had a near-death experience on more than one occasion, and only skilful manoeuvring has kept the lights on. So when Deep speaks of the virtues of patience and persistence, he speaks from experience.

'In India,' he says, 'I don't believe you will see even the semblance of a business in four to five years. Maybe things are changing, the ecosystem is getting more fertile, maybe we are getting somewhere closer to Silicon Valley. But if you turn into an entrepreneur, please hold the faith. Some of the best businesses have not seen the light of day because some entrepreneur gave up too early.'

Sacrifices are an occupational hazard

Entrepreneurship comes with attendant opportunity costs. Choosing an entrepreneurial pursuit is also choosing to abstain from the pursuit of other opportunities that might come your way. The time and effort that you would invest in building a startup might well be invested elsewhere, even, perhaps, more productively.

A regular job might be more financially rewarding. Startups are predominantly structured such that payoffs come only at the end. Along the way, you might, at least for a time, end up earning substantially lesser than you would in a regular job. You might not earn anything at all if you decide not to take out money from the startup.

When Nykaa founder Falguni Nayar decided to become an entrepreneur, she gave up a highly rewarding role as the managing director of Kotak Mahindra Bank's investment banking arm. Falguni started her career as a consultant with A.F. Ferguson after graduating from IIM Ahmedabad. After almost nine years at the company, she moved to Kotak Mahindra Bank, eventually rising through the company to lead its investment banking arm.

As an investment banker taking companies to IPO, she had had a ringside view on entrepreneurs building companies from the ground up. Every time she would meet a great entrepreneur and hear them tell their story, she would come away inspired. She had seen entrepreneurs building businesses and succeeding against odds. She saw entrepreneurship, in requiring a founder to forge ahead with conviction and transform ideas into reality, as a compelling pursuit. Eventually, she realized she wanted to embrace this path herself. However, it still took her three years from when she decided to become an entrepreneur to finally quitting her job at the bank.[3] 'It was very tough to give up a successful investment banking career at a growth company like Kotak,' she says.

Similarly, in choosing to build MakeMyTrip, Deep chose to forsake a potentially rewarding career in banking. He forewent a salary for eighteen months when the company was not doing well enough to pay out full salaries. Had MakeMyTrip not succeeded, the opportunity cost in terms of lost earnings would have been significant.

Often, there will be considerations that might weaken your resolve and cause you to sway from your path. Amongst the most insidious of these would be the notion of having taken a wrong turn in life. It could get particularly unnerving to look around and realize that your peers from university who did not choose an entrepreneurial path are doing well.

---

[3] 'India INC Season 2 Episode 6 with Nykaa.' *YouTube*, uploaded by ET Now, 11 September 2017, youtube.com/watch?v=K4Q4jN10wS8.

A corporate job comes with well-defined career steps. In the three years that you spend working on your startup, your batchmate from university who stuck to her corporate job might receive promotions, and seem to be advancing rapidly. And that can give you enough reason to second-guess yourself.

'You got this awesome idea, and you are putting everything into it,' says Deep. 'But you cannot see the green shoots because it has only been one or two years. You are truly, truly working eighteen hours a day, you are working Saturdays and Sundays. That's what it takes. You're not taking anything out. Maybe you'll get funded upfront, that's fine, but that money will start running out. You'll spend so much time trying to raise more money. And it will seem like there is no light at the end of this tunnel. And you might ask yourself, "What am I doing?"'

This is when your university degree can start playing wicked games with your mind, warns Deep. 'Because all your other batchmates have the same degree and 90 per cent of them, or 80 per cent, are in great corporate jobs, and doing really well. And thanks to social media, this gets rubbed in even more. Because you are seeing them holiday in the south of France, and then Wimbledon pictures are coming up. It's so wrong, right?' Deep laughs.

'But if you want to be an entrepreneur, there is no shortcut. And there should not be a shortcut. Because when you will look back after ten years, or eight, or six, you will feel so proud about the toughest times. Even today, I can tell you, without a doubt, the best time in our lives was 2001–03, when we had nothing.'

Quiet on the family front

When TaxiForSure (TFS) founder Raghunandan G was looking to start up in 2010, the ecosystem in India was still nascent.

'Startups were a craze, startups were a fad,' says Raghunandan, or Raghu as he is often called. 'Things were a lot more difficult then. It was very difficult to convince parents.'

Raghu has an infectious joyousness in person, his conversation replete with light-hearted anecdotes, and a self-effacing brand of humour. He and his co-founder Aprameya Radhakrishna had been friends from their engineering days at NIT Trichy. Their subsequent stints at IIM Ahmedabad overlapped by a year. After his MBA, Raghu had started as a consultant with Feedback Infra, an infrastructure-focused consulting firm. Aprameya had joined the real-estate services firm Jones Lang LaSalle in a business-development role. When they decided to start a ride-hailing startup, they had to first accomplish two things. First, decide on how long they wanted to pursue their idea. Second, convince their families.

Once you arrive upon an idea, and decide to start up, you need to give yourself enough time to be able to build a company around it. But how long is long enough? 'There can be a great idea. But you might be too early. Or too late. In order to even figure that out, in order to even give an idea its due, give yourself at least two years.'

'I was married to my engineering classmate, and Aprameya was my engineering batchmate. The first thing my wife said was: "You guys don't really have the courage to do a startup." We asked her to give us at least two years. Our MBA took two years, and we were not really sure what we actually learned. But it took us that long,' Raghu laughs. They told their families that they would devote themselves to the idea for a couple of years. And if it didn't work out, they would go back to regular jobs. 'I was a consultant, and Aprameya was a business development guy. So, for both of us, even a failure would have only made us better. A better consultant, a better business development guy.'

Once that was decided, Raghu wanted to make sure that there was a fail-safe mechanism in place in case things did not work out. 'Getting into a startup is a risky venture. You need not necessarily go all in,' says Raghu. 'It might not necessarily be worth it to go all in. Try to ensure that something else is also happening for the family.' To ensure that their finances remained in order, Raghu and his wife decided that it would make sense for her to take up a job in Singapore while Raghu stayed back in Bengaluru. It would pay better. They would live apart while the startup idea resolved itself into something more concrete.

'You will go through a lot of stress on this journey,' says Raghu. 'Whether it is a successful startup or a failure, the one reality in a startup is that you are going to go through a phenomenal amount of difficulties. That's a reality. Whether you like it or not, you need to face it. But the last thing you want is something else killing you.'

'You do not want to find yourself unable to sustain the journey because there is a concern on the family front,' Raghu says. It is best to not have to experience disquiet on the family front so that you can be completely immersed in the startup. 'You can't really fight two battles at the same time. It is unnecessary to fight both the personal and the professional battles together. Pick and choose which battles you want to fight.'

Build on a foundation of trust

People and relationships matter in business, and especially so when you are an entrepreneur. If you are building a company, it is likely to take many years. You will need partners willing to work with you, and stand with you when you need them. Even if one startup fails, you might look to start another company later on. You will need associates, investors and employees willing to work with you again. The ability to build enduring relationships is critical for an entrepreneur.

'In entrepreneurship, it takes a village to succeed. It is all about relationships,' says Anu Hariharan, a Partner in Y Combinator's Continuity fund. An alumna of NIT Surathkal, Virginia Tech, and Wharton, Anu worked with Boston Consulting Group and Andreessen Horowitz before joining Y Combinator.

'Entrepreneurship is a very lonely endeavour,' she explains, 'a lot more lonely than any other job you might have experienced. When you start, you might be the only person in the company. If you have a co-founder, then it's still just the two of you. You have to start building relationships from that point on.' In order to build an idea into a company, you need to find users for the product. You need people who are willing to join your team, and others who are able to offer you advice or capital to help you build a company.

'As a startup founder, in the first year, you are building relationships with your customers because you have to ask them if the product you have built is truly valuable or not,' Anu says. 'You are building relationships with your network to hire your early engineers. Where do the first ten people for your company come from? From your network. Why? Because no one's leaving their job to come jump on a startup which they don't even know if it's going to succeed or not. So your first engineers are going to come from your network. But then, as a young startup founder, you have probably never hired anybody in your life. So you need to lean on other founders to learn how to hire. To learn how to convince others, you need a set of advisors, you need a set of mentors, people who have done this for a few years.'

Anu points out that one of the reasons Y Combinator's iconic startup accelerator programme is such a valuable experience for founders is that they are able to tap into a set of peer and alumni relationships from day one. You need a community that you can lean on for all the questions you don't know, she says. You might know how to code and ship a product, but not how to set up a company. 'Company building is not just building a product,' Anu says. 'Who is going to give you advice on who's a good lawyer? What are some efficient structures you need to consider? All of that comes from relationships.'

Anu offers the example of Brex, a financial services company that is part of YC's portfolio. Brex provides a corporate credit card and expense-management software for businesses. Its founders, Henrique Dubugras and Pedro Franceschi, started the company when they were twenty-one. Given that they were building a credit-based product, they needed capital on their balance sheet. Lining up investors before launching a product or even soon after launch is not easy. Nevertheless, Brex raised money within twelve weeks of their launch in a Series A round led by Meyer 'Mickey' Malka of Ribbit Capital.

'That was because of the five or six years of relationship that Henrique and Pedro had built with Mickey since their prior startup in Brazil which they had launched at age sixteen,' Anu says. 'Mickey had seen their evolution and was willing to invest. Then, within the first year, they needed a general counsel (GC) and a CFO for the company. How are two twenty-one-year-olds, who have moved from Brazil to San Francisco, going to hire a good GC and CFO? Well, they used their connections from Brazil to get introductions, built relationships with a lot of people in Silicon Valley, and actively reached out to startup founders who were three or four years ahead of them at YC to learn how to look for a GC and a CFO. Their first two hires came from their network. Then they had to form a partnership with MasterCard because they had to lay down the rails for their credit card product. All of this had to happen in the first twelve months,' Anu says. 'How do you do any of this without relationships? You can't.'

Being able to build enduring relationships is exceedingly valuable. However, it is easier said than done. According to Sanjeev Bikhchandani, the first step in building relationships is being able to inspire trust. 'Entrepreneurs have got to have the ability to create trust across the table,' he says. 'Whether with customers, co-founders, employees, colleagues, associates, investors or whoever you talk to, you have to have the ability to create trust.'

However, trust does not flow out of a vacuum, Sanjeev points out. 'You have got to be trustworthy to create trust. If you're not trustworthy, you cannot fake it,' he says. Trustworthiness comes from valuing relationships and commitments that you make. If you make a commitment, it has to be a sincere commitment, with the understanding that you will do your very best to honour it. 'You have to think things over from the other person's point of view, and try to create a win-win,' Sanjeev emphasizes. 'So your co-founders win when you win. Your investors win when you win. You can't win while having someone lose and then say that you've got a great relationship.'

Fight the good fight

During their years of struggle between 2001 and 2003, Deep Kalra and his co-founders, Sachin Bhatia and Keyur Joshi, came close to selling the company.

'We had shrunk to a mezzanine,' Deep says. 'If I raised my hands, I could touch the ceiling. And if I swung my arms and rocked a little bit, I could touch the walls on both sides. We were in a long railway compartment of a mezzanine. The original business was next to a warehouse of Wipro Soap and

Oil. It stank—most of the time it really stank. And there was a dharamkanta[4] right under it. It was so crazy. It was a place in the boonies, at ₹10 a square foot, Okhla Phase 1, the cheapest possible real estate you can probably get in the country.' Things were not going well with the company.

At that point, a company called Cendant was keen on buying MakeMyTrip. 'We'd reached the end. You went back home, and your wife gave you a withering look. Two of us—Sachin and I—were married, we were experiencing that, and the third founder—Keyur—wanted to get married, and prospective in-laws would always look at him and wonder about his prospects. It was really bad,' says Deep, laughing. 'So I told Sachin and Keyur that I was going to have this meeting. I told them if we get $10 million, at that time, I think we should sell. We owned 55 per cent of the company among us and 45 per cent was with angel investors. It was a lot of money in 2002.'

At the prevailing exchange rate, it would have meant almost ₹50 crore. 'We said that would buy us respectability. Keyur would be able to get married, our wives would smile again. *Hamare ghar mein bhi phir chirag jalega* (There would be light in our homes again).'

Deep met Cendant's representatives at Waves restaurant on Aurobindo Marg, next to the IIT Delhi gate. 'They didn't budge beyond five. Maybe they would have gone up to six.' However, instead of feeling disappointed, Deep was strangely relieved. 'I was so relieved. I only later realized, actually I did not want to sell *at all*. I really didn't want to.' But had they offered ten, Deep says they would have sold the company.[5]

---

4   A weighing scale for freight vehicles.

5   Deep shared that the Flipkart founders, Sachin and Binny Bansal, too had faced a similar situation early in the life of the company,

'Other startups have been faced with the same dilemma, and the bottom line is that if you are truly focused you will realize you cannot sell out halfway; you are going to build something amazing,' Deep says. 'The point I am trying to make,' Deep says, 'is it will seem bleak, it will seem crazy, but I would much rather you err on taking a risk than play it safe. So what if you give it one more year, or six months more? It's a marathon, it's not a sprint. It might be a series of sprints, but life or entrepreneurship is clearly a marathon. And it's immaterial today, for me, whether it took me eight years to list my company or twelve. How does it matter at the end of the day? It's immaterial. So, therefore, always err on the side of saying I'm persevering. Hang in there. Don't quit until it has sapped every iota of your self-confidence, strength, sweat, tears, blood and everything. When you are completely ravaged and completely wrecked, and you have nothing else left to give, go see *Rocky 3* and come back again.'

Discipline in depression

During their Okhla Phase 1 days, the MakeMyTrip founders would take calls from the US and sell tickets all night long. Some nights were tougher than others. It would show on their faces. This would demoralize the team.

---

and had almost sold the company. 'This was when Flipkart was still selling books. They came this close to selling the company for 10 million bucks. They were going through exactly the same. Tough, terrible times, nothing was happening. And so the founders agreed to sell. They came back and they had a mentor of sorts who gave them a severe lashing,' Deep says. 'He said what have you guys done, you cannot sell this company right now, you're going to build something amazing.'

'When things get very tough, you can't stop thinking about it. The more you say to yourself "no thoughts", the more thoughts come in, we all know that. So, it would show on our faces, and the rest of the team would pick up on what was going on,' says Deep.

One day, they made a rule: 'Either we would be "in", or we would quit. But if we decided to continue, we would be "in" for a whole month. So, once we were in, we would be in it for a month and we would not question ourselves on what we were doing throughout the whole month. And then at the end of the month we would take stock.'

This did not mean they stopped monitoring their metrics. They simply stopped questioning themselves. 'We all obviously looked at the company's metrics every day, at conversion by shift, conversion by individual call operator. We are creatures of numbers, of course. But we would not take a call with regard to the company until the month was over.'

Given that Keyur was then unmarried, the founders would invariably meet at his place, and their discussions would take place on the terrace over a cheap bottle of alcohol. 'We had this conversation: are we in for one more month? And then if we were in for a month, we were in,' Deep says.

'This silly ritual kept us going for the good part of a year— eight, nine months at least; because instead of those months being 240 or 270 days, they actually became eight or nine discrete months. And we had each other, and we had promised each other. That really helped. It helped us tide through a tough time.'

Their simple stratagem was so effective that they even came up with a name for it. 'We called it "discipline in depression,"' Deep says. 'I think it is really relevant when you are going through a tough time. You need your true north, you need someone to latch on to, you need to cry about your woes, but when you are in, you need to be disciplined.'

Deep narrates a conversation he had had with Heena Sidhu, the first Indian pistol shooter to win a gold medal at the ISSF World Cup finals. The biggest gift you can have for a sportsperson at the highest level is zero memory, Deep shares. 'The target is ten metres away and it's about the size of the tip of a ball pen, and that tip is divided into nine parts and that is the bull's eye; that is how the scoring works. You're going in, you're taking that shot again and again; all you need is a little tremor to start to completely throw you off. The ultimate thing is to have zero memory of your last shot.

'So, if you're going through a tough phase, if you've had a tough month, say we are going to start all over again. And that's how you get out of bad form,' says Deep. 'The only way you get out of bad form is not by wallowing in the bad form, but by believing that you can actually play much better and you're just going through a bad patch.'

Playing the long game

Sahil Barua founded the logistic courier service provider Delhivery in 2011 after spending three years working for Bain & Company, a top-tier management consulting firm. He had studied mechanical engineering at NIT Surathkal, and immediately afterwards entered the MBA programme at IIM Bangalore where he graduated with a gold medal.

Delhivery was initially conceptualized as a hyperlocal express delivery service provider for offline stores, initially delivering flowers and food locally in Gurugram. At the time, the e-commerce segment in India was witnessing explosive growth. Intrigued by e-commerce's potential, the founders decided to focus exclusively on e-commerce companies, providing them logistics services. By 2020, Delhivery was delivering one million shipments a day across more than 2,300 cities.

Looking back on his journey of building Delhivery, Sahil wishes he had known three things before starting up. He says he wishes he had known that getting stressed when things did not go to plan was not worth it. 'Entrepreneurs have a deep and desperate desire for control. For entirely the wrong reasons we believe that we can control the world. And that's not true,' he says. 'The problem is when you start a company you tend to think of yourself as quite important. Over time if you are lucky enough and the company survives, your company beats that notion out of your head. And you realize that not everything is under your control.' What happens as a consequence of trying to control everything is that you take on a tremendous amount of stress on yourself, he says. Once you are under stress, you tend to transfer it to your team. 'They then start running around all over the place. That's what is expected of them,' he says. 'And it doesn't work. I wish I had known that sooner.'

He wishes he had known how important it is to ensure that work remains sustainable in building a company. He says he finds stories of entrepreneurs working 140 hours a week ridiculous; it is simply not sustainable. 'Why are you working 140 hours a week? If the business demands 140 hours a week, something is wrong. How are you going to get 100 people to work those many hours? They have lives, they have other things to do. You have to respect that.'

'But unfortunately, it has become a sort of a meme,' he sighs, 'and we subscribed to that as well for the first four or five years. No vacations, nothing, just work all the time. And then we realized the company could not be built this way. We realized that either we should sell the company and just go and do something else, or if we really wanted to build a large company that lasts for a long time, then we had to think about it differently. It took a lot of time for us to understand that.'

The third thing he wishes he had known is that sometimes it is better to focus inwards on the company, rather than be obsessed with the competition. 'The risks that you think are going to kill you are rarely the risks that are real,' he says.

'In our early phases, when we were growing, we spent a lot of time worrying about what our competitors were doing. If our competitors launched a new service, we would get depressed that we had not launched it. I wish I had known that our competitors shared many of the same problems.'

'The reality is that sometimes it is better to collaborate than to compete. And we really needed to think of the market very differently. We were thinking too small. We were thinking how our competitors and we were these tiny organisms in a pond, fighting for resources. Instead of realizing how massive this entire pond was, we were trying to kill each other.'

'The Indian logistics market is a $200 billion market. There could be thirty Delhiverys in this market, and we all would have enough space to survive. I wish I had known that this "winner-takes-it-all" mentality is not necessary in every industry. We didn't need to have it when we started out. And it would have helped us make much better choices than we did had we realized it at that point. We would have been more careful in marshalling our resources and more worried about customer experiences than we were in our early years.'

Not all tales are fairy tales

Not every startup story ends well. Sometimes there is no light at the end of the tunnel. Sometimes you must know when to stop.

Before he found success with the Urban Company, Abhiraj Bhal had failed miserably with another venture. A graduate of IIT Kanpur and IIM Ahmedabad, Abhiraj had joined the Boston Consulting Group (BCG) after his MBA. After having spent three years in corporate life, the realization had slowly crept up to him that he had spent most of his life chasing after conventional notions of success rather than actually pursuing a vocation.

'Our version of success is a wealthy person working at a great job and wearing an Armani jacket. All our conditioning has been to chase after this image of success,' he says. He realized he had been chasing after this image for a long time, and he wanted to stop. He wanted to spend his life doing something that he found meaningful instead of chasing after an idealized notion of success.

'When I had this realization, I decided I was not going to spend my life solving one problem per year or trying to change my job from one designation to another,' he says. 'Rather, I would spend it on one problem deeply so that it moves the needle. If it took ten years or fifteen years, I didn't mind. Because *building and doing something* is far more satisfying to me than *being* somebody. That was my realization.'

Abhiraj called up his IIT batchmate Varun Khaitan, who too was working with BCG at the time, and told him that he wanted to start a company. Varun was soon in. Soon after, they quit their jobs.

However, they were missionaries without a religion. They did not know what they wanted to build yet. They had resigned from their jobs but were still struggling to find an idea.

They spent time talking to people. They went around meeting brick-and-mortar businesses. Varun's father helped them set up meetings with businessmen in traditional businesses. Some were making tea bags, some were making bottle caps for Coca-Cola. These were all lucrative businesses. However, they quickly realized that building a traditional business was not their cup of tea.

Then during the same time they were going about exploring ideas, they found themselves on a train ride from Delhi to Udaipur for a friend's wedding. They were soon bored out of their wits because there was no mobile connectivity. That's when it struck them that if only there were a device that could create a Wi-Fi loop in the train, and send movie content directly to their phones it would solve the need for entertainment while millions of people travelled in buses and trains in India everyday, starved for entertainment. They decided that it would also be a great match with their skillsets. This would be an electrical device, and they were electrical engineers, after all!

'Just like that, without any study or market analysis, we jumped straight into this idea,' Abhiraj laughs. They were so excited by the idea that they did not pause to seek customer feedback. Nor did not try to understand the market dynamics that could be at play. They were convinced that it was a superb idea. 'It is amazing how confident we were.'

They put together a deck of slides detailing their idea, and the business proposition, and took it around to senior business executives that they had come to know at work. The feedback that they received was uniformly positive. 'Every conversation told us that we were on to something big. We were excited,' Abhiraj says. They hired an engineer and started building, calling the company CinemaBox.

Soon after, they realized that their device could not be installed on trains; Wi-Fi systems were not allowed on trains at the time. 'We had not done even that basic research.' They wangled a meeting with a member of the Board of Railways and pitched the idea to him but that did not lead anywhere. So they were finally left only with buses. Soon, they realized even that might not work.

In offering an on-demand entertainment streaming solution in buses, Abhiraj and Varun were simply acting as middlemen. They neither owned the content, nor the transportation layer. 'You get ₹100 from the customer; ₹33 goes to the content owner, ₹33 goes to the bus operator and ₹33 comes to us. But we realized that the two sides could eventually squeeze us out. We didn't own the customer, and when you don't own the customer, you have no pricing power. There was a possibility we might be squeezed all the way down to zero, with each of the other two market players, the content owner and the bus operator, splitting the ₹100 between them. We would potentially get nothing. It was never going to be a large company. This realization was constantly sinking in.' It was a small market contrary to early expectations, and it was going to be very challenging to build the company.

'Between an archaic entertainment industry, and private air-conditioned bus operators, it became clear to us this was not going to succeed. There was no real competitive advantage. This was going to be a struggle. And after all this struggle, at best, this was going to be a lifestyle business. This was a really hard realization for us.'

Despite their misgivings, they found it hard to quit. They had already invested nine or ten months and a considerable amount of their savings in trying to build the business. In addition, they were stuck with the idea that as entrepreneurs, they should not quit. 'The larger entrepreneurial ecosystem has these stories where you have to go on and on. Even when there is no light at the end of the tunnel, you need to continue and light will come eventually. You have to believe as an entrepreneur. Those are glorious stories,' says Abhiraj. 'You think, maybe I am not able to see what this could become.'[6] So, they persisted. They explored partnering with Netflix, they explored building an offline business by loading content into kiosks. The writing was on the wall, however. 'For us, the tipping point came with the realization that even if we did it for three or four years, at the end it would be a lifestyle business. It would not have impacted anybody's life.'

The 'why' is very important, Abhiraj says, echoing Sanjeev Bikhchandani. 'I didn't want to do a startup just so as to work for myself. In fact, the day you start as an entrepreneur, everybody's your boss. The first employee is your boss. The guy who cleans the office is your boss, and asks whether you'll be able to pay the salary. When we quit BCG, we wanted to work on something we were really passionate about. That could have deep impact. This lifestyle business was not going to create deep impact or add value.'

---

6   Deep Kalra admits it can be difficult to let go. He spent two years of his life trying to build a bowling alley company with AMF Bowling. 'There is a fine line between stubbornness and perseverance. And the irony is you will probably only know later in the day which one it was. When you are in the moment, there is nothing but stubbornness,' he says. 'When I look back, there are at least three occasions when I should have given up much earlier in my life. But I could not tell because I was in that moment, I was living that moment, I was right there. In AMF Bowling, I wasted two years of my life. I can say today, no regrets. But perhaps I should have been practical; perhaps I should have said I should move on.'

'The thought experiment that I use is if your company shuts down, will somebody out there feel that they had been stabbed in the back? Today, if Urban Company shuts down, thousands of service professionals who completely rely on us would feel betrayed. Their households run because of us. They would actually feel somebody had stabbed them in their backs. CinemaBox would not have been that company.'

Finally, better sense prevailed. 'One fine day we opened a bottle of Old Monk, finished it, and decided to quit. The next day we shut shop. That was my first business, CinemaBox.'

Summary

- **Before starting up, ask yourself 'why'.** Ask yourself what drives you to choose to start a company. Having an overarching sense of purpose will propel you forward; when in doubt, your 'why' will become your guiding star.
- **Great things take time to build.** A startup may take several years to build and might take up a large portion of your working life. Be prepared to play the long game to build a company that will last.
- **When building a company, sacrifices are an occupational hazard.** These might include financial sacrifices, when the startup might not be churning much money, or personal, such that commitment to the project might leave you with little time for family and friends.
- **The difference between success and failure might lie in your willingness to persist.** Setbacks and frustrations are par for the course. When faced with adversity, be willing to continue moving forward.
- **Having a strong support system is crucial.** During a tumultuous startup journey involving many setbacks and

sacrifices, it is the stable relationships around you that will fortify you, and allow you to carry on.

- **Not all tales are fairytales.** Not all startups succeed. In some cases, it might be futile to persist. Occasionally, it might be better to lay one endeavour to rest so that another might begin.

2
The Idea

BEFORE THERE CAN BE a business, there must be an idea. It is the foundation on which you would build the edifice of your startup. Eventually, that idea will grow and evolve, and hopefully transform into a living, breathing company. But when you start, there is very little that you have apart from the idea itself.

While every startup begins with an idea, the converse is not necessarily true. Not every idea leads to a startup. How do you find an idea that is inherently viable and can be built into a startup?

Look for customer insights

'If you are looking to be an entrepreneur, and figuring out what to do, I think you should start by trying to get some customer insights about some unsolved problem, and then see if you can address it,' says Naukri.com founder Sanjeev Bikhchandani.

In 1989, Sanjeev was one of the students coordinating the campus recruitment process at IIM Ahmedabad. He could observe, at close quarters, the premium that recruiters placed on talent, as well as the inherent uncertainty linked to the hiring process for both recruiters and interviewing candidates. He could see senior HR executives at highly reputed companies coming to blows over talent. For Sanjeev, this insight eventually led to the foundation of Naukri.com.

Upon graduation, Sanjeev joined Hindustan Milkfood Manufacturers—now GlaxoSmithKline—as the brand manager for the popular milk drink Horlicks.[1] There he would see that every time a new edition of the business magazine *Business India* would come in, everybody in the office would read it from back to front. *Business India* was the number-one medium for job advertisements at the time; the magazine carried these at the back. Once they had read through the advertisements, his colleagues would have animated discussions about job openings, even the ones who were not really looking for jobs.

He realized that job opportunities clearly formed a high-interest category of information; after all, his colleagues were primarily interested in only that section of the *Business India* magazine. He realized that there was a huge but fragmented database of jobs out there. If someone were to organize it, and make it available, it would become a valuable resource. However, the internet was not yet a reality in 1990, and it was not obvious how this problem could be solved; the idea simply sat at the back of his mind.

---

[1]   Sarika Malhotra and Sukalp Sharma, 'Right Man for the Job', *Financial Express*, 30 December 2011, financialexpress.com/archive/right-man-for-the-job/893653

'Seven years later, when he saw the internet for the first time, he joined the dots, and launched Naukri.com,' Sanjeev says. 'So if you base your business idea on a deep customer insight, the likelihood of your success multiplies manifold,' he says.

Yashish Dahiya stumbled upon a customer insight that eventually led to the founding of Policybazaar through a conversation he had with his father.

Yashish is an IIT Delhi and IIM Ahmedabad alumnus who co-founded Policybazaar in 2008 as an insurance comparison website. Before starting the company, he had run an online travel company called ebookers.com in Europe. The company had been sold in 2005, and Yashish had returned to India.

Once, during the course of a conversation, Yashish came to know of an insurance policy that his father had invested in. It offered 2-3 per cent annual returns as well as tax benefits; his father was quite happy with it. By 2008, Yashish's parents had been investing substantial amounts in similar policies. This made Yashish look deeper into these products, and seek to understand how they operated.

He soon realized that there were two key stakeholders—the agent selling the policy, and the company which would have created the product—and the products were highly profitable for both. For each successful sale, about half of the principal investment would be taken by the agent as their commission. The other half would be invested in the stock market by the company offering the product. The stock market at the time was growing a lot faster than the promised return on the product; a part of the gains on the investment would be directed to offering returns to the policy holders. If a holder cancelled a policy before a period of three years, then a large part of the principal would be forfeited, creating an ever-larger profit for the company.

Such insurance policies were being purchased by a large number of people in India. Yashish realized that the industry existed because those buying these policies were not educated as to how these products operated. When Yashish understood how such policies worked, he was initially annoyed at the thought of his father having been inveigled into investing in them. However, he soon realized that this also offered a brilliant opportunity. A platform that could assist users to make informed decisions while buying insurance would solve a real customer problem. This is how Policybazaar was born.

Getting startup ideas

Arriving at an idea that can solve a real-world customer problem is a non-trivial proposition. TFS founder Raghu offers three possible approaches for arriving at solutions which can become ideas for startups.

The first is to look at the problems you might be facing and see if you have any viable solutions. In this, Raghu echoes Y Combinator founder Paul Graham who holds that the way to get startup ideas is not to try to think of startup ideas. Instead, it is to look for problems, 'preferably problems you have yourself.'[2]

Any given real-world problem can be classified either as an unmet demand or a latent need. An unmet demand exists when a market already exists, but there is a potentially better solution than those that are available. The idea itself might not be so revolutionary that it leads to the formation of a new industry,

---

2   Paul Graham, 'How to Get Startup Ideas?', *www.paulgraham.com*, November 2012, paulgraham.com/startupideas.html

but it might be disruptive enough to alter the workings of an existing industry.

Raghu attributes WhatsApp's successful penetration of the Indian messaging service market to its ability to provide a solution that served an existing demand in a more convenient fashion for its target customer segment. Incumbent technology companies already offered messaging platforms at the time. The market segment was closely contested by Yahoo! Messenger, Google Hangouts and Facebook Messenger. Nevertheless, WhatsApp succeeded where the others failed to take off. What allowed them to succeed was that they only asked for a phone number, not an email address. 'India is one of those very few countries across the world where people are on the internet without an email ID,' Raghu says. 'That single insight gave them the entire market.'

TFS, too, did not create a new industry. It simply disrupted the existing taxi industry by offering customers the ability to book a taxi using a smartphone. 'People were already using taxis,' Raghu says. 'There was already a market for people to use taxis. TFS came up with a solution that would make it a lot more convenient for people to book tax. We didn't create the market; we didn't build the market. When we were ideating, the market existed. But we had a better solution than what existed in the market.'

On the other hand, there are startups that tap into a hitherto unknown latent need among customers, and thereby lead to the creation of a new industry. A latent need is, by definition, not immediately observable and not explicitly known. There is no glaring hole or readily observable unmet need in the market. However, every once in a while, an idea or a product comes along that captures customer imagination in such a way that it leads to the rise of a new industry. The iPhone was such a product, entirely upturning the smartphone paradigm as it existed at the time. 'An idea or product that addresses a latent need is rare. It requires both deep customer insights, and an ability to imagine what might appeal to customers, if offered,' shares Raghu.

The second approach to arrive at ideas is to look at emerging areas of technology. Using these technologies, can you build applications that can address certain problems? There might be ideas that did not make sense earlier, because the technologies were not viable or the economies did not add up. But with time, these ideas might have become more viable.

Raghu gives the example of startups based on virtual reality. While early breakthroughs in virtual reality were made in the 1980s, for the longest time, the technology was not mature enough or accessible enough for a startup to be based on it. With the advent of smartphones, virtual-reality-based startups have become more viable.

Being familiar with the leading edge of rapidly changing fields makes it easier to notice technology-driven solutions to customer problems. According to Paul Graham, if you are at the leading edge of a field that's changing fast, you are more likely to notice opportunities that others might miss. 'If you look at the way successful founders have formulated their ideas, it's generally the result of some external stimulus hitting a prepared mind,' he says.[3]

The third approach is to examine startups that are doing well in other markets, and replicate them. 'When you look at something that might be working elsewhere, you should try to figure out what is the problem that it is essentially trying to solve,'

---

[3]   Paul Graham, 'How to Get Startup Ideas?', *www.paulgraham. com*, November 2012, paulgraham.com/startupideas.html

says Raghu. The problem that a given startup solves might not
even exist in the Indian market. Or even if it does, it might vary
significantly in shape and form, thereby immediately defeating the
prospect of directly applying the solution to the Indian context.
It is therefore crucial to customize a solution to the needs of the
local market. 'Figure out if that problem is also prevailing in
Indian markets and whether the solution is a right fit for Indian
markets, or something needs to change,' Raghu says.

In starting Nykaa, Falguni Nayar took inspiration from
beauty stores in the US. Both of Falguni's children were studying
in the US; in her frequent visits to the country, she had become
a loyal customer of the beauty giant Sephora.[4] The beauty
industry in the West was huge, with entire floors of high-end
department stores dedicated to cosmetics and other beauty
products; she realized that it was only a matter of time before
it picked up in India.

Buying beauty products in India had hitherto made for a
poor experience. In contrast to their Western counterparts,
Indian women still had to visit neighbourhood stores for their
beauty needs. These mom-and-pop stores, mostly staffed by
male owners, sold cosmetics alongside other knick-knacks.
Assortments were limited, displays poor and there was no
opportunity to sample products. A reliable retailer of branded
cosmetics did not exist in India.

Falguni decided that an Indian version of Sephora was a
timely idea; there was a clear opportunity in giving customers
easy access to high-end beauty items, complete with tutorials

---

4   Anu Raghunathan, 'India Mints New Billionaire Woman As
     Nykaa Founder Grooms Her Beauty Retailer For An IPO', Forbes,
     4 August 2021, forbes.com/sites/anuraghunathan/2021/08/04/
     india-mints-new-billionaire-woman-as-nykaa-founder-grooms-
     her-beauty-retailer-for-an-ipo/?sh=22878fa81b54

and testimonials. However, instead of looking to replicate Sephora's brick-and-mortar-first model, Falguni decided to set up an online retailer first; it would be less capital intensive and somewhat easier to scale. She started Nykaa as an e-commerce platform, eventually adding high-street stores once the brand became established.[5]

Similarly, while Flipkart took inspiration from successful e-commerce businesses in developed markets, the founders needed to tailor their approach to e-commerce for the Indian market. Flipkart was founded in 2007 by Sachin Bansal and Binny Bansal, batchmates from IIT Delhi who had both worked at Amazon. They had both realized the potential of an e-commerce business in India while working at Amazon. But for the e-commerce platform to be successful, it had to be tailored for the Indian market.

When Flipkart started offering cash-on-delivery (CoD) in 2010, it was one of the earliest online retailers to embrace this innovation.[6] At the time, only 0.5 per cent of the Indian population used credit cards.[7] Credit cards and online banking were still nascent; most customers did not have a means to shop online. CoD allowed consumers to buy online and pay in

---

5   Mallika Kapur, 'Falguni Nayar: The Beauty Entrepreneur', *Mint*, 24 March 2017, livemint.com/Leisure/EMOmjllb5hPv8Se8T62ZaK/ Falguni-Nayar-The-beauty-entrepreneur.html

6   Goutam Das, 'Cash-on-Delivery a Necessary Evil for E-commerce Companies', *Business Today*, 16 February 2014, businesstoday. in/magazine/cover-story/story/cash-on-delivery-impact-on-e-commerce-companies-customers-134631-2014-01-29

7   Tanya Dubey, 'These Disruptions Made by Flipkart Over Ten Years Helped It Lead the E-commerce Sector', *Business Insider*, 2 June 2017, businessinsider.in/These-Disruptions-made-by-Flipkart-over-Ten-Years-Helped-it-Lead-the-E-commerce-Sector/ articleshow/58951257.cms

cash only when the product was delivered. It was an industry-defining innovation that played a major role in popularizing Flipkart, and driving adoption.

While the three outlined approaches can help generate ideas, Raghu stresses upon the importance of combining them with wide-ranging discussions with peers that can drive deeper understanding and insights. 'Ideas do not usually come when you are sitting alone or trying to ideate. Ideas originate from discussions. You just cannot get into a meeting with the agenda of getting an idea. Ideas happen,' he says. 'As you take part in conversations, something or the other is going to click within you. You can't sit alone and start looking at ideas.' Discussions lead to the distilling of thought, and can drive the uncovering of customer insights.

Riding the wave of macro trends

Girish Mathrubootham started the cloud-based customer engagement company Freshworks on the back of deep immersion in the enterprise software-as-a-service (SaaS) ecosystem.

Girish had joined software development company Zoho in 2001 as an engineer. Nine years later, he was the vice president of product development in the company. During the time he spent at Zoho, he built wide-ranging expertise in the development of enterprise information technology service systems. He had been building IT helpdesk systems, which enabled enterprise clients to offer technical support to their customers since 2004. He understood the enterprise IT service management market inside out. He had also had a ringside view to cloud-computing developments taking place within Zoho. This placed him really well to tap into opportunities created by global developments in this sector.

In the middle of 2010, he stumbled upon a discussion thread on the technology-focused social news website Hacker News that piqued his interest. Zendesk, at the time the largest customer-service support company, had raised their prices by up to 300 per cent. Their existing customers were livid, and were tearing into the company on discussion forums. For a customer-service support company, they did not seem to have very happy customers, Girish found himself thinking.

Zendesk's prices made it unviable for startups and smaller companies who would be forced to resort to alternative providers. Many of the alternative providers could not offer the same level of functionality as Zendesk could, especially as the startup expanded. However, over time, as customers got locked into alternative ecosystems, it was hard to make the switch back to Zendesk.

Scrolling through the discussion thread on Hacker News, one particular comment caught his eye. One user had written that there was still a huge opening in the market. If a competitor could come in, offering the right functionality at the right price, they could take away all of Zendesk's and its alternatives' customers.

Girish had already started thinking that someone like him, with a background in having built helpdesk systems, could start a company in this space. That comment was like a slap on his face, he says. It made him wake up to the very real potential in the market. 'Here was an opportunity sitting right in front of me,' he says.[8]

---

[8]   Girish Mathrubootham, 'The Freshdesk Story of Where and How It All Started', *Freshdesk Blogs*, 18 March 2011, https://freshdesk.com/general/the-freshdesk-story-blog

Girish understood that the SaaS segment of the enterprise application software market was growing rapidly. From 2009 to 2010, the segment had grown by almost 16 per cent, and it was expected to grow by as much again in that year.[9] As the technology had matured, adoption was becoming more widespread. In addition, Girish understood that a massive transition to cloud-based services was already underway. Microsoft CEO Steve Ballmer had publicly announced that the company was betting its future on the cloud; they were 'all in'.[10] Oracle and IBM had committed to the cloud too.[11]

Girish decided that he would start a company that would deliver cloud-based customer-support services, delivered through the SaaS model.

He was thirty-six years old at the time, had two kids in school, and in March of that year, had taken out a home loan. His situation in life did not necessarily make him very well-suited for entrepreneurship, he says. That did not deter him. However, the very same day, Girish pitched his idea to his friend Shan Krishnasamy who had worked with him for over eight years. Soon Shan was on board and joined him as his co-founder.

Girish had learnt relatively early in his life that it was a lot easier to take on a macro trend that was working, and ride that wave, than to go against the trend. Many years earlier, at the

---

[9]   Tyler Thia, 'Global SaaS Market to Hit US$9B in 2010', *ZDNet*, 15 December 2010, zdnet.com/article/global-saas-market-to-hit-us9b-in-2010

[10] Denise Dubie, 'Microsoft's Ballmer: "For the cloud, We're All in"', *CIO.com*, 4 March 2010, https://www.cio.com/article/2420002/microsoft-s-ballmer---for-the-cloud--we-re-all-in-.html

[11] John Rymer, 'Oracle Likes Cloud Computing after All', *Forrester*, 1 March 2010, go.forrester.com/blogs/10-03-01-oracle_likes_cloud_computing_after_all

height of the dot-com boom in 1999, Girish had got his first taste of building a business.

He was working as a programmer at HCL at the time. Computer programming was the flavour of the moment; everybody wanted to learn to programme. His friends, dissatisfied with instructors in Chennai at the time, had beseeched him to teach them. He had agreed. Within a month, his programming classes had grown from three students to fifty. When the dot-com bust happened later, however, his students disappeared. The situation was so bad, in fact, that it was difficult to convince people that Java was still relevant, he says.

Having learnt his lesson, when it came to building products for Freshworks, Girish resolved to focus on riding the wave of existent trends in the market. They would build a cloud-based service. They would build products that already had traction in the market—a customer-support software, an IT helpdesk software and a customer-relationship management software. These were products that enterprises already understood, and needed. They would not seek to build products that did not yet have traction in the market. They would take product categories that were already witnessing growth; only, they would build better than what the market had to offer at the time.

There was already an identified need in the market, but existing players could not serve that need well. There was a huge opening in a market that was expanding rapidly. With a product that offered high functionality at an affordable price point, Freshworks rode the wave of market forces to drive exponential growth.

Within three years of their founding, they were serving 5,000 enterprise clients across eighty countries.[12] Within eight years,

---

[12]   Preethi Chamikutty, 'A Fresh Idea, a Fresh Business and Like A Breath of Fresh Air', *YourStory*, 5 April 2013, yourstory.com/2013/04/

they were a unicorn, valued at over a billion dollars.[13] When Freshworks got listed on the Nasdaq in September 2021, it was valued at over $12 billion.

Seeking customer feedback

How do you know that an idea is one worth investing time and effort into? The pursuit of every idea comes attendant with an opportunity cost; in choosing one path, you choose to forgo another. How then do you know which road you must take?

According to Raghu, during early stages of startups, founders invariably start questioning themselves, the idea, and the product. It, therefore, becomes imperative to invest time in the beginning to calm any doubts.

While evaluating an idea, it is important to ask if the problem even exists for a large enough customer base, and does the proposed solution offer a legitimate remedy? Seeking customer feedback and assessing product-market fit is central to addressing this question.

After graduating from IIM Ahmedabad, Raghu and Aprameya would continue to meet, and when they did, the talk would often veer to startup ideas. However, they would always dismiss the ideas that they got. They were either not 'big enough' or 'not great', Raghu says.

During one such conversation, they stumbled upon the TaxiForSure idea. They had spent three years in their respective

---

        culture-series-a-fresh-idea-a-fresh-business-and-like-a-breath-of-fresh-air

[13]   Jason D. Rowley, 'Freshworks Joins the Unicorn Club with $100M Series G Co-led by Sequoia and Accel', *Crunchbase*, 31 July 2018, news.crunchbase.com/news/freshworks-joins-the-unicorn-club-with-100m-series-g-co-led-by-sequoia-and-accel

jobs by that time, and they were cribbing to each other over glasses of beer. While their jobs were very different, what they had in common was that they both were required to travel a lot. Every city that they would go to, finding a cab was always difficult. 'It just so happened that both of us arrived at the same crib at the same time,' Raghu laughs. When they realized that both of them were facing the same issue, they realized there could actually be real potential in solving the problem. 'Thankfully, one of us had the presence of mind to put it down on a tissue paper, and thankfully we found the tissue paper the next morning, otherwise there would not be a TaxiForSure story,' he quips.

However, before they set out to build TFS, Raghu and Aprameya wanted to be certain that they would not set off on a fool's errand. They carried out extensive market research, and sought customer feedback for their idea. First, they wanted to be certain that the problem was large enough for them to build a startup around it. They wanted to understand if there was a large enough segment of the population that sought to hire cabs on demand, but was finding it difficult. To test their idea, they prepared an online survey enquiring about this problem and sent it to their friends.

The survey responses came back and they indicated that this seemed to be a universal problem. However, they reasoned, there might have been an implicit bias in their sample selection; given that so many of their friends were business school graduates, or worked in consulting, or business development, the sample might not be representative of the larger population. This was perhaps only a problem for a niche segment, potentially too small to build a viable business around.

They refined the survey questionnaire, and began administering the survey to strangers outside the Delhi and Bengaluru airports.

As it happened, their earlier findings were validated; the difficulty in hiring cabs on demand seemed to be a major concern. However, once again, they were apprehensive, wondering if this might be a problem restricted only to frequent fliers.

They refined their survey further, coming up with a questionnaire that had ten close-ended objective questions, and five open-ended questions, designed to elicit more detailed responses and explanations. They hired a set of college students, asking them to administer the survey to people visiting malls. This would be a sample free of implicit biases linked to the two of them. They gathered around 3,000 responses—a large enough sample to help come to definitive conclusions. Around 92 per cent respondents had claimed that they could not find cabs when needed; clearly, this was a real problem.

Until this point, they had only tried to gauge if the problem itself was real. Once it was clear that it was so, they sought to understand if the solution they proposed would be accepted. They went back to many of the survey respondents who had claimed this was a problem for them, especially those who had taken the time to fill out answers to the open-ended questions. They explained their concept of an app-based taxi-on-demand solution. When they did, they received an overwhelmingly positive response. This was validation offered directly by those they believed were their future customers. This was finally enough to convince them of the potential of their idea. When customers tell you that an idea is amazing, only then can you be sure that there is potentially value in your idea, Raghu says.

There was one additional filter their idea had to pass through, though. They went to the most critical of their friends, in Raghu's words, their 'annoying friends', and explained their idea to them. We all have such friends, he says. 'Whatever you do, they keep cross-questioning, whatever you do, they are never happy,' he laughs. But, he says, you need to have such friends because they are the ones who make you evaluate your idea in and out.

As they engaged with their friends, they kept refining their idea based on the feedback they received. Every time one of their proposals was shot down, they would go back to the drawing board and try to come up with a solution. This depth of thinking and research served them in good stead later on. 'None of the investors asked us the kind of questions that our annoying friends asked us,' Raghu says. 'Which was beautiful because we had such strong fundamentals.'

Raghu says there are two ways to respond to criticism. One is to assume that the person being critical of you does not have your best interests at heart. The other is to welcome feedback. There are those who will tell you only what you want to hear, Raghu says. 'That is not going to help you. Because life is brutal. It is going to come after you in a way you would not really expect.' It is better to go to a trainer, and learn from the trainer, than to come up short later when reality hits, he says. It is much better to face questions at the outset so that you may find ways to resolve them than to go forth without adequate analysis, only to come up short later on.

While Raghu and Aprameya might have initially received favourable responses to their idea, this is not always the case. After Abhiraj Bhal had shut down his first startup, CinemaShop, he and his co-founder, Varun Khaitan, had gone back to the ideation stage. They had been joined by Raghav Chandra who too had tried to start up, only to run his company to the ground in six months. The three of them would get together in Abhiraj's living room, and spend time throwing out ideas for discussion.

On one occasion, Abhiraj's wife asked him to have three wall hangings put up in their home. He assumed that this would be easy enough, and arranged for a carpenter to visit. However, the carpenter did not show up at the appointed time. Neither did the next one that he called up. Abhiraj arranged for a third person; he found the house with much difficulty, but was without his tools. He fixed a time to come back later with his tools.

Later, when Abhiraj, Varun and Raghav got together, they started discussing the problems they had faced in getting reliable providers of home services. Amongst the three of them, they had, collectively, tried to find help for home services over forty to fifty times over the last six months, and had been routinely left underwhelmed. Abhiraj had spent the entire day trying to find a service provider, was willing to spend money, but had still not succeeded. They decided that the existing state of affairs in the home-services industry could not continue; this was an industry ripe for disruption.

It was a massive industry, albeit one that was completely fragmented. It would eventually be organized by a company built on the internet. 'There will be somebody who will build Amazon for local home services,' they reasoned. Why couldn't it be them?

They put together their concept of an internet-based service provisioning startup on to a set of slides, and set out to garner feedback, especially from business executives, those with years of experience in running real businesses. However, what they heard was far from encouraging. Almost all of those they discussed the idea with suggested it was a really bad idea. Some did not understand what they had sought out to do, Abhiraj says. Others responded that given that a service like JustDial—a company that provides local search services—already existed, it was perhaps not viable to build another one.

Initially, Abhiraj was dejected. But eventually he came to the realization that perhaps they had stumbled on to something that others could not see. Eventually, this gave way to happiness. 'I was happy since I was seeing something others weren't seeing,' he says. 'Because if it were so simple and so apparent, probably multiple people would have already done it.'

In addition, unlike Raghu and Aprameya, they had not yet gone to their actual customers. They had not sought out feedback from a large enough base of potential customers. Had they done so, they would have perhaps already heard differently. Ultimately, it is customer feedback that is sacrosanct, especially if carried out over a large sample size. In the absence of it, if Abhiraj remained sanguine, that was perhaps not uncalled for.

When they did eventually seek out much wider feedback, not only did theirs seem like a viable idea, they discovered that they had stumbled upon what could be the perfect two-sided marketplace. Finding reliable service professionals with relative ease was clearly a problem for those seeking services; however, the other way round held true as well. Many service professionals were dependent on middlemen and contractors; this ate into their margins.[14] Through offering a marketplace, there was clearly an opportunity to build a viable business.

Validating potential: The Delta 4 framework

While a proposed solution might create value, is there enough potential in it to build a startup around it? FreeCharge and CRED founder Kunal Shah's Delta 4 framework offers a way to gauge the potential value in an idea.

A serial entrepreneur, Kunal founded the online payments company FreeCharge in 2010. FreeCharge was acquired by

---

[14] SeedToScale, 'Abhiraj Singh Bhal and Abhinav Chaturvedi—Untold Seed Stories: First 500 Days of Urban Company', 2 October 2020, https://www.seedtoscale.com/content/untold-seed-stories-first-500-days-of-urban-company

Snapdeal for $400 million in 2015, at the time the largest acquisition in India in the consumer internet space in India.[15] In 2018, he founded CRED, a high-trust community of individuals, merchants, and financial institutions. CRED rewards members for responsible financial behaviour, such as paying credit card bills on time, with premium products, services, and experiences.[16]

The Delta 4 framework rests on the premise that humans are constantly striving to move from a state of lower efficiency to a state of higher efficiency. The past, therefore, always represents a state of lower efficiency, the future a state of higher efficiency. Humanity moves towards a state of higher efficiency through inventing goods and services that enable this shift.

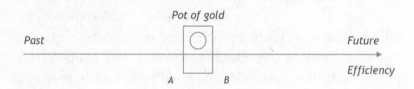

According to Kunal, between a prevailing state A and a more efficient state B lies a pot of gold, the inherent value in enabling humanity's shift to a state of higher efficiency. Any solution that enables this shift from A to B to take place captures this pot of gold.

---

[15]   Patanjali Pahwa and Ashish K. Mishra, 'What Happens to FreeCharge?', *The Ken*, 1 June 2019, the-ken.com/story/what-happens-to-freecharge/

[16]   Tenzin Pema, 'After 3 Years "on the Sidelines", Kunal Shah Finally Reveals His New Venture Cred', *YourStory*, 6 November 2018, yourstory.com/2018/11/kunal-shah-reveals-new-startup-cred

Each of the states A and B can be assigned an efficiency score between 1 and 10, based on a survey of a large sample size of target users. Then if solutionA corresponds to how a given problem is solved in state A, and solutionB how the same problem is solved in state B, the difference, or the delta in efficiency (Δe) can be calculated as

$$\Delta e = avg.\ of\ efficiency\ scores\ for\ solutionB - avg.\ of\ efficiency\ scores\ for\ solutionA$$

According to Kunal, the potential of an idea to create value can be evaluated by measuring the delta in efficiency scores between the existing solutionA and the proposed solutionB.

Kunal illustrates efficiency scoring with examples. Consider booking a railway ticket in India. Historically, one had to get to a railway station, line up in a queue and buy a ticket at the counter. It was a time-consuming process, unlikely to feature amongst a set of positive user experiences. Once the Indian Railways' web portal came online in 2002,[17] travellers could book tickets with a few clicks. It was a superior solution, one that rapidly enabled a shift to a much higher state of efficiency; by 2020, 80 per cent of railway tickets were being booked online.[18] SolutionB, in this case, was clearly superior to solutionA.

---

[17]   Kopal Cheema, 'How Online Train Booking Platforms Are Gearing up for Indian Railways' Privatised Future', *Inc42*, 30 November 2019, inc42.com/features/how-online-train-booking-ticket-platforms-are-gearing-up-for-indian-railways-privatised-future

[18]   Shine Jacob, 'Covid-19 Impact: Railway Move to Halt Operations Set to Dent IRCTC Earnings', *Business Standard India*, 14 April 2020, business-standard.com/article/indian-railways/railways-plan-to-stop-operations-till-may-3-set-to-dent-irctc-earnings-120041401734_1.html

Table 1: Illustrative example of efficiency scoring across solution alternatives

Solution Alternatives: Old vs New	SolutionA	SolutionB
Railway ticket booking: Railway station ticket counter vs online portal	2	6
Cab booking: Legacy cab services vs online apps	2	6
Buying apparel: Brick-and-mortar vs online store	6	2

Similarly, if asked, frequent users of online on-demand cab-booking applications such as Uber, or TaxiForSure, are likely to score them higher than the earlier method of booking cabs through traditional service providers. Modern applications afford a superior user experience, often at a lower price.

On the other hand, buying apparel online is not strictly a higher efficiency solution for every consumer segment. It might be more difficult to make a purchase without the option of trying on a piece of clothing as one could in a brick-and-mortar showroom. There could be an issue with the fit, realized only once the item is delivered, necessitating a return later. In this case, efficiency scoring might not necessarily reveal a clear delta with the alternative. As Kunal points out, simply going digital, or building an app, does not make for a more efficient state.

According to Kunal, when the difference in efficiency scores between two states is equal to, or greater than, four, three things happen:

1. **The shift from state A to state B becomes irreversible.** If the railway-ticketing portal does not work one morning, users

are unlikely to immediately rush to the railway station to book tickets.

2. **Users develop very high tolerance for failure, or shortcomings in the new solution.** Even when the railway-ticketing portal is down, or slow, users continue to select the solution over the alternative.

3. **The new solution creates a unique bragworthy proposition.** A large number of early adopters become evangelists for the solution, catalysing its wider adoption. Early users take pride in having discovered a new, more-efficient method, and tend to advocate its use to others, until there is a shift of most users from the earlier state to the new, more-efficient state.

Together, these drive customer stickiness, and widespread adoption, both crucial for a startup to succeed. In the absence of Delta 4 differentiation, there is lesser likelihood of an idea driving value, of the startup succeeding.

In certain cases, however, even a Delta 4 innovation might not be enough to create disruption. The following are four such situations:

1. **Microconfigurations:** In many cases, there is a high degree of customization that has been carried out to an existing state. If switching to a new state, even if it offers a Delta 4 improvement, means losing these customizations, then many users might be unwilling to make the switch. Kunal offers the example of a trusted driver who has been with him for a long time. He has become familiar with Kunal's idiosyncrasies, and understands his preferences well. This makes him irreplaceable.

2. **Network effects:** Certain solutions are more persistent simply because these have already been embraced by a large

base of users. Kunal offers the example of the spreadsheet software Microsoft Excel which almost has a monopolistic hold on the market. What makes it hard to dislodge is its widespread adoption and popularity. While one user might make the switch to a competing software, his colleagues and counterparts might not be familiar with the alternative, and find it difficult to work with. This ensures that Excel continues its hold over the market.

3. **Supporting ecosystem:** If a Delta 4 solution does not have a supporting ecosystem in place, it will fail to get traction. For instance, a cab-booking app in a country without smartphones will fail to take off.

4. **Affordability:** If affordability is a major constraint, then even a superior solution might see weaker adoption. For instance, between trains and flights, trains win out simply because they are more affordable.

5. **Learning effort:** If the learning effort required to move to a new solution is very high, that creates a barrier to adoption. For instance, if someone has spent years learning English as a language, and developing a grasp over its vocabulary, even a new language comes with Delta 4 differentiation, it might be difficult to make the switch.

6. **Branded lanes:** In certain cases, an existing solution associated with an efficiency shift can come to enjoy very powerful brand recognition. In these cases, it might be more difficult to dislodge. For instance, Google has become synonymous with search over time. Even if a better search engine might come around, Google's brand recognition is likely to help it create user stickiness.

According to Kunal, the best startups are those that succeed in creating both Delta 4 differentiation and powerful network effects.[19] This ensures rapid adoption as well as defensibility against a potential alternative that might come along in the future.

Before you start to build, try to gauge if your product or service is truly Delta 4.

Taking the plunge

Building often starts in earnest when founders decide to start working on their idea full time. Raghu advises arriving at this decision only once an idea has received some form of validation, especially from those who are likely to be actual customers of the product or service.

While Raghu and Aprameya got the idea of TaxiForSure in early 2010, they decided to devote themselves full time to the pursuit only much later in October, after their idea had been refined extensively, and validated by a large customer survey. 'We didn't quit [our jobs] when we got the idea. Only when customers loved the idea did we quit,' he says. It is only when customers tell you that your idea is amazing that you can be sure that you are on to something that could potentially be big, he says. They formally launched the company in June 2011.[20]

Nevertheless, Raghu admits that the decision to commit to your idea cannot always be perfectly rationalized. On many occasions, it is driven by a feeling in the gut. He offers an

---

[19]   Rishi Gaurav Bhatnagar, 'Kunal Shah's Delta-4 Theory', *Kunal Shah Talks*, 1 May 2020, kunalshahtalks.com/post/kunal-shah-delta-4-theory

[20]   Anand Daniel, 'Market Opportunities—The TaxiForSure Case Study', *YourStory.com*, 29 May 2018, yourstory.com/2018/05/market-opportunities-the-taxiforsure-case-study

analogy: How do you know if your romantic partner is the right person for you? 'Do you have a formula for it? You just get a feeling,' he says.

Entrepreneurship is similar. Before you take the plunge, there are likely to be apprehensions. 'But somewhere deep inside, you think this is the correct move. And you jump in,' he says. 'That is what entrepreneurship is about!'

Summary

- **Start with customer insight.** Great companies are built on the foundation of deep customer insights. Before you start building, as yourself what problem you are solving for customers.
- **Look to tap into broader trends shaping an industry.** Successfully tapping into macro trends will allow you to expand rapidly as market forces multiply your efforts. On the contrary, pushing against industry trends is unlikely to serve you well.
- **Seek customer feedback on your idea before you start building.** Before you start up, try to validate that the problem that you are looking to solve is one that is faced by a large number of people. Testing for this would help you understand whether the market for your product or service actually exists, and can support a large company. Then, try to understand if the solution itself resonates with potential customers.
- **Explore the existing set of solutions available for the problem you are trying to solve, and examine whether the proposed alternative is a substantial improvement.** The Delta 4 theory suggests that if an alternative is better than the existing solution by at least four points in terms of an

assigned 'efficiency score', an irreversible adoption of the new solution can take place.

- **In deciding to start a company, you have to trust your gut.** No amount of external validation can help you determine if, and when, you should become an entrepreneur. Ultimately, the answer lies within.

3

The Team

A T THE IDEA STAGE, a startup is but a vision. It needs a team to bring it to being, to build it, refine it and take it to market, to build an organization around it.

According to TaxiForSure founder Raghunanandan G, the market that a startup is seeking to serve is of paramount importance. A large market that can be successfully tapped and offer unbounded growth is crucial to the promise of a startup. The product is the means to serving the market; building and getting the product to the market is the raison d'etre of the startup. The team, however, is what makes the product possible in the first place.

Superlative success is only met in the presence of a great team. 'When a great team meets a great market, then something special happens! That's where the unicorns are really born,'

Raghu says.[1] If ideas are a dime a dozen and execution is everything, it is the founding team that first makes execution possible. Having the right team in place lies at the very core of a successful proposition.

Sharing the load

Startups require a tremendous amount of sweat and toil. They demand a diversity of skillsets, rarely possessed by a single individual. Moreover, startup journeys are rife with ups and downs; companionship helps ease the load. Having co-founders on the journey with you is likely to make it both easier and more enjoyable.

It's extremely difficult to run a startup. And if you are alone, it becomes a lot more demanding,' Raghu says. 'Not that one can't do it. It's probably not worth it.

It's better to do it with someone with whom you want to work.' As Y Combinator founder Paul Graham points out, a startup with multiple co-founders generates a powerful sense of esprit de corps, binding the team together, allowing them to continue pushing forward. This is missing when there is a single founder.[2]

The absence of others with a similar degree of skin in the game can also quickly suck out all the enjoyment that might

---

[1] Raghu references what is called Rachleff's Law here, named after legendary venture capitalist Andy Rachleff: 'The #1 company-killer is lack of market. When a great team meets a lousy market, market wins. When a lousy team meets a great market, market wins. When a great team meets a great market, something special happens.'

[2] Paul Graham, 'The 18 Mistakes That Kill Startups', *www.paulgraham.com*, October 2006, paulgraham.com/startupmistakes.html

otherwise stem from seeking to solve a problem, or build an organization together. If you are doing it with someone, it's a lot more fun, Raghu says. 'It is better to have a group of co-founders and have fun while you're building the startup.'

In the presence of one or more co-founders, there is an opportunity to distribute responsibility. Having a co-founder reduces key-person risk for the company, ensuring that operations are not paralysed in the case of illness, or emergency. It also allows for greater flexibility for each founder, making it easier to fashion individual roles so that they are in alignment with aptitude or interest. 'For instance, you don't want to deal with government authorities,' Raghu explains. 'Then the co-founder can pitch in and deal with them. As far as the government is concerned, they are speaking to the founder. They would prefer that rather than speaking with an employee.'

However, having too many co-founders is not advisable either, Raghu clarifies. 'You don't have to have a cricket team! Two or three is a good number.' When there are too many co-founders, a lot of time might get wasted in resolving differences between the founders, he points out. If there are many decision centres in the company, it might become harder to take decisions quickly. In addition, he says, even if you get a great exit, you are not going to make enough money. If equity is distributed among too many founders, it would reduce the payoff for any single founder. This would in turn reduce motivation to continue with the company through adverse situations.

Finding partners in crime

Most startup founders find co-founders among those they might have studied or worked together. While there also exist examples of a solo founder hiring a team of co-founders very consciously from among people they might not have personally known from before this is typically rarer. Since a co-founder would determine the company's direction, it is important to select one with great thought and care.

'The most important role of a co-founder is to be there for you when you are down, when you get punched in the gut,' says Y Combinator Partner Anu Hariharan. 'That's what you need from a co-founder.' Mutual trust, therefore, is of paramount importance; it is important to be able to believe that your co-founder will continue to stand with you, and if required, pick you up, when the chips are down. Often, such trust is forged through shared experiences. 'You have to have an extreme level of trust. That comes only with time. If you are picking a co-founder, it is ideal to have known them for a few years,' Anu says.

Anu notes that it is also important for individuals to have worked together at least on a side project before deciding to start a company together. 'Ideally, you should have done at least a side project with them so you really understand how well you work together,' she says. In fact, she points out, when Y Combinator tours universities as part of their outreach efforts, they recommend first year students to take the four years at university to do a lot of side projects with a few friends who have similar interests. This can allow them to understand who they can work with well. Starting a company with somebody who you might only have socialized with across four years at university, but not necessarily worked together with, does not necessarily work out. 'Many times, people take the shorter route, which is saying we are good friends, let's try to do something together. It doesn't always work. There may be a fifty-fifty chance of it working out, but I would say not even fifty-fifty. At YC, it works out less than 20 per cent of the time,' Anu says.

In offering an example of a founding team that works well together, Anu brings up Groww, an online investment platform that allows investors to invest in mutual funds and stocks. The founding team consists of Lalit Keshare, Harsh Jain, Neeraj Singh and Ishan Bansal. All of them had worked at Flipkart before founding their startup. Lalit and Harsh were part of the same team at Flipkart, had worked closely together and knew each other well. They needed someone to take care of engineering. Neeraj, who had worked as an engineer with them, joined as the chief technology officer (CTO). Since they were building a company that was to offer a finance-based product, they needed a strong CFO from the start, which is how Ishan joined. Having known each other and worked together at Flipkart, there was a high degree of trust among the four individuals which helped them come together.

In addition, in deciding upon a co-founder, it is important to find someone who has the same ambition for the company, and is equally determined to make the company successful, Anu says. It is also vital that they be able to prioritize the company over their individual selves, if needed. Anu offers the example of Pedro and Henrique, the co-founders of the financial services company Brex. 'Soon after starting the company, they stood in front of the entire company at an offsite event,' Anu narrates, 'and said, look, we ourselves are twenty-one, there's only so much we know, there's only so many people that we can coach at scale. What is important is we put Brex first. We will find all the help in the world that we can for you, for us, for everybody. But when we realize we're not the right person at a point in time to lead a function, we have to bring people in who know how to lead that function and scale. Because at the end of the day, there's only one thing that matters, the company needs to be successful.' Anu points out that the in the case of Airbnb, co-founder Nate Blecharczyk was prepared to do whatever was required of him to make the company successful. He started off as the first engineer, then became the CTO, then head of

China and then the chief strategy officer because it was what the company required of him. 'For a co-founder, the company has to be like their baby. They have to always be prepared to do what is required to make the company successful,' Anu says. 'And if the founding team doesn't do that, the employees will smell it.'

Finally, when looking for a co-founder, it is also useful to have complementarity of skills. 'You don't want both co-founders doing everything because then everything is going to break. You want to divide and conquer,' Anu says. Co-founders should be able to take up different functions within the company. For instance, one founder could carry out fundraising while the other oversees engineering and continues to build the product. 'However, it is not strictly necessary,' Anu says. 'As co-founders, you should all be open to wearing multiple hats.'[3]

Select for values

While complementarity of skills is useful, it is critical to have compatibility in terms of values. It is values that determine the long-term complementarity of founders, and determine whether a startup will grow sustainably.

TaxiForSure founder Raghu suggests that when it comes to the founding team, values are a lot more important than skills. 'What you need to look at are the core values of the person you are trying to build your founding team with. Do they have the necessary drive? Are they curious? Are they passionate? That's what essentially matters. If someone is passionate, if someone

---

[3]   Sampath Putrevu, '[The Turning Point] How Three Colleagues Identified the Friction in the Way India Used EMI and Solved It with ZestMoney', *YourStory.com*, 14 December 2019, yourstory. com/2019/12/the-turning-point-zestmoney-emi

has the drive, they will acquire the skills required to succeed. Just because someone has the right skills, they will not necessarily acquire the drive and the passion and the curiosity. So don't try to build a co-founding team which only has the right skills.'

According to Raghu, there is often a tendency to over-index on skills, especially technical skills.[4] However, the skills needed to run a company evolve over the course of the company's growth. Values and inter-personal equations are more enduring. 'The necessity of skills is overrated. You would probably be using those skills for one or two years, not more than that,' he says. 'The reality is, once a startup gets to a particular stage, you, as a founder, will not be building products or writing code or carrying out marketing.' Instead, these things will start getting taken care of by the larger team. 'You will be building the organization, focusing on building the culture of the company, on addressing HR issues, on fundraising, and such,' he says. Skills that may be extremely important for the founding team may not be required once the startup gets to a

---

[4] 'That's essentially what we do at college as well,' Raghu says. 'We focus more on strategy courses, we focus more on operations courses, logistics courses. We don't focus much on HR, organizational behaviour, and other such courses,' he says, referencing the fact that courses on softer skills are often underrated in Indian business schools. 'But whether you are part of a startup, or you are part of a corporate, you get to a stage very soon when you will not be doing strategy, you'll not be doing operations, you'll not be doing logistics. You'll essentially be building organizations, trying to motivate the team to achieve something in life, hiring people, letting go of people, addressing HR issues, and things like that. But we focus more on accounting, strategy. You can get people to do all that for you. But no one else is essentially going to help you build the organization, drive the culture of the company, deal with HR issues and so on.' That is something that the founders have to do.

more mature stage. 'The problem with us is we give too much onus to something in the short term, and miss the big picture,' Raghu says. 'But you are not necessarily going to have a co-founder only for the first one or two years. This co-founder has to last the life of the startup. That is more important.' For that, intrinsic traits, such as inherent curiosity, a certain drive for success, a sense of integrity, a perspective informed by a compatible set of ethics, matter a lot more than skills, he says.

He goes on to say that while a co-founder with the right skill set will solve short-term problems, bigger problems might emerge with time if they do not have the right intrinsic values. 'You are essentially married to the co-founder,' he says. 'As the company matures, you need to be able to continue working together for the company to succeed. It would be difficult to replace the co-founder at a later stage. It would create far too much chaos in the company.' However, if the co-founder is not fulfilling the needs of their role once the company has grown bigger, and is not able to work together well, then that is not an ideal situation.

Raghu's advice therefore is to not go for a co-founder simply because of certain skills that you might be missing at the outset. 'What you really need to ask is: what are the kinds of skills that would essentially build a strong foundation? After that, every other skill can be acquired,' he says.

Instead, Raghu advises looking at the values of potential co-founders and how these might interact with yours. 'Your value systems essentially have to converge. The co-founders must share the same ambition, but not always the same aspiration,' he says. He illustrates this with a pertinent example. 'If you look at most startups, you hear one person's name more than that of the others. One person ends up becoming the face of the startup, and gets most of the media coverage. If each of the co-founders have the same aspiration for media coverage then it starts leading to conflicts. And one might not be so broad-minded to express such an aspiration, but the conflict will start showing itself in different ways.'

According to Raghu, a majority of startups in India have failed because of co-founder conflicts. Not because the market was bad, or the product was bad, or because they were not able to raise funding. In fact, he says, often one of the reasons for not being able to raise funding is that investors sense conflict between founders, and choose to not invest even though they might not reveal this as the reason.[5] 'The problem with Indian venture capitalists is they don't tell the co-founders that this is the problem,' Raghu says.

During the course of building the startup, there will, undoubtedly, be crises and periods of uncertainty. These could make it very stressful to continue running the company. It is important to have a co-founder that you can rely on and continue working with during such periods. 'You just have to look at the other person and consider whether you can live with that person in their worst moment,' Raghu points out. 'And also vice versa: whether they can put up with you in your worst moments. You are being pushed to the wall and the way you are going to behave, the way you are going to react, will they be fine with that?' There will, invariably, be testing times. What will determine whether the startup endures, or falls along the

---

[5]   Anand Daniel, partner in the venture capital firm Accel India, confirms this. 'One of the biggest reasons we have seen startups flounder is due to [bad] chemistry between co-founders. If the chemistry is not good, then it is a red flag.'

wayside, will be the founders' ability to put up with each other at their worst.

'Something somewhere is not falling into place, something is really bothering you, and one day you take it out on the team or on your co-founder. As long as your co-founder can be understanding, and give you space, it will be possible to deal with such situations.' However, if you get together with someone who makes it a lot more difficult for you by not being understanding while you are already in a stressful situation, it can become difficult to continue working together over a long period of time. 'So don't invest in skills, figure out whether you will be able to deal with that person during their worst crisis or not,' Raghu says.

Distributing equity

Equity distribution amongst the founding team must be decided upon with great care and a view to the long-term success of the startup. It has to be carried out with transparency and deliberation, with all co-founders getting on the same page.

While multiple factors bear looking into before deciding upon equity distribution, including the source of inspiration for the startup and how the team envisages the role of each of the co-founders, the ultimate distribution must be one that is arrived at with consensus. When equity distribution is not carried out thoughtfully, it can easily burgeon into misunderstandings and discontentment. Often, this can provide the powder and spark that can result in the startup breaking up eventually.

Unless there is a clear justification for differential stakes, Delhivery founder Sahil Barua suggests that it might be better to start with a more equal split. 'Most companies where I have seen unequal stakes, there has always been a very weird founder dynamic. Where companies have had three, or four, or seven founders, whatever the case might be, one always becomes an alpha founder if they don't have that level of equity in the company. What tends to happen over time is that if you were to talk to different members of that team, they would not be able to describe the business in the same way. They would not have the same understanding of the business.'

Delhivery started with almost an equal distribution of equity amongst the founders as well as a clearly articulated role for each co-founder, and hence has been able to overcome such a situation. 'At Delhivery, if you talk to me or any of the other co-founders, you ask them what is it that Delhivery does, what is your strategy, what are your plans, what do you think is important when you run this business, you will pretty much get the same answer from every one of us. I think that dynamic does get messed up, especially as the business gets larger. The last thing you want to think about is who is putting in how much effort. It's just not the right way to do it.'

It is also ideal to finalize equity distribution early in the life of the company. Delaying it could drive uncertainty, with co-founders wondering what their share in the company might be. As former president of Y Combinator, Sam Altman, says, it is better to have the discussion early than to let it sit there and fester.[6] An early-stage team needs a fully invested team, focused on building the company instead of wondering about their place in it.

---

[6]   Sam Altman, 'Lecture 2: Ideas, Products, Teams and Execution Part II', *How to Start a Startup*, startupclass.samaltman.com/courses/lec02

Division of roles

Division of roles within the team must be carried out based on an analysis of individual skill sets, a shared understanding of ways of working together, and on who gets their energy from pursuing which activity.

At Delhivery, responsibility across the five co-founders got split based on an individual's inclination as well as the experience that they had had previously. Kapil Bharati who had a tech background became their CTO; Bhavesh Manglani and Suraj Saharan both had experience with operations and took up operations at the company; Mohit Tandon became their point person for managing partnerships with other companies. This left Sahil with the task of managing the team. In addition, Sahil also took charge of the company's finances as well as modelling the optimal logistics network for the company. 'I had no specific skills is one way to look at it, so that's where I ended up,' he says.

According to Sahil, it helped, from the standpoint of splitting responsibility, that none of them was an expert in what any of the others did. And as the company grew, each person's expertise became more and more refined. 'We could not manage each other's jobs. So, by definition, we had division of labour,' says Sahil. The founders had been close friends since long before they started the company together, and they had an easy camaraderie amongst them. 'There was not much jostling within the team to prove our worth. There was no question of stepping on toes.'

At the outset, they arrived at a simple mechanism to resolve decision-making deadlocks. In the case of a deadlock, Sahil would cast the deciding vote. And they stuck to that. 'That's something that we've been pretty respectful of as a group,' Sahil says.

On the matter of division of labour, TaxiForSure founder Raghu cautions that when an individual is assigned responsibility for a part of the company, that allocation must be absolute. Responsibility cannot be tokenized and distributed across multiple individuals. 'Collective responsibility becomes nobody's responsibility,' he says. Having said that, when the need arises, there must be easy fluidity within roles at the early stage. 'When there is problem, it's all hands on deck, regardless of who has taken up which responsibility. A co-founder cannot be sitting and waiting for a crisis to blow over, simply because, say, marketing is not his or her domain, while the other co-founder is slogging.'

Finally, especially at this stage of the company, the founders must remain open to having disagreements, even with clearly delineated responsibilities. In fact, Raghu points out, disagreements must be normalized, that they are actually healthy and desirable. Disagreements can diversify perspectives, generate new ideas and drive growth. 'We had fights all the time, as there should be. If there are no disagreements, if there is no creative tension, you are not going anywhere,' he quips.

Building an early team, brick by brick

Even before they had a team or even a product, Raghu and Aprameya started to meet potential investors. During such meetings, as Raghu and Aprameya walked them through their idea, investors evinced interest and said that they addressed an interesting problem. But invariably, they would be asked if they could demonstrate any traction that they were witnessing. At this stage, they did not have any product to speak of. They had an idea which they found promising, but had not executed it. And so, they would demur and seek more time.

Raghu and Aprameya soon realized that convincing investors required definite proof of concept. They had to build a product first and get real users. While both were graduate engineers from NIT Surathkal, their subsequent two-year management education and post-MBA roles had put paid to their software development skills. They were in no position to build a product themselves. They needed individuals with the technical skills to translate their idea into a real product.

They immediately scrambled to find batchmates from their undergraduate days with strong engineering skills. 'We were engineers who had done an MBA,' says Raghu. 'Our engineering friends who had not made that choice were in technical roles. We thought they would help us.' They were quickly disabused of the notion. 'We realized that all my engineering friends in Bangalore were married and had kids,' explains Raghu. 'We had our education loans, they had their housing loans. They wanted us to pay the EMIs [Equated Monthly Installment].' With Raghu and Aprameya having left their own jobs to pursue their idea, this was not a viable proposition. Their next move was to seek aid from siblings and cousins. That did not work out either. They found themselves with a promising idea, interest from investors conditional upon demonstrating traction, but no team to translate their idea into a product.

They began to look for collaborators by attending startup events, alumni events and conferences such as those organized by The IndUS Entrepreneurs (TiE); anybody who could help them build the first version of their product. During one such event, they were introduced to an engineer who had recently exited his company and was looking for an employment opportunity. He eventually came on board, and started building the first version of their product.

With an engineer on board, they began working on the product in earnest. He worked part time with them, on a salary that Raghu and Aprameya could pay out of their savings. They started around seven in the evening and worked till midnight.

The only language that he knew well was Python, in the Django framework. So the product was built on Python Django. They did not fully explore potential alternatives or whether it was the right product decision, and whether the platform was flexible enough to meet scalability demands they were likely to face if the product did well. 'There was not much research done,' says Raghu. They were relieved that they could start building the product. In the end though, it worked out well for them. It turned out that Python Django was the right platform for the product; its framework lent itself perfectly to rapidly building a secure website that was both scalable and easily maintainable. It took them close to forty-five days to build their first website. They finally had a product.

However, their new hire had not joined as a full-time employee, and eventually left after a disagreement. Raghu and Aprameya were back to being a twosome.

Around this time, Raghu was travelling to meet his wife who was then working in Singapore. His flight was delayed by half an hour. He started to search on the internet for engineers who could code in Django. He stumbled across Django Gigs, a platform for job postings for Django developers, sent a short mail describing their plans to all the thirty-eight people who came up in his search for India coders. By the time he landed, three had responded. One of them was willing to come on board full time if they could match his existing salary. Neither of them was receiving a salary at this point. It was a difficult proposition, but they agreed.

He became their first permanent employee, and a perfect one at that. He was committed to the organization and was willing to wear multiple hats. He carried out product upgrades, received customer calls and took on other ad hoc responsibilities in the office. This allowed Raghu and Aprameya to focus on business-development activities. More importantly, he understood their business, and was willing to challenge their assumptions, instead of simply taking orders. Raghu notes that they made amazing progress with their work after he joined.

A well-functioning early team can turbocharge a startup's growth. On the flipside, a poorly functioning team can be crippling. This is why Flipkart founder Sachin Bansal cautions against hiring a 'B team' early on, even if it might mean holding out slightly longer before putting together a team. 'We were resolved to do the job ourselves rather than hire somebody who was not better than us,' Sachin says. He does, however, acknowledge that recruitment is often the biggest challenge for an early-stage startup. High-quality talent can be expensive, and startups are often unwilling, or unable to pay well.

Hiring their early team was not easy for Flipkart. They were cash-strapped, and their cubbyhole office did not inspire much confidence either when prospective candidates chanced upon it. 'The first software engineer we interviewed was from Amazon,' Sachin says. They had connected with her over LinkedIn, and asked her to come down to their office for an interview. She had agreed. 'I remember our first office was really shabby. If you have seen chawls in Mumbai, it was almost like that. So Binny is on the phone, trying to give directions to the software engineer, and I am chasing away the dog. Then she called and said she could not find the place, and she was gone. She probably saw the place from outside, and left,' he laughs.

Notwithstanding such setbacks, they sought to fill the company with great people, he says. And when they erred in hiring, they were quick to make amends. 'From very early on, we were selective with our hiring. If the person was not working out well for the company, we let them go very quickly,' Sachin says.

Talent might have been elusive, but the Flipkart founders were unwilling to lower the bar. That, in their minds, was not the solution. They were convinced of the potential of the market they were seeking to serve; they quite rightly believed that the e-commerce market in India was going to be one of the largest in the world. And they knew they had to have a winning team in place.

Summary

- **Sharing the load makes for an easier journey.** Starting up is often easier in the presence of one or more co-founders. A startup often demands a diversity of skills that is rarely possessed by a single individual. Moreover, having a co-founder creates a sense of camaraderie that can push the company forward in times of adversity.

- **Select for values when choosing a co-founder.** While skills might be useful, complementarity of values amongst founders is a lot more important. It is what determines whether the founders are able to work together effectively over the long term to build the company.

- **Ensure there is skin in the game.** Ensure that equity distribution amongst founders is carried out with fairness and transparency without disproportionate concentration in a single individual. This will make certain that every founding member is invested in the success of the endeavour.

- **Decide on specific roles within the company** for every team member. Every person in the need must be assigned a specific responsibility and must be accountable. Role allocation can be carried out based on individual skill-sets, personal aspirations and shared understanding of ways of working together.
- **Build an 'A' team.** A well-functioning early team can set up a company for rapid expansion. A poorly functioning team can hobble a company at the outset itself. While it might be hard to hire high-functioning team-members initially, do not settle for a 'B' team.

4

The Product

THE PRODUCT IS WHAT customers interact with, what they pay for. It is the startup idea distilled and manifested. A startup is defined by the product that it takes to market.

The act of building a product can be broadly split into three stages: creating a minimum viable version of the product that is likely to be embraced by a small set of users in the identified target segment, launching it to the market, and thereafter iteratively improving the product based on user feedback. In this chapter, we focus on the first stage, with the subsequent two stages covered in the next chapter.

Find your niche

Product-market fit lies at the heart of a successful startup. It is what determines whether the product is likely to be enthusiastically embraced by a loyal set of users, or only receive tepid attention at best. The former is the path to rapid growth, the latter is more likely to lead to the startup eventually fizzling out.

In the early days of a startup, it is especially important to focus on a small segment of the market where it might be easier to achieve Product-market fit. According to renowned entrepreneur and venture capitalist Peter Thiel, it is always a big mistake to go after a giant market on day one.[1] In a large market, there is going to be too much competition from the outset. Instead, he advises going after a small market, and then expanding. When Amazon first opened, it only sold books. But, Thiel says, it was online, and it offered a new way of buying books; gradually, they could expand to other forms of e-commerce, and then beyond.[2]

When Freshworks started, they realized that they could succeed more easily if, instead of targeting the same set of enterprise clients that established SaaS companies were going after, they identified a niche that had relatively lower competition.

The SaaS model typically works on building one product, and going after revenue expansion through a sales-driven approach. It is contingent on hiring more and more salespersons, and setting them large targets. According to

---

[1] Peter Thiel, 'Lecture 5—Competition Is for Losers', *How to Start a Startup*, startupclass.samaltman.com/courses/lec05

[2] Entrepreneur and investor Sam Altman concurs when he says that it is better to build something that a small number of users *love the product*, than a large number of users who just *like the product*. He asserts, 'It's much easier to expand from something that a small number of people *love* to something that *a lot* of people love, than from something a lot of people *like* to a lot of people *love*.' Sam Altman, 'Lecture 1: Welcome, and Ideas, Products, Teams and Execution Part I', *How to Start a Startup*, startupclass. samaltman.com/courses/lec01

Freshworks' founder Girish, when the company started, for a typical sales representative at a US SaaS company would lie in the range of $140–200 thousand. The typical annual sales target would lie in the $1–1.4 million range. This could be achieved with two to three deals with mid-market or large enterprise clients with a deal size of $50–100 thousand per month. The salary and target structure incentivized going after larger clients.

An India-based SaaS company's economics could be entirely different. The salary range for a typical sales representative would be $25–30 thousand annually, one-sixth to one-eight that in the US. A SaaS company could set a monthly target of $30–40 thousand per representative, and still be highly profitable. Moreover, such a target could be achieved not only by pursuing a small number of high-value clients, but also with a larger number of small ticket price clients. A salesperson could execute 20–25 deals a month, with an average ticket price of $1,500, and still meet their target.

This was not simply a matter of having a cost arbitrage, Girish says It was a new way of going to the market which opened up a new set of customers who were on no one else's radar earlier because they couldn't be served by the prevailing economics of US-based SaaS companies. While US-based SaaS companies were going for 'elephant hunting', Girish explains, Freshworks decided to go for 'deer and rabbit hunting', targeting a set of much smaller clients. This differentiated approach early on paved the way for their success.

Electric vehicle company Ather Energy was founded by two engineering graduates from IIT Madras, Tarun Mehta and Swapnil Jain. Tarun and Swapnil had spent a lot of time during their undergraduate days tinkering in engineering labs. Building physical products excited them. In their final year at IIT Madras, they chose to work on a project on electric vehicles. During the course of their research, they realized that most people in India were still using lead acid batteries, not lithium-ion ones. Since it seemed that nobody was building lithium-ion battery packs in India, they started exploring the idea of building a company that would.

However, they soon realized that there were not enough electric vehicles being used in India for the battery packs to find a market. So they decided to build an electric vehicle instead of just a battery pack. More people in India bought two-wheelers than cars, they reasoned, and so decided to focus on building two-wheelers. The vehicles would run on one of the cleanest forms of energy. So they named the company after the Greek word for 'pure'.

Explaining the electric scooter market, Tarun says, 'In 2012, a typical electric scooter had a top speed of 25 km/hr, ran on a 250-watt battery giving about 0.3 horsepower, resulting in poor acceleration. Batteries were lead-acid and would run out of juice in 5,000 km resulting in the need to change the battery in eight to twelve months, and required six to eight hours of charging.' This did not make for a happy experience. However, the vehicles were priced relatively inexpensively at ₹30,000–35,000. This was cheaper than a typical petrol scooter.

'We spoke to the people who were building these vehicles, we spoke to dealers selling the vehicles. Their thesis made sense. They said, "Look at China—exactly the same vehicle with sales of 30 million every year." This is twice the sale of the overall Indian two-wheeler market. We are talking about the same vehicle which is cheaper than the petrol version and six to eight times cheaper to run. What's wrong with this thesis? Why won't everybody who can't afford to buy and run a petrol two-wheeler buy it?"' However, sales of electric vehicles made up less than

0.1 per cent of the Indian two-wheeler market. What explained this dichotomy between what the electric vehicle manufacturers were projecting and the actual demand in the market?

According to Tarun, while their thesis seemed sound on paper, they were going after the wrong customer segment. 'Their definition of a prospective consumer was pretty simple: someone from a low-income segment who wants a very cheap, probably safe vehicle. It could have probably sold if the lower-income segment had trust in the product, if electricity availability was not a problem for that, and if they could believe the requisite infrastructure was available to charge these vehicles. But none of this was true at that point.' This persuaded Tarun to probe further.

'At that time, the people who were actually looking to buy electric vehicles were those who probably had a Honda car parked in their garage. They were not looking for the cheapest two-wheeler in the market. What they were looking for was a good story,' he says. What electric vehicle manufacturers were telling prospective buyers at the time was that the product was environment-friendly, but they would need to compromise on speed, quality, reliability, comfort and looks. On top of that, the buyer will 'look like a dork riding that scooter,' Tarun quips. 'It was a disaster sales pitch and that was the reason electric vehicles were not selling a great deal.'

Tarun realized that, at least in a short run, the Indian electric scooter market will not grow the China way—by the government mandating the usage of electric vehicles and banning petrol scooters—and will probably grow the US way. 'If you look at the US, clearly the only thing that was working was this very cool vehicle—Tesla. Nothing else was taking off.' In looking at Tesla, Tarun realized that they had to go after a higher-income segment with an aspirational product if they were to sell electric vehicles in India.

Having refined their hypothesis, they went back to prospective customers of electric vehicles that they had come to know during their research. 'We asked them: What if we built a vehicle that would give 3x speed, 20x more power, have a 10x longer battery, lighter than their petrol scooters and have more storage space? The only catch here was that we decided to charge 35 per cent more than the average two-wheeler. The first five people we met were ready to pay ₹85,000 upfront for the scooter.' This formed the premise for their product. They would build an electric vehicle that offered superior specifications, and would be offered at a premium price. They would look to target a niche, and expand outwards once they had captured the niche.

Build subject matter expertise

Once you have honed in on a customer segment that would value your product, the next step is to understand the broader ecosystem within which their needs exist. Successful founders develop an exhaustive understanding of each individual component of the customer problem they are trying to solve, the business ecosystem in which it exists, and the modus operandi of existing players. Being the foremost subject matter expert is the first step in coming up with a compelling solution.

When the founders of logistics service provider Delhivery were starting out in 2011, they had decided they would focus on serving e-commerce players. Between 2009 and 2011, online commerce had seen explosive growth in India. Flipkart had raised their first round of investment in 2009, and since then even relatively young startups had been attracting investor interest. The founders had identified logistics as a common crucial challenge that every online retailer would invariably face.[3] However, before they could start building a solution, they had to understand what it was that existing players could not provide. So they went to every e-commerce company they could to better understand the market landscape.

What founders of e-commerce companies told them was that their biggest problem, as a B2C company, was that they were essentially outsourcing their consumer experience to their logistics partner. During this time, the logistics partners of choice were the traditional incumbents. When the retailers shipped a box, it would take three to five days to get to the consumer. They did not have a way to track their shipment along the route. Delays in order delivery, and the lack of a robust tracking mechanism, meant a suboptimal customer experience.

However, that was not the only issue that they were facing. At the time, the vast majority of orders in India were being paid for using the cash-on-delivery mode. Traditional retailers had not built systems to get this cash back to the retailers, this was not a solution that their business had been built to provide. This often meant delays, which in turn adversely impacted the retailers' ability to keep their operations running smoothly in a cash-dependent ecosystem.

Next, the founders went to one of the incumbent logistics players in the market, telling them that they wanted to start a business in transportation. Perhaps through hubris by virtue of being the dominant player in the market, perhaps through

---

[3] Anu Thomas, 'Missing Package? Delhivery's New Software to Automatically Correct Inaccurate Addresses', *The Economic Times*, 23 August 2017, economictimes.indiatimes. com/small-biz/startups/missing-package-delhiverys-new-software-to-automatically-correct-inaccurate-addresses/ articleshow/60185972.cms

poor judgement, the company opened up their operations for inspection. 'They actually opened up all of their systems to us, and they said we were welcome to visit all their hubs and distribution centres. So, we went and looked at them,' says founder Sahil Barua.

What their market research revealed was that the traditional logistics providers were simply unprepared to fulfil the needs of e-commerce companies. 'We realized that existing players in India at that point were simply unaware of what was coming their way through e-commerce,' Sahil says. Their operations were not digitized, and they continued to offer handwritten waybills when orders were placed. This meant delays in processing orders; often, a shipment would not have moved even eight to ten hours after the order was placed. This also meant that the companies could not instantaneously provide information on the expected delivery date and the shipment status.

'If you have ever bought things online, you would realize that does not align with what customers expect,' Sahil says. 'The second somebody makes a purchase online, they want to know when they are going to receive their shipment. They actually expect both the e-commerce company as well as the fulfilment partner to have real-time information on this.'

To the Delhivery founders, there seemed to be three problems that, if they were to solve, they could gain market share at the expense of the traditional logistics players.

The first problem was that the existing players simply failed to recognize the value of cash in the economy. Logistics companies had never dealt with cash until the e-commerce boom started. All of them were designed to operate based on prepaid modes, getting paid for shipments and then delivering them.

'This was the first time that someone was saying, you take my products one way and bring my cash back the other,' says Sahil.

'What the logistics companies really missed was that while one part of their business was transportation and warehousing, there was another part which was actually a payment gateway; a giant offline payment gateway which over time would have to transact billions of dollars of cash annually with complete fidelity.' It was a system they were completely unprepared to build.

The Delhivery founders, on the other hand, were fully clued in early on with regard to the importance of solving the cash-management issue. Over and over again, they had heard from founders of online retailers that 90 per cent of their cash volume was from delivery; 'you need to figure out how to bring this cash back to me,' the retailers had urged. And so they designed to solve it at the outset itself. They decided to build a payment gateway on top of their operating servers right at the start.

The second problem that they identified was that the incumbent players were simply not equipped to provide real-time operations. 'None of the existing courier companies at the time were equipped to provide real-time information. They were still operating off old manual systems which they had built in the late '90s, without understanding that they now had the tools to offer real-time updates,' says Sahil. This was a technology problem which could be addressed through available technology solutions. They decided to invest heavily in technology and automation. Not only did this help them provide a better customer experience, but over time also drove better network speed, and reliability, while reducing costs.

The third problem with incumbent players was in the engineering of their networks. 'Typically, the larger a logistics company and the greater the diversity of products it handles, the more it moves towards a hub-and-spoke model,' explains Sahil. 'The challenge with the hub-and-spoke model is the number of times a parcel is handled as it moves through the network, because you are trying to move it through a specific set of aggregation points. The trouble with this model in e-commerce is it slows you down and increases the cost at which you operate.'

E-commerce companies in India, most of them startups themselves, were already bleeding money to acquire customers and build scale. They could not afford high costs. 'So one of the major challenges we had to recognize was that we were going to operate in an environment in which our customers were dramatically cost-sensitive,' Sahil says. Instead of a traditional hub-and-spoke model, they decided to use a distributed model where every branch could function like a hub as well as a processing centre. They could route packages directly to the customer, avoiding parking it in the hub.[4]

Their close examination of both of the needs of their potential customers, as well as how their competitors operated, empowered the founders to build significant competitive advantages into their operating model. In fact, Sahil goes to the extent of describing their future customers and their competitors as their first set of business partners. 'Our customers because they helped us by defining needs for which we were able to co-develop solutions with them, and our competitors because they actually helped us figure out how to grow our business in the first place.'

The insights that they gained in the early days of building their company laid the foundations of their eventual success. In developing a deep understanding of the market in which they were looking to operate, they set themselves up perfectly to win.

---

[4] Goutam Das, 'Coolest Start-ups: Supply-Chain Enabler Delhivery Is Rising Rapidly', *Business Today*, 13 April 2014, *businesstoday*, in/magazine/cover-story/coolest-start-up-in-india-2014-delhivery/story/204527.html

Lead with a minimum viable product

The minimum viable product, in the words of Eric Ries, author of *The Lean Startup,* is that version of a new product (MVP) which allows a team to collect the maximum amount of validated learning about customers with the least effort.[5] A minimum viable product would be one that would only contain critical features, with the objective being to gather feedback from customers, and iteratively build a better product.

The term was first coined in 2001 by Frank Robinson, CEO of SyncDev, a California-based company, focused on developing new products, markets and businesses through a lean product-development process. It was later popularized by American entrepreneur Steve Blank, and Eric Ries. A focus on MVP development is a core element of the lean startup movement that aims to shorten product-development cycles and rapidly discover if a proposed business model is viable.

There are three core principles of the lean method:[6]

1. Instead of engaging in months of planning and research, the lean method notes that early on in the life of a startup, a founder is only likely to have a series of untested hypotheses with regard to the business model. The lean method encourages founders to summarize their hypotheses in a framework called a business-model canvas, essentially a diagram of how a company creates value for itself and its customers.

---

[5] Eric Ries, 'Minimum Viable Product: A Guide', *Startup Lessons Learned,* 3 August 2009, http://www.startuplessonslearned. com/2009/08/minimum-viable-product-guide.html

[6] Steve Blank, 'Why the Lean Start-up Changes Everything', *Harvard Business Review,* May 2013.

2. It emphasizes the importance of repeatedly engaging with potential users, purchasers and partners for feedback on all elements of the business model, including product features, pricing, distribution channels and affordable customer acquisition strategies. Releasing a minimum viable product is a core element in receiving such feedback.

3. Lean startups practise agile development which focuses on iterative, incremental development instead of long development cycles. The objective is to create a series of minimum viable products that may then be tested. Agile development eliminates wasted time and resources by developing the product iteratively and incrementally.

According to Eric Ries, the idea of a minimum viable product is useful because it allows a company to build a product that aims to solve a core problem for early adopters of the solution. Even if there are certain features missing in the solution, such early adopters are likely to be more forgiving. And so, building a minimum viable product 'allows you to ship a product that resonates with early adopters, some of whom will pay you money or give you feedback'.[7] Based on such feedback, the team could then start the development cycle over again, testing redesigned offerings and making either small adjustments (iterations) or more substantive ones (pivots) to ideas that aren't working.[30]

Building an MVP not only allows for rapid improvements based on customer feedback, but also helps create conviction in the inherent feasibility of the product. 'Though every product has magic in it, you can't be sure of the magic on paper,' Tarun

---

[7]   Eric Ries, 'Venture Hacks Interview: "What Is the Minimum Viable Product?"', *Startup Lessons Learned*, 23 March 2009, www.startuplessonslearned.com/2009/03/minimum-viable-product.html

says. 'To me, the biggest point of building an MVP is discovering the magic for yourself, because you've got to sell that magical story many times over to many people, to team members that you will hire, to investors that you will bring in, everybody. For you to be able to sell that magic, you need to experience it yourself first. The MVP helps you do that. Otherwise, you're working on borrowed statements and visions, and that's hard.'

An MVP signals a willingness to go beyond a mere paper plan. As a manifestation of the core product idea, it can drive real and immediate credibility in the eyes of external stakeholders. In the case of a hardware player like Ather, an MVP can allow you to stand apart from the crowd especially when you are approaching investors. Not every potential competitor exploring a similar idea is likely to have gone to the trouble of building an MVP. 'I believe we got the first three rounds of funding because we were the only ones in the electric vehicle ecosystem who had built an actual vehicle. A few others, I do believe, were considering the idea, but never built an MVP,' Tarun says.

In his book, *The Startup Owner's Manual*, Steve Blank states that there are three key questions that a startup team must look to use the MVP to answer:[8]

- Do we really understand the customer's problem or need?
- Do enough people care about the problem or need to deliver a huge business?
- And will they care enough to tell their friends, to grow our business quickly?

---

[8]   Steve Blank and Bob Dorf, *The Startup Owner's Manual: The Step-By-Step Guide for Building a Great Company* (Wiley, 2020), p. 189.

According to Blank, in building the MVP, you must start by asking yourself what you want to learn, and what is the simplest test that you could run to learn this. And then you should think about how to design an experiment that could help carry out this test.

Ideally, an MVP should be easy to build and modify. In fact, Blank argues that for a startup with a web- or mobile-based product, the MVP could be as simple as a landing page with the product's core value proposition, a summary of the key benefits and a call-to-action inviting users to learn more, answer a short survey or pre-order.

In the case of service-provider startup Urban Company, their MVP was a fairly skeletal website which users could get on and place orders. The team would then work with service professionals to fulfil these orders. In releasing their MVP, they were looking to understand whether the pricing that they had in place would work for the service categories they were looking to carry. The MVP, as Urban Company founder Abhiraj Bhal describes it, was only a slightly improved version of a Google form. They had coded it on JavaScript, and put it out, their philosophy having been 'let's launch it, and learn from it'.

In building their first MVP, Abhiraj says that they erred on the side of 'putting a pretty embarrassing product out in the market', and choosing to learn from market feedback rather than trying to get a perfectly built product launched. 'I think our first product was excruciatingly embarrassing,' he laughs.

They continued iterating with a series of MVPs over a period of two months, exploring new categories, dropping others. Initially, their model was built on generating leads that would be serviced by service partners. Through a process of iteration, they eventually pivoted to a full-stack, fully controlled marketplace model for Urban Company.

Building an MVP for a hardware product can be more challenging. It is likely to require working with physical materials, and may take more time and energy. However, even in this case, the objective of building the MVP is not to build a prototype for the final product, but to test initial assumptions about potential customers, and the market.

In the case of hardware products, Steve Blank advises first reaching out to a set of fifty target customers, sharing with them an assumed list of problems that you believe they have, and getting them to talk about whether you're missing any problems, how they would rank the problems, and which are must-solve rather than nice-to-solve. Blank suggests summarizing the discussion with two key questions:

- What's the biggest pain in how you work?
- If you could wave a magic wand and change anything about what you do, what would it be?

Only after gaining a complete understanding of the customer, Blank argues, should you expose the product to a potential customer for the first time. While this approach is not fundamentally different from that for software products, it acknowledges the inherent physical constraints placed by hardware in exposing the product to customers.

According to Tarun, the biggest mistake they made in building the MVP was spending time on including features that were fundamentally extraneous at that point in the product journey. They had started tinkering in a lab at IIT Madras in early 2013, putting together their MVP. Looking back, Tarun believes they took too long in coming up with what should have been a fairly rudimentary MVP.

'I don't think we truly understood what we were really doing with an MVP,' he says. 'To some extent, we were actually a little lost, thinking that this is likely to be the final vehicle, which was, in retrospect, extremely naive.'

They ended up building features that Tarun says could have been easily skipped at that stage. 'We built a frame, got the wheels, chose suspensions, tested them out, started assembling all of them together, did a whole bunch of tests and quite a few simulations,' he rues. 'Then we put the entire vehicle together. We built a few batteries, put the batteries in there, got a few motors, assembled the motors. Then we built the transmissions, started with the chain transmission, then a belt transmission, put all of that together and ran the vehicle.'

'Before you kickstart the MVP, you are often confused about what you're really testing for. In our case, I think all we were testing for was a fast electric scooter. A really fun scooter with a dashboard on your dial. That's it. Nothing else needed to be tested.' Features such as structural rigidity, or the strength of the vehicle, or what will happen in a crash, aspects that they spent a lot of time on, were not integral to what the MVP was meant to accomplish. 'What we needed to put together was a fast-enough motor and slap a nice Nexus 7 tablet on to the dashboard. That should have been our MVP. We could have just picked these things off the shelf to do the bare minimum MVP.'

Having learnt the hard way, Tarun's advice is simple: 'Just be aware that you want to build an MVP. Define the set of things you are testing for, and their timelines. Having a list of things that you are looking to test really helps.' The implication is straightforward. The MVP is not necessarily an early version of the product. It is only meant to be a means to test initial hypotheses. It is not advisable to sacrifice practicality for perfection at this stage.

Focus on three key product attributes

Once you have identified features likely to be favoured by customers and start building your product, it is ideal to only focus on the most critical features initially. In terms of prioritizing between features, Paul Buchheit, the American computer engineer who created the ubiquitous email service Gmail, offers direct and uncomplicated advice. He suggests prioritizing three key attributes for the first version of the product—just three—and getting them right.[9,10] 'Get those things very, very right, and then forget about everything else. Those three attributes define the fundamental essence and value of the product—the rest is noise.'

Buchheit uses the original iPod as an example. According to him, it had three key attributes: (1) It was small enough to fit in your pocket; (2) it had enough storage to hold many hours of music; and (3) it was easy to sync with a Macintosh computer.

When he was building Gmail, Buchheit took a similar approach. It had three core attributes, around which the product was built: (1) it was fast; (2) it stored all of the emails a typical user was likely to have—at the time 4MB quotas were the norm; and (3) it featured an innovative interface based on conversations and search. Gmail's product design deliberately eschewed secondary and tertiary features: there was no 'rich

---

[9] According to Buchheit, this applies to a greater extent to consumer products where the purchaser is also the user. For markets that prioritize a long list of features, it is potentially more important to integrate as many features as possible.

[10] Paul Buchheit, 'Paul Buchheit: If Your Product Is Great, It Doesn't Need to Be Good', *Paul Buchheit*, 9 February 2010, paulbuchheit. blogspot.com/2010/02/if-your-product-is-great-it-doesnt-need. html

text' composer, and the address book only offered minimal functionality.

Focusing on core attributes forces higher prioritization of those attributes that create the greatest value for customers. In essence, it helps define your unique value proposition to customers. This drives more streamlined product design, and according to Buchheit, enables the development of more innovative products, rather than products that simply contain a lot of features: 'By focusing on only a few core features in the first version, you are forced to find the true essence and value of the product. If your product needs "everything" in order to be good, then it's probably not very innovative ... Put another way, if your product is great, it doesn't need to be good.'

Build what the user needs, not what the user wants

According to Paul Graham, product design begins by asking, 'who' is a product meant for, and what might they need from it. However, he writes, 'making what works for the user doesn't mean simply making what the user tells you to. Users don't know what all the choices are, and are often mistaken about what they really want.'[11]

In building their product, Ather was mindful of the distinction between building what the user might claim to want, and what they are likely to need from the product. Even if a customer claimed that what they really wanted was a certain feature, if the team did not believe in it, they would not build it into the product.

---

[11] Paul Graham, 'Design and Research', *www.paulgraham.com*, January 2003, www.paulgraham.com/desres.html

This is not to suggest they did not take into account customer feedback in first identifying what it was that customers needed. Even before Tarun and Swapnil had left their jobs to commit to Ather full time, they had taken pains to track down electric vehicle enthusiasts in India, and sought to understand what it was that they wanted. They had met thirty to forty early adopters of electric vehicles in Chennai and Bengaluru, and carried out detailed customer interviews which would often stretch to as long as two hours. They had probed into their selection criteria for existing products at the time, and their user experience over the period of ownership. How had the manufacturer responded if components did not work? What was the vehicle experience like when there was a pillion rider? What had happened when they had tried to sell the product? They had taken time to understand their target customer.

Even afterwards, when they were designing the MVP, they had engaged closely with customers. They had welcomed feedback. But once they had finalized upon what they believed they needed to build, they hunkered down. Thereafter, they scheduled customer feedback sessions only when they believed that they needed feedback on something that they had already developed.

Not all feedback is likely to be constructive and actionable, especially before the product has even launched. 'Once we've launched and people are using it, then we should be listening to users' feedback. But feedback from potential customers is way too early,' Tarun says. 'They have no skin in the game.'

Tarun had noticed that often they would get very strong feedback from customers during open house events, on pricing, on specifications, on design, on storage. However, a lot of this feedback seemed to be unreliable. They were afraid that they would go off in a direction that was suboptimal for the product. This is why they decided to stop gathering feedback until after the product had actually launched. Tarun says that they spend a lot of time listening to customers now, given that the product has launched. 'Because now,' he says, 'who we listen to are actual users, people who use the scooters day in and day out. So to understand their usage and what problems they face and what joys they have, that's very important.'

Customer feedback is vital. It is equally vital to understand when it might be most useful. Unless approached with great thoughtfulness, customer feedback can drive a team to distraction, consume precious time and resources and lead to a product that is a hotchpotch of features that individual customers might have desired, but which makes for a whole that is lesser than the sum of its parts.

Differentiation through design

Product design determines how customers first interact with the product. It informs the first impression of the product. Often, it is a core element of what makes customers fall in love.

According to Tarun, in the case of consumer products, often a big part of the purchase decision is how the product makes customers feel, the emotional response it elicits. Purchase decisions are not entirely objective and rational. This is especially true in the case of early adopters of the product. In the absence of an established brand name, product design, the Ather team hypothesized, could create the kind of emotional response in early adopters that would drive them to purchase their vehicles.

Tarun buttresses his argument with an example of how customers purchase cars. 'If I think I like the look of a certain car, let's say that's a Honda Polo, I will come up with enough reasons to justify why the Polo is a better hatchback than many other hatchbacks.'

Purchase decisions are not entirely driven by an objective assessment of superiority in terms of product specifications. 'If objectivity won the day, there will be only one car that dominated the entire hatchback market. It clearly isn't that way,' he says. While they were building in superior product specifications compared to existing electric scooters in the market, on their own, they might not necessarily be enough to win. A beautifully designed product was going to evoke a much more powerful response from early adopters, they argued.

Furthermore, design was going to be a key element in countering commoditization in the market. While product specifications were going to be important, eventually competitors might be able to catch up on these. When that happened, they did not want to have a common-looking vehicle that could not be differentiated.

Their decision to lead through design was also driven by a desire to adopt a development approach that was differentiated from the industry status quo. Before they set out to build, they spent time speaking to industry veterans, including industrial designers who worked with scooter designs. A common refrain that they heard was that scooter design was relegated to putting a skin on top of the chassis that the engineering team had put out. 'And it seemed very easy to say, oh, that's bullshit,' Tarun says. 'You don't need to be a student of design to see that.' It intuitively seemed like the wrong approach for a consumer product. At Ather, they decided to switch the sequence. They were going to design their scooter first.

Before they had even incorporated the company, they roped in an industrial designer whom they knew. They sat down with them, described in great detail what they were trying to build, and let them come up with a set of sketches of what the vehicle should look like. 'This was in 2013, before we had incorporated; at this point, we had no idea how exactly we were going to build this vehicle. But what we saw looked beautiful, a seven-inch screen dashboard was right up there, and it caught our eye.' They loved the sketches.

They took the sketches, and made these the constraint around which the engineering team had to work. 'Instead of saying "Engineering, do your job, and Industrial Design will put up a wrapper around it," we said, "Here's the wrapper, here are the specs that you want to do—now fit everything inside this wrapper,"' Tarun says. Over the next four years of engineering the product, they stayed true to the original design. The scooter that rolled out in 2018 had, at best, only minor variations with the original sketches. 'Conceptually, actually from most perspectives, it was exactly the same thing, down to the exposed frame and the colour of the exposed frame,' Tarun says.

One could argue that letting design lead engineering made their job more difficult. Indeed it did, says Tarun. But it also allowed them to clearly differentiate themselves in the market. 'It led to a vehicle which many people now feel is one of the most beautiful scooters in the Indian market,' he says.

Tarun believes this was an important element in driving customer acquisition early on. I think there has to be something that your early adopters absolutely fall in love with, he says. In the early days of a product, Tarun believes, there needs to be a certain element that both the team and early customers can anchor themselves to. It would be hard to even start up if you don't find the early set of people who resonate strongly with something in your product, he says. If people find your product to just be broadly adequate, you will not generate enough traction. There needs to be a clear differentiator that creates an anchor, whether it be the lowest price, the best performance metrics, or the best design. In the case of Ather, their anchor was their design.

Embrace adaptability in product development

Product development, in the case of Ather, was a particularly complicated process given that they were looking to build a smart electric scooter, a hardware product with a software soul. Early on in their development cycle, they decided to integrate elements of the agile development methodology.

The agile method, which originated in the software development industry, emphasizes breaking down product development work into small increments that minimize the amount of upfront planning and design. Each iteration, or 'sprint', is carried out within a short time frame, and involves a cross-functional team. At the end of the iteration a working product is demonstrated to key stakeholders, and based on the feedback received, a new iteration cycle begins. Overall, the agile method minimizes risk and allows the product to adapt to changes quickly.

While the agile methodology served Ather well, it also came up short in certain cases. While the agile method emphasized upon cross-functional teams and integrated development, in practice, this was not always possible.

The hardware-development cycle was one year long when they started, much longer than the development cycles for most software. This was less of a concern in the case of the embedded software which would sit on top of the hardware, and control core processes. Its development cycle was tied more closely to that of hardware. However, there were other software applications that would require much shorter development cycles, in line with classical two-weeks-long agile sprints. This would hold especially true for customer-facing softwares such as the mobile app, or the user interface micro-apps that would sit on the dashboard. Product development cycles for hardware components, and the vehicle software, they realized, had to be separated.

Even under the 'software' umbrella, individual components had differing requirements. The cloud development team could not work in the same manner as the mobile app development team. In some cases, there were hardware dependencies; these teams could not move as quickly as other software teams could. They realized that software development was too broad a categorization. Instead, they shifted to having development cycles that were written separately for each element, with often very different time frames. This willingness to tailor development cycles, as needed, allowed Ather's teams to be far more effective.

Adaptability can also serve a company well when product development gets affected due to dependencies on development partners. In the case of Ather, one year before they were to launch, one of their key suppliers of the battery cells that they had used in their vehicle battery packs went bankrupt. They had built their own battery pack on top of the supplier's technology and product architecture. They had even designed their manufacturing lines accordingly. Now they would have to quickly transition to using an alternate supplier.

This meant moving to a type of cell which had a very different form factor. This meant that everything from the assembly of the battery packs to its mounting had to change which, in turn, meant that the entire assembly process had to change. Even all of their process parameters had to change, and as that happened, software algorithms too had to be completely re-written. That they had constantly looked to integrate flexibility and adaptability in their processes allowed the company to overcome this setback.

Development processes can often break, and may need to be re-engineered. Adaptability is the first step towards resilience.

Pricing the product

According to entrepreneur and venture capitalist Michael Dearing who worked on product pricing at eBay, pricing is 'at the very heart of the economic engine of any product that aspires to become a business.'[12]

A business needs cash to continue operating. This can only come from one of three sources: internally generated cash, that is, cash flow from operations; debt from lenders; or equity investment from shareholders. Given that the supply of debt or equity is finite for any business, Dearing suggests that cash flow from operations is the only permanent and renewable source of life for the company. Given this context, product pricing is central to a company's survival since, as Dearing writes, 'pricing—especially relative to variable costs, asset intensity and fixed overhead—is a primary determinant of whether internally generated cash is a positive or negative number.'

There are two core approaches to product pricing: cost-plus pricing, and value-based pricing, both based on work done by

---

12   Michael Dearing, 'Three Ideas on Pricing', *Medium.com*, 11 September 2016, medium.com/@mcgd/three-ideas-on-pricing-6a90c2910a97

Harvard Business School professors Robert J. Dolan and John T. Gourville.

The cost-plus pricing approach starts with the overall cost of developing, building and taking the product to market, and then adds a gross margin on top. It ensures a certain profit on each unit of sale. However, it also has real drawbacks.

According to Rice University professor of marketing, Utpal Dholakia, first, it can discourage efficiency and cost containment.[13] Profits are linked to the margin added on top, and not to the underlying cost structure. Therefore, there is no clear incentive to address inefficiencies and reduce costs. Second, because sales volume often has to be estimated beforehand, and fixed costs allocated to each unit based on the forecast, the cost-plus price can easily be too high or too low. This could easily hold true in the case of a logistics company such as Delhivery, which might have fixed costs linked to warehouse assets, or a hardware company such as Ather with fixed manufacturing costs. Third, and perhaps most importantly, cost-plus pricing ignores both the customer's willingness to pay and the competitors' prices. When these factors are ignored, a pricing decision risks being completely off base. Nevertheless, the cost-plus pricing approach is simple to implement, and can offer a useful starting framework, especially in the presence of limited information. The value-based pricing approach on the other hand builds on the perceived value of the product to the customer, or how much value the customer thinks the product delivers. The gap between the price and the perceived value to the customer from purchasing the product is the incentive to

---

[13]   Utpal M. Dholakia, 'When Cost-Plus Pricing Is a Good Idea', *Harvard Business Review*, 7 December 2018, https://hbr. org/2018/07/ when-cost-plus-pricing-is-a-good-idea

buy. The larger this gap, the easier it is to have customers want to use your product.

Unless your product is entirely novel with no available alternatives, its perceived value is unlikely to be independent of competition. In arriving at the perceived value of a product, customers examine the product not only on its own, but also in relation with the pricing of competing products, and alternatives. This must be borne in mind when implementing value-based pricing.'[14]

In pricing their electric scooter, Ather utilized elements of both pricing strategies. Ather started by predicting the cost of building the vehicle, and then adding a gross margin of 15–20 per cent on top. They also looked at the pricing of the competition. The benchmark they looked at was a mass-market scooter. However, the value provided by a high-tech fast electric scooter was higher than the mentioned scooter. Ather calculated the price of the scooter at ₹1.25 lakh, a 50 per cent premium over the mass-market alternative. This was the price that they initially released with in 2018.

However, they soon realized some of their initial cost estimates were not holding up, and this was eating into their margins. Moreover, they realized that as a premium product, they should add a higher gross margin on top. So when they relaunched the product in 2020, they revised the pricing structure, increasing pricing by 20–30 per cent depending upon specifications.

---

[14] Utpal M. Dholakia, 'A Quick Guide to Value-Based Pricing', *Harvard Business Review*, 8 September 2016, https://hbr.org/2016/08/a-quick-guide-to-value-based-pricing

According to Michael Dearing, there are two other pricing concepts that are widely applicable:[15]

1. Good–better–best assortments give you a bigger market. According to Dearing, offering 'a range of options from a range of options from low price to high price, with functional and aesthetic differences along a spectrum' or good–better–best assortments allow for expansion of the customer base.

    Offering multiple products at similar price points can allow a company to cater to a range of tastes. A consumer product which comes in different colours with minor variations in prices can be a good example. Another approach involves offering versions at multiple price points. This allows a company to price-discriminate, based on how customers value different features. Some who don't see the value in a high-end version of a product might be willing to pay less for a stripped-down model. For instance, Ather offers multiple variants of its flagship electric scooter, with feature differences, and at different prices.

2. Offering optional add-on features and pricing them separately lets users optimize perceived value. According to Dearing, optional features can help arrive at a more optimized configuration. Offering optional features allows three things to happen:
    • users become participants in prototyping and iterating your product design, allowing you to get real-time feedback on what features and functions users value;

---

[15] Michael Dearing, 'Three Ideas on Pricing', *Medium.com*, 11 September 2016, medium.com/@mcgd/three-ideas-on-pricing-6a90c2910a97

- users' perceived value of the product goes up, which is likely to drive up customer satisfaction and retention; and
- in such cases where add-ons are highly valued by users but may be offered inexpensively by the company, there is a large incremental margin opportunity.

Product pricing strategy is an essential piece of the startup puzzle and often notoriously tricky to get right. However, getting it right early ensures sustainable cash flows, strong customer acquisition and a path to scale.

Summary

- **Find your niche.** When you start, focus on identifying a small segment of the market that you can dominate. Focus on this segment, build product-market fit, and then expand outwards to capture a larger share of the overall market.
- **Building subject matter expertise is the first step in coming up with a compelling solution.** Successful founders develop an exhaustive understanding of each individual component of the customer problem they are trying to solve, the business ecosystem in which it exists, and how existing players operate.
- **Lead with a minimum viable product.** Instead of looking to build a full-fledged product, first try to create an initial version that can be used to gather feedback from customers. Look to build iteratively in creating a better product.
- **In building the first version of the product, focus on three key attributes and get them right.** Identify three key attributes that are likely to define the fundamental essence and value of the product. Focusing on three core attributes

forces higher prioritization of those attributes that create the highest value for customers.

- **Differentiate through design.** Design is often a core element of what makes customers fall in love with a product and therefore influences purchase decisions. It can also counter commoditization in the market.
- **Build what the user needs, not what the user wants.** While receiving customer feedback is important, during the product development phase not every input might be useful. Before launch, the user has not actually purchased or experienced the product. Instead of building everything that potential customers ask for, focus on what they might actually need.
- **Embrace adaptability in product development.** Break down product development into small cycles to minimize the need for exhaustive planning and design upfront. Plans can often go awry, and mayhem might follow. Build adaptability into the process to address unforeseen eventualities.
- **Optimal product pricing has a major impact on the cashflow of a company.** Cost-plus and value-based approaches are the two most widely used methods for determining pricing. In determining your pricing strategy, look to understand what each approach might imply, not only in terms of unit economics but also with regard to the perception of the product and its competitive positioning.

5

The Launch

ONCE YOUR PRODUCT OR service is ready, it is time to launch it into the world. Everything up until this point would simply have been for what will come next.

Once the product or service has launched, the most important objective for the startup is to get as many customers as possible. After all, the raison d'etre of any company is to get customers to use and engage with its offering. As they do, they will offer also offer feedback. Listening closely to early customers and engaging in a process of continuous refinement will lead to a superior product which is likely to be more widely embraced.

A multiplicity of hats

At launch, the team would typically consist of the founders, and perhaps, a few early employees. With only a limited number of human resources at disposal, assigning and distributing tasks is not an option.

'When you are small, you should be doing everything yourself,' Flipkart founder Sachin Bansal says. During Flipkart's early days, the founders would attend to every aspect of the company.

When they first launched the website, and were looking to test it, Sachin reached out to a friend from his undergraduate days to place an order. When Flipkart launched, it only sold books. 'It was 10 p.m. on 15 October 2007. We had just finished writing the code. We could place the order ourselves. Or we could get somebody else to place the order. I reached out to a friend from IIT who was then studying at IIM Ahmedabad.' At the time, the founders had a limited set of books that they could ship. Hence, Sachin told his friend to place an order for a specific book.

'And at around 11 p.m. he placed an order. But he did not place the order for that book. He placed the order for two other books,' Sachin laughs. 'We spent all of the next day looking for those two books.' Sachin says the act of looking for those books and shipping them was the biggest source of learning from them in their early days. In trying to find those books, they met distributors. They learnt about the logistics element that would be required in shipping items. 'We learned which industry we were in,' he says.

In the early days, the founders would attend to every detail themselves. 'I did everything from picking up books, to packing them, to fixing the generator, to daily customer support calls, to whatever else was needed,' Sachin says. 'Customer support calls used to be my personal phone number—sometimes I would get calls at 2 a.m. at night.'

After finishing his tenth grade, Ritesh Agarwal moved to Kota in Rajasthan to enrol in a coaching centre to prepare for the entrance exam to the Indian Institutes of Technology. He would travel to nearby Delhi over weekends, often attending business events and conferences taking place in the city. He would lodge at small bed-and-breakfast establishments.

After finishing his twelfth grade, he moved to Delhi for good. He wanted to be an entrepreneur. He had realized that finding good but affordable accommodation in India could be quite difficult; even clean sheets, and an option of breakfast was not always available. At seventeen, he founded Oravel Stays, offering a listing of budget hotels that users could book from. Eventually, this evolved into OYO Rooms, a marketplace for branded budget hotels.

While working on this platform, Ritesh chanced upon a small, fifteen-room guesthouse in Gurugram near the Huda City Center metro station. It was a ramshackle establishment with dismal occupancy, and the owner busy with another business.

Ritesh went to the owner with a simple proposition: if he were to be given the reigns to the guesthouse, he would increase the occupancy to at least 80 per cent within six–seven months. He also told him that if they made a profit, they would share in it, but in case they made losses, these would only accrue to Ritesh: *nafa hua to dono ka, nuksan hua to mera* (if we make a profit, we will share it; in case of a loss, I will bear it in its entirety).

Ritesh says the guesthouse owner probably took him for a naive, young boy, flush with money who is likely to burn it in two–four months, and then scoot; he had no belief that the establishment could make any revenue at all. The terms of the deal were loaded in his favour, and he agreed to the proposition. With the agreement in place, the first priority for Ritesh was to make the property more appealing to customers. He went to Sadar Bazar, the largest wholesale market for household items in Delhi and bought decorative items and furniture for as cheap as he could get. 'For 35,000 rupees, we got the property up to an acceptable condition.' He cleaned it up, removed the furniture that was not required and put up the OYO signage. Called the OYO Rooms Huda City Centre, this would be the first in worldwide marketplace for branded budget hotels. Having refurbished the establishment, Ritesh started working at the hotel himself, doing everything he could.

'For close to three months,' he says, 'I would do absolutely everything at the hotel. I was the guy who was transforming the hotel; I was the guy who was doing food-and-breakfast; I was doing front-office work; and I was also the guy who was spending time with the guests.' Not only did it help him understand what customers were looking for, but also how to optimize operations. When OYO looked to scale rapidly later, these formative experiences would serve him well.

Expanding reach

Customer acquisition is fundamental to growth. The AIDA model provides a framework to guide a company's efforts. The model can be viewed as a simplified rendition of a sales funnel: prospective customers travel across the funnel which culminates in a sale.

The steps proposed by the AIDA model are as follows:

- **Awareness:** Initially, customers need to become aware of the offering. Efforts need to be directed to ensure that potential customers are aware that the product or service exists.
- **Interest:** Once aware of the offering, customers should be able to understand how it benefits them, thus piquing their interest.

- **Desire:** Customers must be led to develop a positive disposition towards the offering, convinced of its benefits.
- **Action:** Once a customer has formed an intention to purchase the product or service, they must be supported in carrying out the act.

Customer acquisition can be carried out through both marketing and sales. While the former is a pull-based approach, designed to drive greater awareness, the latter is designed to push the product or service to potential customers and achieve sales conversion. As author and investor Jessica Livingston notes, sales and marketing are two ends of a continuum: 'At the sales end your outreach is narrow and deep. At the marketing end it is broad and shallow.'[1] While marketing channels focus to a greater extent on generating awareness and interest, sales channels focus on driving conversion.

After launch, it is vital to actively make efforts to reach potential customers and driving use. It is not prudent to build and release the product or service and expect customers to flock to it. At the point of launch, most potential customers will not be aware of the offering. They would need to be directed towards it through skilful marketing and sales efforts.

Freshworks founder Girish Mathrubootham says that you need to make efforts to get noticed when you start a company. 'If you are a startup, it's not enough to build quietly and hope that customers will come. They will not come,' he says. Creating an outstanding product or service is not enough. You have to make sure that people sit up and take notice, Girish says. Not

1   Livingston, Jessica (2014). 'Why Startups Need to Focus on Sales, Not Marketing', *Wall Street Journal*, 3 June, https://www.wsj.com/articles/BL-232B-2715.

only do such efforts help acquire early customers, they can also be important in generating interest from investors.

Soon after their founding, Freshworks participated in the Microsoft Bizspark India Startup Challenge that sought to recognize promising startups. When they won, they received a $40,000 grant. Girish says that it was akin to oxygen supply for the company at the stage, for it came without debt or equity-related riders and allowed them to experiment. At the time, they needed to prove their business, and determine the right marketing channels. They spent the money over the following two months to identify the best-suited marketing channels to scale the business. They ran experiments on online marketing platforms offered by Google, Facebook, and LinkedIn, and succeeded in acquiring seventy customers. With this, they started receiving interest from investors. Soon after, six months after launching, they received an initial investment of $1 million from Accel Partners.

Effective public relations campaigns can also play a major role in expanding reach. Girish holds that most startups misunderstand what public relations implies, imagining that it is limited to putting out press releases. Instead, he says, it involved telling a remarkable story that can make people sit up and take notice. According to Girish, often, many startups do not invest enough in creating powerful public relations campaigns. As a result, they miss out on opportunities to expand reach and strengthen brand recognition.

The day after Freshworks announced the investment from Accel, the company became the subject of a dispute on the social media platform Twitter. At the time, the Freshworks team used the platform to identify customers who were unhappy with Zendesk, the most significant player in the customer service software market. They would encourage such users to try Freshworks. The company at the time was called Freshdesk, and based on this, first a noted industry analyst, and then the CEO of Zendesk accused them of being 'a rip-off'.

Instead of engaging in an extended dispute on the platform, Freshworks set up a website called ripoffornot.org. They explained their position, noting that many companies in the segment shared the same suffix, and that many of them had in fact been started before Zendesk. In addition, they encouraged users to sign up for a trial, and decide for themself as to whether the accusation was valid or not. It became a defining moment for the company. 'At that time Zendesk had 20,000 customers, we had 200 customers. But by attacking us they put us on the same plane and from that point onwards we never let go of that slot,' Girish says. Ensuring that the startup was mentioned in the same breath as the industry leader became a concerted part of their public relations strategy. They would ensure that if there were an article on Zendesk, it would mention their company, and if there were coverage of Freshworks, it would also mention Zendesk. They were offered an opening to catapult to a higher level of brand recognition and made sure that they did not let go of the opportunity. 'We latched on to the small opening that was given to us, and stayed the course,' Girish says.

Freshworks also brought to bear their skill in mounting an effective marketing and public relations campaign when they launched a customer relationship management product in 2016.

One of the lessons that Girish had learned during his days at Zoho was that a company could build brand recognition by positioning itself as a direct competitor to the market leaders in a certain segment. This realization had been driven home when he was part of the team building an enterprise IT management software suite called ManageEngine. Zoho's solution would compete with software suites from IBM,

HP, BMC, and CA Technologies, the four companies that dominated the IT management software segment. While Zoho had had a comprehensive solution, and could go up against the major players, what ended up happening was that each of the elements within their software suite would get relegated to a small sub-segment of the market, competing with niche players. The company was not seen as a competitor to the major players. 'We were not being spoken of in the same league,' Girish says. This was a concern.

Girish points out that in B2B markets it is important to be seen as a leader; it is a key element in being invited to participate in sales processes. 'Not B2B market is a winner-takes-all market, users will always evaluate two or three different softwares before choosing one,' he says. 'But if you do not feature in the list of solutions that are to be evaluated, you are not going to get many calls to participate.' In order to change this, Zoho came up with a 90:10 principle: they started advertising that Zoho's solution offered 90 per cent of the features that the Big Four players were offering at 10 per cent of the price. When they did, they increasingly started being seen as a key player in the segment. This was a valuable lesson for Girish; a well-designed marketing campaign positioning a smaller player against large incumbents could yield favourable results.

Therefore, when Freshworks launched their CRM offering, Girish understood that they could build brand recognition early on by positioning themselves against the San Francisco based company Salesforce, the most important player in the segment. They chose to do so at the 2016 Dreamforce event. Organized in San Francisco by Salesforce annually, Dreamforce is the biggest technology conference in the world, typically hosting more than 150,000 attendees. Leading up to the conference, they had seventy buses, decked up in cheeky ads highlighting concerns that customers faced with Salesforce's offering, and carrying the line 'Sorry we didn't launch earlier'. The campaign ensured that their product got noticed immediately. If you want to be noticed, you go after the biggest player, Girish says.

However, in developing audacious campaigns, there is one underlying premise that a company needs to bear in mind. The most important point, Girish says, is that the product has to be world-class. An audacious campaign will deliver results only when built around an outstanding product that could measure up to any claims that might have been made.

Balancing acquisition and retention

To drive growth, it is crucial to focus on both acquiring new customers and retaining existing ones. A company cannot focus on one at the expense of the other, and continue to grow; it is fundamentally unsustainable. If the needs of existing customers are not adequately met, they will stop being active. This will only serve to weaken, even cripple the offering.

TaxiForSure founder Raghu says that the only way to grow rapidly is to continually onboard new customers, while making sure existing customers remain active. 'That's the only way you can do exponential growth,' he says. In fact, he argues that if a company had to choose between the two, for want of resources perhaps, it might even be better to have greater focus on customer retention rather than customer acquisition. 'It is better to retain existing customers than to go after new customers,' says Raghu. 'To acquire new customers, you have to spend money. If you are losing existing customers while acquiring new ones, and spending money to acquire them, it is more expensive to drive acquisition than to focus on driving retention.'

Over the first three years after its founding, OYO Rooms had grown rapidly. They had grown to become the largest marketplace for budget accommodation in the country, with associated properties present nationwide. However, in the beginning of 2016, they realized that dissatisfaction with the service was growing amongst customers. While they continued to expand, and acquire new users, customer satisfaction ratings were showing a sharp decline. This was a worrying sign. Declining satisfaction could eventually lead to users abandoning the platform. They realized that they needed to set things right.

There were two metrics that OYO tracked at the time. The first was what they called the 'unhappy percentage'. It was the percentage of users who would give a rating of 1 or 2 after using the service. When they had first started, it used to be in the low single digits. Now this was steadily increasing. The other metric that they tracked was their TripAdvisor score. From a peak of 4.1 in 2014, this had declined to 3.7. They decided to double down on offering outstanding customer experiences. For the first six months of year, they would primarily focus on improving customer experience.

They structured their efforts around meeting three core objectives. First, ensure that OYO's five promises to customers were being met: clean washrooms, spotless linen, air-conditioned rooms with television, free breakfast, and free Wi-Fi. Second, through making their technology platform more robust and deepening adoption, ensure that bookings and check-ins could be carried out without friction. Third, focus on delighting customers even if it meant going above and beyond what was strictly required.

Over the following six months, focusing on these three objectives, they managed to turn around the situation. Their unhappy percentage value halved, and their TripAdvisor score rose to 4.4.

Ritesh says that you need to maintain a healthy balance between growth and consolidation. He offers the analogy of a race run over several stages. 'You will always have that period in which you will run really, really fast,' he says. 'Then you might need to slow down a little, gather energy. You say let me get some juice, let me jog for a while, let me ensure I am going to survive till the end of the race. And once you are alright, you can once again sprint like there is no tomorrow.'

Building an identity

As marketing guru Philip Kotler notes, 'The art of marketing is the art of brand building. If you are not a brand, you are a commodity.'[2] A company's brand is a promise of a certain standard of delivery. It symbolizes the company's core values, its product principles and the user experience it delivers. Effective branding is a powerful driver of a company's value.

On building a brand, Abhiraj Bhal asserts that for a service-focused startup, your brand is synonymous with the service that you deliver. 'In the initial years of your operations, your brand is basically your product or your service—they are the same thing,' he says. If you are able to deliver on the promise you might have made to customers, you start building your brand. 'People remember Urban Company's brand because of the service experience that the service professionals deliver, not because of some very fancy brand campaign that we'd

---

2   Philip Kotler, 'The Art of Brand Building', *11 Powerful Marketing Quotes from Philip Kotler*, emeraldgrouppublishing.com/archived/promo/11-most-powerful-quotes-about-marketing-philip-kotler.htm

run.' And so, your entire focus should be on making a great product or service because that will lay down the foundation for building a great brand.

For a product startup, brand building could be a means to communicate certain attributes of the product itself. When Ather Energy were looking to communicate what their product stood for, they focused on the message that it was a well-engineered technology product rather than simply a vehicle. Ather's brand positioning emphasized upon the 'intelligence' of the product, the integration of its hardware and software. Founder Tarun Mehta says that they also looked to emphasize that the vehicle was a product that the team members would themselves like to use, that it was a reliable product built with very deep customer focus. Therefore, they adopted taglines such as 'Built for us' that emphasized unity between the company and the customers. Doing so allowed early customers to identify with the team and the brand, serving the company well.

Poor branding can irredeemably mar a product's prospects. This was the case with Tata Nano, a highly anticipated car that was supposed to lure India's burgeoning middle class with its cheap price tag, which upon release saw few customers. Prior to its release, it was being hoped that the car would allow families that could only hitherto afford a two-wheeler could purchase a car.

However, these hopes were soon dashed. While the car had a lot going for it, from good engineering to great initial publicity, the company had not anticipated that the brand would get marred by its positioning as a cheap car. It was not seen as an aspirational product, and customers stayed away.

Products tend to transform over time, teams transition and customers evolve. But once a brand has been created, it becomes an enduring identity, enduring at its core. Creating a powerful brand creates enduring benefits over the life of the company, and is worth investing effort in early on.

Metrics do not lie

Performance tracking enables a deeper understanding of how the company might be performing. Metrics communicate progress, or the lack of it, and enable you to plan course correction whenever required. Metrics provide benchmarks that could then be built upon, and improved upon. They would be your North Star, your guiding light, pointing towards the true north, objective and unbiased. Selecting and tracking certain metrics, and then arriving at target values for these, provides direction for the company.

When Falguni Nayar started Nykaa, she was convinced she wanted to build a company with strong underlying unit economics. E-commerce businesses in India that were raising money at the time were prioritizing gross merchandize value, the total value of merchandise sold on the platform, instead of the actual revenue for the company. GMV growth was a key metric that potential investors would examine; e-commerce platforms were driving up GMV values through heavy discounting.

Instead of focusing inordinately on GMV though, Falguni wanted to prioritize healthy unit economics. She was not averse to raising capital. But the time she had spent in investment banking had taught her the importance sustainable growth. 'I come from a discipline of understanding a company's financial numbers and having a clear view of what's a sustainable model and sustainable number that a business needs to have to trade well in equity markets,' she says. She focused on ensuring that the underlying unit economics and cost structure of the business were sustainable; 'I want to grow but with the right metrics and cost structure,' she would tell investors.[3] Prioritizing sustainable growth over growth at all costs has served Nykaa well. By the time it launched its IPO, Nykaa was already a profitable company.

It is imperative that you choose the right set of metrics. These metrics must comprehensively communicate the health of the business and the progress you might be making in extremely specific ways. These must be aligned with your strategic focus, comprehensively map each aspect of your strategic focus and truly represent what the company is trying to solve. This must be done with a great deal of thought and care. For instance, if your strategic focus is to become the lowest-cost logistics provider, as was the case with Delhivery, you need to ensure that you are examining every possible facet of transportation cost.

Delhivery's customers valued low-cost, accurate and timely delivery. The team chose metrics based on what their customers valued the most. The first was precision of service. So, if they promised to deliver an order within a certain timeframe, for what percentage of the time could they meet their service guarantee? They strove to ensure that in 99 per cent of deliveries, the guarantee was met. Not only did they measure this metric at an overall level, they measured it across every lane through the entire network. And so, if a product was to be delivered from Delhi to Mumbai in twenty-four hours, the service precision along the lane had to be in line with their target performance value.

The second metric they measured was cost efficiency, which they defined as the cost per unit for delivering an order which, therefore, fed into the price that they charged their customers.

3   Deepti Chaudhary, 'Nykaa: Adding Gloss to the Beauty Business', *Forbes India*, 28 August 2018, fortuneindia.com/enterprise/ nykaa-adding-gloss-to-the-beauty-business/102337

'So, we started out strategically,' explains Sahil, 'with a simple road map, deciding we have to be the cheapest player in this space over the next ten years and that we have to build a model that becomes materialistically cheaper than anything a competitor could develop. Today, our cost structure is about 70 per cent lower than that of any of our competitors in this space. But, it's come out of specific design choices in the network.'

In addition to monitoring the overall cost, the team set out to measure if they were the most cost-efficient at each stage of the service. From a transportation standpoint, there are three legs to the delivery of an order. The first is when the order is picked up, the second is the middle mile, and then there is the last mile—from the distribution centre to the customer. Delhivery decided that overall, they had to be most cost-efficient across all three, as well as within each leg individually. This was a strategic call because they reasoned that this way the competition would seek to unbundle delivery. 'If you are the cheapest player in the space in all individual parts as well as the sum, nobody can compete with you on even one single element of the service,' says Sahil, 'and then, you can open out each of those three.'

Apart from core metrics, Delhivery also tracked auxiliary metrics which could enable them to monitor different elements of their operational matrix. They tracked return rates, cash-handling time, amount of cash handled and fidelity of cash service, amongst others. These metrics allowed them to increase efficiency in operations, by further reducing the time taken. But their core metrics were based on their strategic focus. Metrics that dovetail perfectly with the startup's core strategy enable it to chart progress in a highly visible manner. These metrics must demonstrate high fidelity with target values. If that is not being achieved, you have to obsess over why that is so.

The use of data and metrics is not just limited to tracking success, but also showing the way, 'We are data-directed versus being purely data-assisted. The data tells us this is the way it should be done, not just that there are five ways to do it and you can choose one,' he says. Such data-directed strategy helps make business decisions, such as the decision to locate distribution centres closer to consumers for delivery staff to spend less time on road and more time on knocking doors. The business impact was immediate. 'We went from doing eighteen parcels per head a day in September 2014 to doing thirty-seven parcels per person per day by June 2016, which was huge in terms of the unit economics.'[4]

The other key aspect of measuring growth is to understand how many people are truly using your product. If you examine the stories of some of the biggest startups, it is striking how many of them prioritized usage over registrations. When Facebook started, MySpace was the largest social network around and they were tracking registered user numbers. Facebook, on the other hand, decided to put out monthly active users, the premise being that Facebook needed users to be active on the site and not just in the form of registered users, some of whom could be dormant.

Dormant users add little value. Neither are they likely to drive new users, nor force improvements in the product by providing a continuous feedback loop. In fact, dormant users could well lend a false sense of confidence to founders. Spending on marketing could lead to initial usage. But if it does not translate into repeat usage, and founders continue to mistakenly focus only on the number of registered users, it could

4   Aparna Piramal Raje, 'The Intellectual Courier', *Mint*, 8 October 2017, livemint.com/Leisure/PjKgD12aLwWoYbztMBD4iI/The-intellectual-courier.html

paint a false picture as to the growth of the company. Active users are a more meaningful metric because they create value for advertisers and other users. Similarly, WhatsApp focused on the number of messages sent through its service. Instead of looking at total page views, LinkedIn focused on profile views, or how many people were using LinkedIn to search for and find other people, and the number of people who were being viewed on their platform. Twitter focused on how many people were looking at their timeline, reading tweets or tweeting.

Tracking customer-centric metrics is critical, at least in the beginning when you are trying to figure out the product-market fit. These metrics tell you whether your product is suited to the market, or if changes are required. They tell you whether your customer loves your product; if they don't, they will leave it for another or find alternatives. Investors, too, judge your startup based on customer love, because the more the number of people who love your startup, the higher is the propensity for growth.

You might not be the typical customer

Before understanding what the customer wants, you need to first find your customer. However, you must not confuse yourself with your customer.

When Raghu and Aprameya started out, they were convinced that if they built a product that they would themselves use, they would succeed. In fact, they had hit upon the taxi for hire idea driven by a personal need for such a service. 'We felt that we were the customers for the service,' says Raghu, 'we used taxis all the time.' They believed they were truly representative of their target demographic, and that their needs and expectations would be that of a typical customer. They would build the service as if they were building it for themselves. 'So when it came to customer experience, or deciding upon customer-side features, we would put ourselves in the customers' shoes and decide what we needed to do. That was the worst thing that we could have done.'

While they might have started out as typical customers, over time they had ceased to be so. They had become too familiar with the underlying setup, with workings on the supply side and with the driver's psyche. They had become insiders, assimilated within the entrenched taxi-hiring ecosystem.

'As a customer, you don't know anything about the supply side, or about taxi drivers. The moment you come to know a little bit about how the typical driver operates, you cease to be an average customer,' says Raghu. 'We knew exactly why a driver would reject a certain booking, why a driver would want additional charges, what a driver might be willing to agree to, and what not. Once this sense of understanding had become ingrained, we would ourselves decide that certain things were possible, and others were not.' They were no longer functioning as typical customers. 'As customers, our expectations had reduced. But a typical customer does not have any understanding of how a driver functions. They expect that their driver will do everything that is humanly possible to serve them. It took us some six to seven months to realize that we were not the customers.'

Obsess over customer feedback

After Raghu's epiphany that they themselves were not the customers, they had to chase down their actual customers, go to them and understand what they really thought about the service and what their expectations were. They set up interviews with customers and focus group discussions, deriving customer insights. Focus group discussions, or FGDs, are a widely used form of participatory research, occasionally resembling semi-structured group interviews, but typically promoting discussions within the group, with the researcher playing the role of a facilitator. Raghu and Aprameya had learnt of FGDs during their MBA course. They invited selected groups of customers to discuss the service and their needs as users. Then they went back to the drawing board. 'That is where the MBA helped,' Raghu laughs. 'We could use FGDs well, and they were significantly useful.'

Thereafter began the customer obsession phase. They would obsess over customer feedback, going so far as to monitor individual users and their repeated usage. They regularly got on calls to understand how their users had come to learn of the service, what they valued the most about the service and what changes they would like to see. They obsessed over repeat usage and referrals. 'We kept calling them shamelessly,' says Raghu. 'In a consumer business, what you especially need to measure are repeats and referrals. If you don't have either, then there is no consumer business.'

A focus on customer feedback need not be limited to the initial stages of a company. Even as a startup matures, or as its operating model evolves, these values continue to hold paramount importance. Deep Kalra of MakeMyTrip not only embraces this philosophy, he ensures it is upheld across the organization. Deep is a strong believer in directly going to customers and understanding their needs and perspectives. It matters little that MakeMyTrip has grown into a behemoth, with a multibillion-dollar valuation.

When on flights, Deep talks to the passenger sitting next to him, plying them with nuts and foodstuffs, in the hope that it could lead to an insight that could improve their product. Every month, he goes to the market himself, visiting customers, and visiting the properties of up-and-coming competitors, so that he can better understand how the market might be evolving. Not only does he do it himself, he ensures that the entire senior leadership does it too. 'The top hundred guys in the company have been mandated that one day in the month is go-to-market day. And if it's a weekday, go ahead and do it on a weekday. The amount I learnt in those visits is unbelievable. It's amazing the learnings you get if you're willing to ask.'

'But,' he cautions, 'talk to real customers. Getting a theoretical set of customers sitting in your office never works.' He also warns against delegating market research beyond a point. Only when you talk to a customer directly, when you are in that moment with them, will you understand why they make a certain choice, and why they don't. 'Somewhere along the way,' says Deep, 'the moment you get senior, you start saying the marketing flunkies will go and do the work, they'll come back, the marketing agency will package it, and I'll just see the executive summary. That executive summary is very dangerous because while it prepares you enough to sound knowledge about the market and consumer behaviour, it doesn't give you customer insights. Consumer insights are gained only through first-hand interactions, they tend to get lost in translation.'

Iterate; if required, pivot

Continuous iteration lies at the core of any product that eventually becomes successful. No matter how carefully you might have analysed the market, developed the idea, designed the product, it has to be an improbably rare product if it does not require further iterations.

Even four months after launching their website, things were not moving as fast as Raghu and Aprameya had hoped. An investment of 5 lakh rupees from an alumnus of their undergraduate institute, NIT Surathkal, allowed them to invest in Google AdWords and Facebook ads. These ads helped them inch to eight rides per day in October from four to five in September. However, after this initial bout of traction their growth was again becoming stagnant. Then they stumbled upon an insight which made them rethink their market.

While combing through their growth metrics in mid-November, they came across a particular customer who had booked fifty rides in October. They could not understand why. So they called up one of their empanelled drivers. 'He told us that this was a pregnant woman and she had requested multiple rides,' says Raghu. They had hitherto not realized that pregnant women could be a target demographic. In truth, they did not fully realize it at that point either. But they were willing to follow through on a hunch. In any case, they were clutching at straws at this stage.

So, the next day at 6 a.m., we went and stood in front of maternity hospitals and distributed pamphlets,' recalls Raghu. They told anybody who would listen that TFS was the best taxi service for pregnant women. The women had many questions. Raghu and Aprameya patiently answered their questions while making copious notes on what they were uncovering about their clientele's needs. '"Will the driver keep calling me and asking me for directions?" someone asked. We said no and made a note of it. "Will the driver drive fast?" We said no and made a note of it. "Will he keep honking on the road?" "Will he open the car windows?" "Will he put on loud music?" "Will he speed over speed bumps?" We told them no, the driver will not do any of these things.'

They went back, and quickly laid down ground rules for TFS drivers serving pregnant women. 'There shall be no speeding, all the windows shall be closed, the air-conditioning shall be turned on, so on and so forth.'

As it turned out, their hunch was right. Pregnant women, as it proved, could be persuaded to become loyal, and often lucrative, customers, as long as they could ensure reliable service that set a high bar on quality. More importantly, they could generate powerful network effects. 'Pregnant women become regular customers for six to seven months, to go to yoga classes or aerobic classes with other pregnant women. So there were a significant number of referrals,' says Raghu. They had looked at the data, teased out an insight and had immediately acted upon it. 'Overnight, we moved from eight rides per day to forty-five,' says Raghu. 'We never saw the days of the tens and twenties.' Thereafter TaxiForSure sustained the explosion in growth.

Many a time, a simple iteration is not enough. A deeper course correction might be needed, to the extent that the underlying business model might need to be changed. A 'pivot' might be inspired by feedback from customers, the discovery of a new customer insight, or even fundamental changes to the market. Irrespective, pivots are carried out in an attempt to build a more robust business, with a stronger value proposition.

'Flipkart initially started out as a price-comparison engine. It was not supposed to be an e-commerce company,' founder Sachin Bansal says. 'What is a price comparison engine? People compare prices, and then ship the order.' However, Sachin and Binny Bansal realized this was not going to fly. 'We thought, let us go to the market and understand what people need from a price-comparison engine. We talked to people—our friends and family—to understand their expectations. But it was very hard to have that conversation with them because if you have never shopped online, how will you imagine a price-comparison engine? Then we woke up. Clearly, shopping itself was an interesting opportunity.' Shopping online involved elements beyond comparing prices. The Flipkart founders realized that there would be value in offering an integrated end-to-end experience to customers including managing an inventory of products, managing logistics for delivery to customers, and enabling simplified payments. Flipkart switched from being a price-comparison engine to a marketplace.

It is difficult to understand how effective a product is in solving a customer problem until it is put to use by customers. Only after launch does this become evident. Based on feedback received from customers, the company could choose to refine the product, or pivot to a new model.[5]

Speed is a premium

Sam Altman says that many founders spend a lot of time talking about grand plans, but they do not necessarily get things done. The best founders, on the other hand, may work on things that seem small but they get them done extraordinarily quickly.[6]

'The speed with which a founder moves is directly correlated to the success of the startup,' Y Combinator Continuity Fund Partner Anu Hariharan says. 'We have seen this a lot across data on Y Combinator startups. Speed is all that you have in the early days. It is the only weapon you have against incumbents. They cannot ship fast. It is also one of the key weapons you

---

[5] Hoffman Reid, 'If There Aren't Any Typos in This Essay, We Launched Too Late!', *LinkedIn*, 30 March 2017, linkedin.com/pulse/arent-any-typos-essay-we-launched-too-late-reid-hoffman

[6] Sam Altman, 'Super Successful Companies', *Sam Altman's Blog*, 16 January 2014, blog.samaltman.com/super-successful-companies

have against competitors. It is critical to move fast, learn and iterate.'

The speed at which a company moves is the speed at which improvements happen, Anu explains. It is only possible to understand who wants a product, what works and what is broken once it has shipped to users. The longer it takes to build and ship a product, the longer it takes to make improvements, and achieve product-market fit.

Speed is also critical for ensuring the continued viability of a startup in the face of limited personnel and resources. Anu offers the example of the fintech startup Brex. In the middle of the COVID pandemic, the company realized that they needed to shift their focus from one vertical to another. Once the decision was reached, the founders immediately moved to reprioritize resource allocation. It was a hard decision for the founders. Not only were they updating the company's strategy in the middle of a pandemic, the move also meant potentially letting go of a part of the original team. 'It was one of the hardest decisions they have made,' Anu says. 'But the thinking was that they had new information and they had to tailor their course based on what they had learned about the market.' Delaying the decision would have only hurt the company's prospects.

Once a product has launched and becomes available to customers, it also becomes available to competitors, making it easy to copy. Unless a startup continues to execute at lightning speed, it can fall behind, with competition walking away with customers.

This becomes especially risky given that many industries operate under a winner-takes-all model. As a result, capital tends to flow to market leaders. If a company is able to move quickly and take a lead in the market, it is likely to attract more capital which in turn can fuel further growth. Moreover, a first-mover advantage for one company may also starve competitors of capital because once an investor has already made an investment in one company, it will not invest in a competitor.

Policybazaar CEO Yashish Dahiya says that being nimble is extremely important, especially when dealing with competition. 'Competition wipes out companies which have been set up over a period of time within a few years. I think companies have to be prepared to respond very, very quickly,' he says. He offers the example of Yahoo's demise. Had Yahoo responded to Google when the search giant was still in its infancy, they might have survived, he says.

At Policybazaar, they pay very close attention to what competitors might be doing, and are prepared to move really quickly in response. He offers the example of a competitor who combined a two-wheeler insurance with a dengue care product. A two-wheeler insurance was not lucrative on its own, offering only fifty rupees per transaction. However, the combined product could generate four hundred to five hundred rupees per transaction as the dengue care product offered a much higher margin. When Policybazaar came to know of this, decided to build their own product which could offer the same benefits. Within a week, they had put together their own product, and released it into the market. Even the competing firm was impressed, Yashish says. They could not believe that Policybazaar could respond within seven days with competing product.

Adhering to quick decision-making and executing with agility requires a formulated approach. Decentralization was the formula adopted by Raghu to ensure speedy execution. He embedded this in TaxiForSure's psyche. 'If anyone approached me for decision-making, I asked them, "What would you do?" Most of the time, we went ahead with what they had decided, because we had already thought that their decision would be our decision. Every time anyone came to us, we asked them the same question. After a while, they stopped coming to us and took their own decisions. So, only the important things, things that could have a huge impact, came to me. I know some other founders who still take a call on what Diwali gift has to be sent. But because we followed decentralization, such things never reached us.'

'With whatever we have done, we never worked towards making the right decision. We always made the decision and then worked towards making it right. The worst thing that anyone can do in a startup is to sleep over a problem or a decision. Normally, we would make very, very quick decisions and if things were not working, we would change the decision and move on.'

Summary

- **Be prepared to don a multiplicity of hats.** Early in the life of a startup, often in the absence of a large team, a founder might be required to attend to a plethora of demands. Be prepared to attend to every aspect of the company early on.
- **Invest in building a brand.** Effective branding is a powerful driver of a company's value. It symbolizes the company's core values, its product principles and the user experience it delivers.
- **Acquisition of new users must not come at the cost of losing existing users.** Focusing on acquiring new users at the expense of existing users will not allow for growth that is sustainable. While seeking to acquire new users, ensure

that the needs of existing users are being met so they do not churn out.

- **Identify the most critical metrics for the company and track them rigorously.** Tracking metrics enables a deeper understanding of how the company is performing. Metrics communicate progress, or the lack of it. Identify the most relevant set of metrics for the company and track them rigorously.

- **You might not be the ideal customer.** The needs of the customers might differ from those of the founders and the team. In refining the product, you should look to receive feedback from actual customers.

- **Obsess over customer feedback.** Customer feedback will guide as you to what the product might lack, and how it might be refined. Customer insights will also be vital in integrating new features into the product. Collecting customer feedback must be an integral part of the product development and improvement process.

- **Iterate, and if required, pivot.** It is difficult to understand how effective a product is in solving a customer problem until it is put to use by customers. Look to refine the product based on the feedback received from customers. If a superior use-case emerges that the company could be adapted for, look to pivot.

- **Speed is a premium.** The speed at which a company moves is a key determinant of success. Moving too slowly can be perilous for an early-stage startup, leading to delays in achieving product-market fit as well as allowing competitors to surge ahead.

6

Raising Money

RAISING MONEY IS NOT necessarily integral to a startup's growth. Not every firm needs to, and many companies have managed without external investments to drive growth.

Raising money, however, can often allow a company to grow far more rapidly than it would have otherwise. Not only does it offer financial resources that can be directly invested to drive expansion, it also lends a sheen of credibility to the company. External validation can be leveraged for both hiring talent, as well as strengthening brand recognition amongst potential customers.

However, raising money will come with attendant expectations with regard to the trajectory of the company. An entrepreneur would be well served to take these into account before committing to the path.

Bootstrapping versus raising money

Delhivery CEO Sahil Barua says that when they started the company, he and his co-founders did not fully appreciate the fact that 'the thing that makes business work is capital.' 'So as a consequence,' he says 'in the beginning perhaps it was harder for us than it should have been. Capital as a means of strategy is something we learnt much later, as the business scaled up.' Capital is the life blood of business; in the absence of capital to fuel its operations, a business will fold quickly.

Bootstrapping implies running a company without relying on large influxes of capital from external sources. Entrepreneurs would survive on the back of internal cash flows through selling the company's product or service, and their own savings. Raising money from external investors typically implies large capital infusions, carried out in exchange for a significant equity stake in the company.

Most startups start out being bootstrapped. Eventually, as they look to scale, their expenses increase. Raising money from external investors can meet these needs. Most startups eventually need to choose between continuing to bootstrap and raising money.

According to Steve Blank, serial entrepreneur, and author of *The Startup Owner's Manual*, there might be two key reasons for raising money:[1]

- You have a killer idea that is only partially validated, and you need money to get to product-market fit, or

---

[1]   Steve Blank, 'How to Raise Money—It's a Journey Not an Event,' *VentureBeat*, 22 February 2020, https://venturebeat.com/2020/02/22/how-to-raise-money-its-a-journey-not-an-event/

- You (think) you have product-market fit with real customers and real revenue and need money to grow and expand.

According to Rajan Anandan, managing director at Sequoia India, choosing between bootstrapping and raising money depends on two factors: the nature of the startup's business, and how much capital the founders are willing, and able, to put into the business.

Rajan was a Partner at McKinsey & Company before leaving to head Dell in India. Later, he headed Microsoft in India, and Google across India and Southeast Asia. As part of the leadership team at Sequoia India, he co-leads its Surge programme that focuses on investing in early-stage startups. He is also a prolific angel investor, having backed a large number of successful startups at very early stages.

The nature of the startup's business is a key determinant of whether it could continue to operate without needing to raise money. There are two elements to this: the nature of the product, and the nature of the industry.

If a product lends itself to being built with a small team, and the startup is able to secure revenues that can help meet its expenses, it might not need to raise money for a long time.

Rajan offers the example of a hypothetical company that is building a B2B software product. It could potentially lend itself to being built by three co-founders: one could be a very good product leader, one an engineer and the third responsible for go-to-market and distribution. They could find a set of early customers to co-develop the product with, such that they get paid while they are still coding the product. Once they release the product, their income streams could expand. In such a case, the company could continue to be bootstrapped for a long time. 'Theoretically, this company could be built over ten years and become a very large company, and could never raise any capital,' Rajan says. It might take them longer to scale than if they were to raise money, but they could still survive, and grow. 'If you can do it with a very, very lean team, and you can start getting customers to pay you very early in your startup journey, the higher the likelihood that you can actually bootstrap the company,' he says.

On the other hand, if the product requires a long gestation period before it can ship, if there needs to be a team in place beyond the founders, such that you need fifteen to twenty people to build the product, then bootstrapping might not be sustainable. Then you would need to raise money.

The industry that the startup is operating in is an equally important factor in determining whether fundraising will be required. If you are in an industry in which monetization takes time, then external capital infusion will be required. Similarly, if it is a competitive space, and other firms already have a lot of resources at their disposal, then you will need to raise money. If your competitors are looking to capture a large share of the market through aggressive promotions, you will need to raise money so that you are able to counter them. 'So the industry that you pick, and the type of business that you want to build, makes a huge difference,' Rajan says.

Beyond the nature of the business, what determines whether, and when, a startup will raise money depends upon how its founders approach the business. Every business requires some level of capital; if the founders are able to continue building without needing external infusions, then they might not need to raise money.

According to Anand Daniel, Partner at Accel, founders should first think through whether they would be willing to build their company within a specific period of time that aligns with the investment cycle of institutional investors.

Anand first started investing in startups when he joined a venture capital firm for a summer internship during his MBA at MIT. Prior to that he had spent a little over seven years at Intel in both engineering and management roles. He joined Accel in 2010, and has continued at the firm since, focusing on investments in consumer technology, online marketplaces, and healthcare technology.

Venture capital firms especially have an investment cycle that requires an exit within ten years. Founders need to consider if they want to build over a period of ten to twenty years, or are willing to build towards an exit for their investor within ten years. 'If it's something that you want to build over ten-plus years, I would encourage you not to think about institutional funding very early,' Anand says. 'There are a lot of companies that go on, get to profitability, and then only raise capital from private equity or growth funds. A lot of companies go down that route. And it's possible in certain industries. If so, that's a great way. Some companies never raise capital all the way through to exit also.'

Anand offers the example of enterprise application development company Zoho. Founded in 1996, Zoho has not raised money from external investors even as it has grown into of the largest companies in its segment; by 2020, it had more than 45 million customers in 180 countries, with an annual turnover of more than $500 million.[2,3] Even though it took the

2   Kritti Bhalla, 'Zoho's Profit Streak Continues as FY20 Revenue Crosses INR 4,300 Cr.', *Inc42*, 22 February 2021, inc42.com/buzz/what-the-financials-zohos-profit-streak-continues-as-fy20-revenue-crosses-inr-4300-cr.

3   Patrick Moorhead, 'ZOHO: The Most Successful SaaS Company You May Have Never Heard Of', *Forbes*, 30 March 2020, forbes.com/sites/moorinsights/2020/03/30/zoho-the-most-successful-saas-company-you-have-likely-never-heard-of/?sh=289760f33b60

company a long time to scale, because it was profitable, it could continue to operate without needing to raise money.

'So all kinds of funding opportunities and ways to build companies exist,' Anand says. 'It is a question of you understanding your industry and what you want to achieve. Once you're clear about that, if you pick an area where you want to grow a company fast and exit in five to ten years, then institutional funding makes sense.'

While bootstrapped startups that could scale successfully exist, they are rare. Far more startups seek to raise money than remain bootstrapped. As a company looks to scale, raising money becomes an important imperative.

Catalyst for growth

External financing for a startup can be obtained through contributions from family and friends, through grants, through winning competitions, and from institutional investors. Institutional investors are typically able to provide larger sums of capital than may be possible through other channels. In addition, beyond the immediate benefits of having access to capital, and media coverage, raising money from institutional investors can allow a company to benefit from their thought partnership, as well as direct, non-financial forms of assistance.

Amongst institutional investors, venture capital firms primarily focus on investing in startups, especially in early stages. As a company grows large, strategic investors investing through corporate venture capital vehicles might also become important. These could be bigger companies in the same space in which a startup is growing, or even in an adjacent space. Private equity funds typically invest in later stages.

'There are various kinds of funding options that are available, depending on which sector you are in,' Anand says. 'As an entrepreneur, it's important for you to figure out, what is the time frame you have for building the company, what is the kind of exit you want, and what are the kind of capital requirements that are needed for what you are building.' Accordingly, you could determine your fundraising strategy.

Institutional investors can offer access to a wide array of resources that can help a startup function better. VC firms can be especially helpful during early stages. Many firms have on their rolls operating partners, highly experienced professionals with domain expertise, who can offer guidance to startups in specific domains, be it in marketing, technology or finance. Startups can tap into expertise in taxation services, and the legal aspects of running a business. Some VC firms can also be especially helpful in hiring talent; they can invite applications on behalf of the startup as well as tap into their network and make introductions.

Telio, a B2B e-commerce company based in Vietnam, was a part of the first cohort of Sequoia's Surge programme through which they invest in early-stage startups. It connects small retailers in Vietnam with brands and wholesalers on a centralized platform that delivers wider choices, better pricing and more efficient logistics. Engineering talent can often be hard to find in Vietnam; Telio was having difficulties in building their engineering team. Once they became a part of the Surge programme, Sequoia India stepped in; their first thirty engineers were hired through the support that the Surge programme provided.

A VC firm can also be a thought partner, and help founders with developing deeper understanding of the segment that they are playing in, Rajan says. It can help founders answer questions such as 'what business do you want to be in', or 'can this space really lend itself to building a billion-dollar company'. It can help refine the company's product strategy, their engineering strategy and their growth strategy 'down to identifying the right channels of distribution for the product', Rajan explains.

Rajan offers the example of InterviewBit which was also part of the inaugural Surge cohort. In their original avatar, they offered a coding test preparation platform, and had built a community of 500 thousand developers who would use their resources to prepare for interviews with technology companies such as Google and Amazon. The founding team was very seasoned in the coding space, Rajan says. Through working closely with the team, Sequoia India helped them refine their strategy, and eventually pivot to an online coding academy model; they are now called the Scaler Academy.[4]

Another aspect that Rajan highlights is the help that they seek to provide to early-stage companies for achieving product-market fit. He says that the hardest thing for seed stage companies is to find product-market fit. 'One of the things we do is we make sure that if a seed stage company has not achieved product-market fit, they should not focus on growth. They should have a very small team until they find product-market fit.' As companies jostle with their model, they seek to help them answer questions like 'how do you find product-market fit?'; 'how do you know when you have it?'; 'how do you know when you don't have it?' and so on.

[4]   Manish Singh, 'India's InterviewBit Secures $20M to Grow Its Advanced Online Computer Science Program', *TechCrunch*, 28 January 2020, techcrunch.com/2020/01/27/interviewbit-secures-20m-to-grow-its-advanced-online-computer-science-program-in-india

Beyond helping with refining strategy, VC firms can provide valuable assistance when a startup is looking to raise capital in a future round. In addition to participating in the round themselves, they can help the startup determine how much would they need to raise, and when should they start. They can help develop the pitch, and refer them to other investors. When Khatabook, a digital credit ledger for micro SMEs, was looking to raise money after being part of the Surge programme, Sequoia offered their help.

However, at the end of the day, a VC firm's involvement is strategic, and not operational, Anand notes. 'We are not running the company,' Anand says. 'We are there more as a sounding board, strategic board, cheering squad,' he says. 'So very rarely you hear, or should hear, about the VCs because it's always a behind-the-scenes job. And we don't do much operationally; it's more strategic, in guiding and opening doors in the case of funding, in the case of hiring, or business development. But it's the CEO's job to go and close.'

No free lunch

While raising money opens up avenues for growth, it comes with attendant challenges. The most immediate challenge that it brings is in terms of the process itself. Fundraising can be an arduous, time-taking process. It can easily distract the team from day-to-day needs at the startup.

According to Paul Graham, raising money has a tendency to suck up attention, diverting it away from the startup itself:[5]

---

[5]   Paul Graham, 'A Fundraising Survival Guide', *www.paulgraham.com*, August 2008, paulgraham.com/fundraising.html

'Raising money has a mysterious capacity to suck up all your attention. Even if you only have one meeting a day with investors, somehow that one meeting will burn up your whole day. It costs not just the time of the actual meeting, but the time getting there and back, and the time preparing for it beforehand and thinking about it afterward.'

Delhivery CEO Sahil Barua says that when he and his co-founders started the company, they underestimated the amount of time it would take to raise capital. 'Most entrepreneurs make this mistake,' he says. 'The assumption very often is I have an idea and I'll just walk up to a VC and I will get $2 million in capital.' It does not usually work out that way. Instead, you need to craft your story appropriately, and deliver it, and 'just repeat that cycle again and again and again'.

He wishes he had known how time-consuming it would be. 'As CEO, for instance, I spent maybe a quarter of my time on investors, boards, board management, making sure that we had adequately capitalized as a company, in thinking about how much more capital we would need down the line, where it's going to come from, and so on. I think founders underestimate that. We underestimated that.' The importance of planning, and adequately allocating time for raising capital, was a realization that only dawned with time. 'Over time, as we built the office of the CFO, as we built the office of investor relations, we started realizing that these things were very high-yield,' he explains.

Rajan Anandan echoes this narrative, admitting that it usually takes a large number of attempts to raise a round for most founders. Raising funding doesn't happen with two or three meetings; founders have to keep in mind that you have to meet a lot of investors because every investor is looking for different things, he explains.

He offers the example of Harsh Jain, the founder of Dream11. Dream11 is a fantasy sports application that allows users to create their own virtual team before a match starts. Based on the performance of the chosen players during the actual match, users accumulate points and are ranked at the end of the game. Based on their rank, they can receive winnings in the form of a share of a common pool of money, collected from participating users.

According to Rajan, Harsh had to take 105 meetings to raise a Series A round. 'That's telling,' he says. 'Founders sometimes get upset because they've had ten meetings and they haven't raised their round and I'm like, well, maybe you're about 10 per cent of the way there,' he quips.

Raising money from external investors also creates more enduring implications. The consequent dilution in the share of the founders has financial implications for the founders, diminishing the size of an eventual payout if the startup were to be acquired, or go public.

It brings additional accountability upon the founders; they are now accountable to their investors who now share in the company's ownership. Founders are expected to adhere to a unified vision for the future of the company, and the growth path that it pursues.

It also has implications in terms of the control that the founders might be able to wield on the company. In case of disagreements over the direction that the company should take, founders are no longer in a position to take unilateral decisions.

In order to avoid disagreements, Rajan advocates upfront and constant alignment between founders and the company's board which would include investors, as well as between founders and the team. 'Making sure that there's very clear alignment on the strategy, where you're trying to go, on the objectives and key results, on the budget and financial plan for the year, that's the first and most important step,' Rajan says.

The next important step is to ensure that there is frequent and transparent communication. 'Why does trust break down? Trust breaks down when both sides don't believe that the other side is being transparent,' Rajan says. 'Or when there's no alignment between interests and objective.'

Rajan holds that communication with the board becomes especially important when things are not going according to plan. 'I've always believed that when things are not going well, you should over-communicate,' he says. 'Whereas, sometimes natural human tendency is that when things are not going well, you kind of go into a shell. But that's really bad because when you go quiet, that's when there's no information, there's no communication, so your investors don't know what's going on. And then, therefore, they start questioning what's going on.'

Even if there is disagreement on strategy, if you can talk through it, and have a discussion with investors, then that would ensure that there is no breakdown of trust. 'At the end of the day,' Rajan says, 'investors believe that founders need to make the decisions.' But being on the board, they also expect to be a part of discussions about the most important, strategic aspects of the company or the major initiatives that a startup is trying to drive.

Ultimately, in seeking to raise money from investors, it is important to remember that when VC firms invest in a company, it is with the understanding that 'number one, these founders want to build very large businesses,' Rajan says. 'And number two, that the markets are large enough to be built large businesses.' Rajan offers an example. If you are building a SaaS company, you could build it into a $20 million SaaS company that generates $8 million of profit each year. If there are two or three co-founders, each of them will make $3 million a year. For most people that's a really good outcome. 'But for a venture capital firm, that is not the reason they invested.'

According to Rajan, founders need to be very real with themselves about whether they want to build a very large business before going to VC firms. 'And if they don't want to be a very large business, or they don't think this market lends itself to building a very large business, they probably should really try to bootstrap for as long as they can,' he says.

Determining fundraising cadence

Startup fundraising events are typically described in terms of the stage in the company's life cycle. According to Anand Daniel, broadly, there are six distinct phases in the life cycle of the startup.

In the beginning, there is the idea stage, or the concept stage. During this phase, there would typically not be any external funding available. During the acceleration stage which comes next, the startup can become a part of accelerator programmes which provide both financial assistance and immersive education, aimed at accelerating growth. Startup accelerators are fixed-term, cohort-based, mentorship-driven programmes that culminate in a public pitch event or demo day for larger investors to invest in the startup. They usually provide a small amount of seed capital, working space and a plethora of networking opportunities, with both peer ventures as well as experienced investors.

During the seed stage, the startup could raise money from friends and family. It could raise money from angel investors, wealthy private investors in startups. It could also be funded by seed-stage-focused VC firms. Beyond seed stage, investments are typically made by institutional investors.

Once you raise capital from institutional investors, the expectation will be to scale the company rapidly. 'The intent is not to slowly, and over five to ten years build a sustainable company. It is to grow the company as quickly as possible into a very large business,' Anand says. Most VC firms will look for an exit within five to seven years. The period is typically extendable, and might not always apply. 'But that's the expectation set,' he says.

According to Marc Andreessen, how much you raise can be determined based on the whether the startup has achieved product-market fit: 'Before Product/Market Fit, a startup should ideally raise at least enough money to get to Product/ Market Fit. After Product/Market Fit, a startup should ideally raise at least enough money to fully exploit the opportunity in front of it, and then to get to profitability while still fully exploiting that opportunity. I will further argue that the definition of "at least enough money" in each case should include a substantial amount of extra money beyond your default plan, so that you can withstand bad surprises. In other words, insurance. This is particularly true for startups that have not yet achieved Product/Market Fit, since you have no real idea how long that will take.'[6]

In determining how much to raise in each round, founders need to define what they would like to accomplish over the next eighteen to twenty-four months. The amount they would need to raise would depend on the nature of the company, the

---

6   Mark Andreessen, 'Part 6: How Much Funding Is Too Little? Too Much?', *The Pmarca Guide to Startups*, 3 July 2007, pmarchive. com/guide_to_startups_part6.html

industry it is operating and the founders who would be setting the vision for the company. If they hit their target, that becomes an opportunity to raise money again, if required.

In the case of TaxiForSure, they were looking to go from less than fifty transactions a month to 500 transactions a month. 'They wanted to do that in a six-to-nine-month window, they needed a million dollars for that,' Anand says. 'That's what we gave, and they hit that milestone ahead of time.' Once they had hit their targets, they could raise money again.

In raising money, investors too need persuading. Most investors will look for a product, and some amount of customer adoption. They would like to understand if the product has achieved product-market fit, or that is still ahead in its life cycle. They would like to understand if the product is experiencing actual growth. For instance, TaxiForSure raised money from Accel only after they had hit fifty transactions a month, and needed money to scale it further.

Founders need to raise enough to have an adequate runway, the duration the company could continue to operate without having to raise money again. According to Rajan, the COVID market environment has especially highlighted the importance of having an adequate runway. Startups have had to face a mix of weakened consumer demand and higher expenses. In raising money, a startup needs to raise enough to be able to tide over periods of uncertainty.

'If you need to raise funding, raise funding so that you have twenty-four months of runway,' Rajan says. 'Because what you don't want to do is be in the business of raising money every six months. It takes an enormous amount of time to raise money, and if you only raise small amounts at a time, you'll end up spending it and would need to raise again. If there are two co-founders, one of them will be raising financing all the time,' Rajan says. 'So generally it's a good thing to think about whether you can raise enough money to give you cash runway for two years.'

Based on how much money a startup is trying to raise, and how they are valued, there is going to be dilution in the founders' equity in the company as investors take a share. According to Rajan, in the first three to four rounds, you should expect 10–25 per cent dilution to take place. As you get to a very large size, the level of dilution with a new round will decrease. 'VCs also want to get to a meaningful level of ownership in a company, he says. 'So usually, you'd see that a series A might be $5–7 million, where the VC gets 20–25 per cent. Similarly, with a Series B. By the time you get to series F, you're, let's say, a billion-dollar company, but you're only raising 100 million, so that could be a 10 per cent dilution.'

Complementarity is key

In selecting which investors to approach, Rajan's advice is to examine the sector focus that an investment firm has as well as the investment stage at which they typically invest in companies.

Given that fundraising can be an arduous process, examining potential complementarity in domains is likely to save both time and effort. For every investment firm there are specific sectors that they invest a lot in, and there are some sectors that they don't invest in, Rajan says. Getting familiar with investment themes historically favoured by a firm will be helpful in prioritizing which firms to approach. If a certain firm focuses on the domain that your startup is operating in, there is greater likelihood of interest in taking the conversation forward.

Rajan offers examples. 'So, for instance, at Sequoia Capital India we don't invest in biotech companies. If you're trying to build a biotech company, coming to us is probably not the best idea,' he says. 'We don't do pure-play offline retail companies. If you're building a business that's a pure-play offline retail concept, that's probably not something we are going to invest in.'

Along with understanding which sectors a firm invests in, you need to assess at which stage of investment a certain firm might come in. If you are an early-stage firm, large private equity firms such as General Atlantic or Warburg Pincus will not make sense, these firms don't do a $10 million deal, Rajan says. These would typically come in at later stages of investment, with larger capital infusions. On the other hand, if you are looking to raise a relatively large amount, seed-stage investment firms will not be interested. 'If you're trying to raise $20 million, going to a seed fund doesn't make sense,' Rajan says.

Given that fundraising can be an onerous process, it is useful to look at VCs that have a history of making follow-on investments in a portfolio company. In the case of firms that do, it makes it easier for the company to raise money in future rounds given that some amount of funding will come from their existing VC investor. While it does not happen every time, in many cases, if you raise capital from a firm, they are going to carry out a pro rata investment in the next round. So if they own 20 per cent of the company, they'll invest at least 20 per cent of the amount raised in the next round.

Anand explains how this typically works. 'At Accel, if we invest $1, we reserve X dollars for that company. What that means is we put in this much, but we're going to put in so much more over a period of time in that same company.' In the case of TaxiForSure, Accel invested in their seed round, and once again in their Series A round along with another VC firm.

Getting a foot in the door

Media coverage is a good way to get noticed by investors. VC firms monitor developments in the startup ecosystem closely, and any coverage is likely to get picked up.

In the case of most firms, you can reach out directly. 'You just write to us. You could find the partners or the associates or the principals, you can send a message on LinkedIn, you can email them, they're pretty responsive,' Rajan notes. Many firms also invite direct applications, especially accelerators and seed-stage programmes. 'At Surge, you just apply online,' Rajan says. 'We look at every application, we take every application seriously.

Being referred to a firm is also a very good way to come to the attention of an investor. It often brings with it added credibility. A referral could come from the founder of one of the portfolio companies of a firm, from other investors, or even from acquaintances. It is especially helpful in reaching out to angel investors who might not have a large team in place, and may not be able to scour the media, or startup databases to identify investment opportunities. 'As an angel investor, I didn't have a team and I used to get too many inbound emails. So being referred really helped a lot,' Rajan notes, referring to a time prior to his stint at Sequoia when he used to invest in startups as an individual.

From the investor's lens

Major VC firms are highly selective, typically investing in less than ten to fifteen startups in a year. According to Anand, in determining whether to invest in a startup, there are four parameters that a firm looks at: team, market, product and business model.

This also evolves based on the stage of the investment. While the team and the market are far more important at the early stages, the product and the business model become more important later.

'At seed stage, what investors are looking for is, is this a very strong team,' Rajan says. 'And is this a space or a market that lends itself to big companies. And if there's traction, if the company has already launched, then you look at early metrics to say, are there early signs that this is an interesting product that customers are going to love?'

'For series A, you need to have some semblance of product-market fit.' According to Rajan, most series A rounds will not happen without product-market fit. 'You have to have strong consumer love, you have to have very strong growth metrics and cohort performance.'

For Series B firms, unit economics becomes crucial. Unit economics describes a specific business model's revenues and costs in relation to any basic, quantifiable item that creates value for the business. For a taxi booking app, a single unit might be a ride in their vehicle. The amount paid by the user would drive their revenues, the cost of acquiring and serving the user would drive their costs. If the value accrued from serving a customer exceeds the cost of serving the customer, then the company makes a profit. Strong unit economics, therefore, implies, either that the company is already profitable, or shows a trend towards profitable growth.

'By the time you get to Series B, generally you have to have pretty decent unit economics,' Rajan says. Especially during difficult market conditions, 'if you don't have strong unit economics, you will not be able to raise a Series B.'

For Series C and Series D onwards, 'you got to have a very strong team, you got to have a large market, you got to have strong product-market fit, you got to have strong unit economics, and you have to have very strong financial trajectory,' Rajan notes. At every stage of financing, the bar for investment rises higher, with every individual component, as well as how they come together becoming important.

a. Market

The market that a startup is trying to serve is the most critical element for investors. The primary question that they try to answer here is does it lend itself to the startup being able to build a large business.

According to Anand, there are two primary filters that investors typically apply:

- Is the market large enough for the startup to offer an outsized return?
- Is it possible to scale rapidly and capture a large share of the market within five to seven years?

'We look at thousands of businesses every year, but 95–98 per cent of them don't pass through to the next level because of the market factor,' Anand says. 'It's not so much the team, it's not the product, not anything else.'

The reason the market that a startup is trying to serve is so important is because of the way VC funds are structured. A VC firm would typically raise money from the likes of sovereign funds, pension funds, and high net-worth individuals to set up a fund. A typical fund will have a ten-year life cycle; VCs will look to generate returns within that period. Typically, a VC firm will look to invest in companies over the first three to four years, and will then work with the investee companies towards an exit in the subsequent five to seven years.

The VC firm will be required to return a multiple of the principal amount to investors in its fund. Typically, for a hypothetical fund size of $100 million, the firm will be expected to return $200–300 million, or more. The firm's returns would accrue from investing in and exiting from startups at a higher valuation. The return from an investment will be a function of the value of an investee company at the point of exit and their share in the company. Suppose it were to invest the entire sum of $100 million in its fund into a single company and held a 20 per cent share at the time of exit, to achieve a return of $300 million, the investee will need to be valued at $1,500 million. For a single company to be so valuable, the market in which the company must be operating must be even larger; after all, except in the unlikely case of a perfect monopoly, the value of a single company could only represent a certain share of the value of the entire market.

However, this is an extreme example. Typically, the entire amount in a fund will not be invested in a single company, and will instead be distributed across multiple investments to distribute risk. A VC firm might make ten to twenty investments from a single fund. Not all of these investments might offer a desirable return; some might even not allow the recovery of the invested capital. Therefore, a small number of investee companies must yield a large multiple on the initial investment for the overall fund to achieve its desired return. VC firms, therefore, constantly look for opportunities in which a startup could become a major player in a large market.

According to Anand, the minimum size of the market that a VC firm looks for depends on the nature of the firm, its industry focus, and their understanding of how a market might evolve. A small angel fund of US$10 million may not have a very large market size requirement. However, larger funds in India might perforce look for very large markets.

Anand says that as investors, VC firms look for companies that will create impact at a very large scale. They would look for consumer companies that could touch 'tens, if not hundreds of millions of lives'. In investing in an enterprise-focused company, they would look for the potential to impact 'tens of thousands of enterprises'. While investing in startups can be inherently risky, it comes with the territory, Anand implies. 'We are absolutely okay with there being risk because as a VC investor we should be willing to lose the money that we invest.' But when a startup is successful, it should be able to return 10x, 50x, or even 100x the initial investment, he says.

b. Team

The team determines the startup's destiny. Especially in case of early-stage investments, when the product is often not fully mature, the strength of the team becomes a key parameter in determining eventual success.

Investors look for a background that indicate a set of founders well-equipped to build a certain company. Rajan offers the example of Chilibeli, an Indonesian social commerce startup focused on fresh foods. The startup had three co-founders, all of them with previous e-commerce experience. One of them had worked with Alibaba, another with Lazada and the third had co-founded an e-commerce startup earlier. 'So the bet that we were making was, these were three co-founders who had very, very extensive ecommerce experience,' Rajan says. 'These were founders who knew e-commerce inside out. They also knew Indonesia deeply,' Rajan says. Chilibeli was trying to build an agent-based e-commerce model where deliveries would be carried out to an agent, and not to every household; this would keep delivery costs low. Given a potentially viable model, and the strong background of the founders, Sequoia Capital India became an investor in the company even before they had launched.

Domain expertise becomes especially important in what Anand describes as 'intellectual-property-led areas'. Such areas are typically highly technical and may require extensive training to be able to solve customer problems. Healthcare is a good example. Mitra Biotech is an Accel portfolio company. Its objective is to advance personalized cancer treatment. Its proprietary platform delivers individualized treatment response predictions to assist with patient-specific cancer treatment selection. The co-founders were both postdocs from MIT, Harvard, who had done years of research there, and founded the company, Anand says. 'If someone from, let's say, no healthcare background, no technology background, in healthcare, had come and pitched the same idea to us, it would have been a lot harder investment decision to make.'

In the absence of a complimentary background or domain expertise, investors would look for unique insights about the market, and the product that a startup is trying to build. According to Rajan, there are two things that founders would typically be asked: 'What deep insights do you have about the space that you're going after and what is the specific problem that you're trying to solve?'

'What we're trying to figure out is what unique insights you have about the space, and, second, based on those insights, what is the product you're going to build' Rajan says. In asking these questions, their objective is to uncover information that will give them confidence that a founder inexperienced in a certain domain will still build 'an awesome product'. 'We're trying to get what unique insights you have about this market, about those specific users,' he says.

However, while the right background and unique insights might be important, the team needs to be able to work together well. 'When we look at teams as investors, what we look for is complementarity,' Anand says. 'It is not necessary that you have five of the same type. I have seen many engineers get together and form a company. Four engineers start a company saying that they are four co-founders.' Even in a technology company that might not always be the best combination of backgrounds. When Anand was a student at MIT Sloan, he too would work on ideas, and look to start up. 'It used to be four or five of my classmates, very similar backgrounds. All smart but not necessarily complementary,' he smiles.

'So when you look at a team, it is very important to understand what business you're building and have complementary co-founders.' He offers an example. For instance, if there are three co-founders, ideally, one should be able to take care of the technology aspects, one of the business and strategy aspects, and the third of operations.

According to Anand, how well a team gels together is also very important. For instance, in a pitch, co-founders might not agree with each other all the time. But they look for signs that might indicate that they are not likely to work together well: are they cutting each other off, are they talking over each other, are they engaging in one-upmanship? While it might not always be obvious, Anand says that they find it important to be observant of these nuances. The objective is to understand if the founders are respectful of each other.

According to Rajan, the other thing that investors look for is the ability to keep building for the long haul: 'Is this a team that's going to stay together for the next ten or fifteen years, go through four or five near-death moments and be able to build an amazing company?'

Investors try to look at the founders' history, for past evidence of having shown perseverance. 'Have they been through very difficult periods in their life? Have they worked through those?' Rajan says. 'Are you somebody who will persevere, despite all the odds, despite it being very, very difficult, keep going at it for ten or fifteen years to make it through?' He offers the example of the cloud data protection company Druva, in which he was an angel investor.

'These guys have pivoted five times, they have changed their business model five times. It just requires a long period of continuously evolving, mutating, pivoting, to be able to get there, and you really need a founding team that is very, very good, but very perseverant, that just keeps staying in the game.'

Finally, investors also look for evidence that the founders will be able to adequately carry out their roles once the company scales. Often they would carry out reference checks on founders. 'We do talk to people who know them to see who will scale up to be CEO, who will say scale up as the technology head, or the various roles we talked about,' Anand says.

c. Product

In evaluating a product, investors will look for the customer insight behind the product idea. A compelling customer insight is likely to drive a superior product. They will also look for its unique value proposition, a differentiating quality that sets the product apart from competitors. According to Rajan, a key question that the Sequoia Surge programme expects applicants to answer is: 'What is the unique consumer insight behind your product that you think other companies in this space just don't get? A unique value proposition will drive a sustainable competitive advantage for the product. Its absence might imply that there is little to distinguish it from competing products, and that a clear competitive advantage might be uncertain.'

In the absence of a released product, investors will impose greater scrutiny upon the market, the team, and the idea itself. If the product has been released, they will look for evidence of 'customer love' for the product. The question that they will look to answer is whether the product or service solves a core problem for its users that drives loyalty towards the product, and repeat usage. They will also look for evidence of the product having reached product-market fit.

Rajan says that for early-stage companies, investors will look for signs that it is an interesting product that customers are going to love. Customer love can be demonstrated through metrics that indicate that the product has a loyal base of users that truly value what it offers.

The retention rate of the product is a useful metric in this regard. The retention rate of a product or service is the proportion of users that continue to use it over a given period. A high degree of retention indicates a product or service that is well-loved by users who keep returning to it. On the other hand, a poor retention rate, or high customer churn, indicates that the offering is losing customers. A product that loses customers faster than it can acquire them will not grow.

The Net Promoter Score indicates the percentage of customers rating their likelihood to recommend a company, a product, or a service to a friend or colleague. If a large number of early users are willing to advocate on behalf of the product, that indicates a high degree of customer love. Other metrics that can indicate customer love can include favourable ratings on the application store, such as the App Store or Google Play.

In the case of seed-stage startups, investors would also like to understand whether it is experiencing actual growth, or traction. Robust week-on-week and month-on-month growth rates will indicate that not only does the product has a loyal base of users, but also one that is growing rapidly.

Detailed metrics tracking will allow for demonstrability of growth, as well as business viability. While each market and sales channel is likely to have different metrics that will need to be tracked, the following is a key list of metrics that may be communicated to potential investors:

- Acquisition: the number of users who interact with your product
- Activation: the percentage of users who actually use the product
- Customer acquisition cost: the cost of winning a customer to use a product/service
- Payback period: the length of time needed to recover the cost of acquisition from a user
- Customer lifetime value: the monetary value of a customer relationship, based on the projected future cash flows from the customer relationship
- Annual recurring revenue: revenue, normalized on an annual basis, expected from customers
- Referral: the percentage of current users who refer new users

Beyond customer love, investors will look for a sustainable competitive advantage, allowing the company to protect its long-term profitability and market share. A sustainable competitive advantage is often described as a moat. The term itself was first popularized by Warren Buffett who, in explaining his investment strategy at Berkshire Hathaway's annual meeting of shareholders in 1995, noted: 'I want a business with a moat around it. I want a very valuable castle in the middle and then I want the Duke who is in charge of that castle to be very honest and hard-working and able. Then I want a moat around that castle.'[7]

According to Buffett, products or services that have wide, sustainable moats around them are the ones that deliver rewards to investors.[8] Investor Pat Dorsey later built on this concept to lay out four kinds of economic moats that an investor might look at:[9]

1. Switching costs: High switching costs keep customers from shifting from one product or service to another. This could either be expressed in terms of monetary value or time value to the customer. If the cost of switching outweighs the benefits, a customer is unlikely to switch.
2. Cost advantages: A company with a cost advantage can produce goods or services at a lower cost, allowing it to

7   'Buffett on Finding the Right "Lord of the Castle",' *buffett.cnbc. com*, 1 May 1995, https://buffett.cnbc.com/video/1995/05/01/ buffett-on-finding-the-right-lord-of-the-castle.html
8   Warren Buffett and Carol Loomis, 'Mr Buffett on the Stock Market', 22 November 1999, *money.cnn.com*, https://money.cnn. com/2006/06/25/magazines/fortune/charity2.fortune/index.htm
9   Pat Dorsey, *The Little Book That Builds Wealth* (John Wiley & Sons, 2008), pp. 23–24.

outperform its competitors. This could be achieved through cheaper processes, location, scale, or access to a unique asset.

3. Network effects: A product or service whose value increases with the number of users on it creates a barrier to entry for new firms which will start with a smaller number of users.

4. Intangible assets: A product or service built on the basis of proprietary technology or regulatory licenses will have a powerful competitive advantage against competitors. Similarly, one that is able to create strong brand recognition and loyalty will see repeat purchases on the strength of its brand value.

A product or service that is able to clearly demonstrate an economic moat is likely to receive higher investor confidence.

d. Business model

In evaluating a company's business model, VC firms look to understand how it will make money. This would imply examining the revenue streams and the cost structure for the company. They will also seek to understand the key customer segments for the company, what is the value proposition that it offers, which channels does it seek to utilize in reaching its target segments, which are the key resources the company would need, and how might it find the right partners, if required.

The business model of the company will inform its unit economics. This would determine whether the company could be profitable as it scales. It is defined as the direct revenues and costs associated with conducting the business, expressed on a per-unit basis. The metric offers a basis for assessing whether the company could be profitable as it scales. Positive unit economics would imply that the business is making more money per customer than it costs you to get one.

In the formative years of the company, the business model might still be evolving, and therefore might be a less important element in the overall assessment. However, as the business matures, there is likely to be much greater emphasis on the business model, and its inherent viability.

e. Bringing it together

Explaining Accel's decision to invest in Freshworks, Anand says that their market potential was very clear upfront. A lot of companies would buy customer support software, and Freshdesk was looking to sell globally from day one. They assessed the market potential to be over a billion dollars.

In terms of the team, the founder Girish Mathrubootham, in their assessment, was a very strong product manager. He had gained a lot of experience in building and scaling SaaS products during his time at Zoho. Moreover, they saw Girish as a team person. They realized that he was a great storyteller who could inspire confidence in not only investors, but also employees. He would be able to manage the team well, they assessed. His co-founder Shan Krishnasamy was a very strong technologist. The founders had a small, but very passionate early team in place. Anand says that multiple things lined up for them to really like the overall team.

While the product itself was not mature in the early days of the startup, the company's product vision was very clear, Anand says. They had analysed the primary player in the market, Zendesk, in-depth, and had a clear understanding of the key features they should build to differentiate their product. In terms of the business model, they were looking to build in

India, and sell globally, while incorporating innovations in their pricing. For instance, they were looking to offer variable pricing models, including a freemium model that could attract early customers. Their unit economics were designed to be viable.

Given that each of the key elements checked out for the company, Accel led the first investment in Freshworks in 2011. They have since participated in every subsequent round.

However, while investors might make use of a framework to drive their analysis, startups are counterintuitive and investment is an art. According to Andreessen Horowitz founder Marc Andreessen, out of 4,000 fundable companies in a year that want to raise venture capital, about 200 get funded by a top tier VC.[10] Of these, fifteen will some day get to 100 million dollars in revenue, and of these around fifteen will generate the lion's share of returns for investors. When investors are looking at startups, they are looking for extreme outliers that would do extraordinarily well. In doing this, Andreessen notes that a great investing firm will look to invest based on 'strength versus lack of weakness' in a startup. Often there might be startups that might tick the boxes in terms of having a great idea, a great team, a great product and a great business model but still not be truly remarkable. Another startup might have serious flaws, but display an extreme strength along one dimension. Andreesen notes that often big winners show serious flaws early on, but missing out on them implies missing out on supernormal returns. 'What we aspire to do is to invest in the startups that have a really extreme strength along an important dimension, and we would be willing to tolerate certain weaknesses,' he says.

---

10   'Lecture 9: How to Raise Money', *How to Start a Startup*, 22 October 2014, https://startupclass.samaltman.com/courses/lec09

Crafting your pitch

The most important skill for a founder is to be good at storytelling, Anand says. It is what allows founders to be convincing, and being able to sell their vision. Good entrepreneurs are also very good storytellers. They can get others excited about their idea. It comes in useful in convincing co-founders to be part of the company, and in building the founding team. It is also very useful in pitching the startup to investors.

Great storytelling begins with brevity and simplicity. VC firms typically employ a small number of people; time is a premium. Paul Graham says, 'Most investors decide in the first few minutes whether you seem like a winner or a loser, and once their opinion is set, it's hard to change. Every startup has reasons both to invest and not invest. If investors think you're a winner they focus on the former, and if not, they focus on the latter.'[11]

Sachin Bansal learnt from his failures in raising funds early in the life cycle of Flipkart. 'You name any VC of any significance operating in India—we had talked to them.' Even Accel, which eventually decided to invest, had rejected them twice. 'It was an enlightening experience,' he says. 'Mostly what we learnt is that you need to simplify your message to the dumbest level possible. If a five-year-old in your family can understand, then it is time to go to a VC. Otherwise, it is too complicated.' He says that investors have limited time, and bandwidth. Within the time given to you, you will have to make them understand. If you are unable to do that, you will get passed on.

---

[11]   Paul Graham, 'How to Convince Investors', *www.paulgraham. com*, August 2013, paulgraham.com/convince.html

Sachin honed his idea down to the simplest possible explanation. 'My idea was very simple: I purchase books for ₹100, sell it at ₹150 and make a profit of ₹50. A very simple business and explanation.' Sachin says that he often comes across entrepreneurs expressing frustration at engaging with VCs who might not immediately grasp the significance of their idea. How much simpler could it be, they ask. Such thinking can be counterproductive. 'Nobody is going to appreciate the real complexities of your business,' he says. 'They have very little time and you have to give them enough.'

According to Rajan, communicating the concept of founder–market fit during the pitch is especially important. 'Why is this team the right team to go build this opportunity at this time? So that's important, he says. Have real insight about who is the user, he says. 'Who is the user you are building for? What is the problem you are trying to solve?'

If you have already launched, Rajan advises that you ensure that your metrics show how you have customer love. This is especially important for very-early-stage companies. 'In very-early-stage companies, what you're looking for is customer love. Do these customers love your product or service?' he says. In demonstrating this, retention metrics can be especially useful, he says.

It helps to have clear and deep insights about these questions. Showcase that the market is large enough for you to build a large business. Then talk about how you're going to build that. At an early stage, we are looking at whether the customers love your product or service or not. Make sure that your metrics show that you have customer love. A few ways to look at it include Play Store ratings, Amazon ratings, retention rate, depending on what kind of product you are selling.'

Pieter Kemps, Principal at Sequoia Capital India, suggests that founders should not seek to oversell when pitching to investors. 'We like founders who are authentic and real. Don't make up stuff to make us believe. Say stuff as it is. Show vulnerability. It is okay to say that you don't know the answer, or are still figuring out, or will get back to us.' When investing in a company, investors look to build a relationship based on mutual trust. Dissimulation is likely to be found out, and likely to undermine faith in both the founder, and the startup.

He narrates the story of a founder pitching to the firm in Bengaluru. 'He was pitching so hard and kept on going.' At the end of the pitch, one of the investors present asked, 'What do you not know about the business?' 'The founder was in an overselling mode and hence could not answer the question,' Kemps says. 'We have to be real about what is working and what is not working. Then only you can address what is not working.'

A good pitch deck, according to Kemps, consists of the following elements:[12]

Title: Define your company in a single declarative sentence.

• Simple, concise one line that states the company at the outset

What has changed: Explain the market and the breakthrough, discontinued shift, or an innovation that opens up a substantial opportunity. Why now?

---

12   Pieter Kemps, 'Tech in Asia x Surge: Anatomy of a Pitch by Pieter Kemps', *Surge*, 16 September 2020, surgeahead.com/tech-in-asia-x-surge-anatomy-of-a-pitch-by-pieter-kemps

- Inflection point including shift in user behaviour, regulatory change, cutting-edge technology are some examples

Pain point: Clear articulation and detailed understanding of the pain point or opportunity this change leads. What are shortcomings of the current solution?

- Understanding of the customer across segments/personas: their behaviour, pain and the gain they are seeking

Solution: Explain your product. How does it solve the problem? How does it deliver value?

- Features, architecture/structure, unique and differentiated, value proposition
- Product demo might be effective way to showcase the product

Business model: How do you create, deliver and capture value?

- Create value: activities, assets and partners
- Deliver: go-to-market, channels and communication
- Capture: monetization, revenue and cost structure

Traction: What are metrics to demonstrate 'success' and how are you faring on those?

- Customer love: retention rate, user feedback
- Growth metrics: growth of customers, engagement, transactions
- Monetization: willingness to pay, unit economics

Future: If all goes well, what will you have built in five years?

- Show the transformation of the company (and the world): compelling vision of how you will grow to additional products, additional geographies, etc.

Market: What does your market look like?

- Detail the total addressable market (TAM) and revenue potential
- Explain the market growth and how it is evolving
- Market dynamics: inefficiencies, layers and players, revenue pools and margin structure

Competition: Who competes with you for the same market, both directly and indirectly?

- How you are different, not just better
- Plan to win

Team: Do you have the team to execute?

- A+ founders: their strong background
- Story of the founders and demonstrate founder–market fit
- Founders' joint history
- Strong second-level team

Negotiating the deal

If an investor is interested in investing in your startup, they will offer a term sheet with the terms of the deal. The terms of the deal, including the valuation of the firm, the extent of equity dilution, and liquidation preferences, will typically be open to negotiation.

Freshworks founder Girish Mathrubootham recommends approaching multiple investors for an investment for it allows for a better understanding of how different investors are perceiving the company. 'The best way to figure out your company's valuation is to get competing term sheets from different VCs. You will quickly get an approximate range if you are dealing with reputed VCs,' he says. Based on a deeper understanding of how the market is perceiving the startup, you are in a better position to negotiate with regard to valuation, and other details. If there is interest from more than one investor, you have greater leverage during the negotiation process. 'If you have only one term sheet, then you don't have any leverage,' he says.

When Freshworks was looking to raise money, it had investor interest from multiple firms. They had received term sheets from multiple firms, and were in a position to decide who they wanted to receive an investment from. In such a position, it is advisable to look at factors beyond just the competing valuations offered.

While the valuation is an important element, it is not the only element in terms of the offering. According to Rajan, beyond ensuring that the terms that you choose are reasonable, if you have interest from multiple investors, you should look to choose the investor who is most likely to be a real partner in your success. The investor will be 'somebody that you're going to have to work with for the next decade,' he says. 'So focus on making sure you have the right firm that you're partnering with, and obsessed less about the valuation,' he says.[13] Whether the valuation is $20 million or $25 million is going to matter less. The question is, are you going to be a $1 billion company or a $5 billion company.' That, he says, is the key thing.

Anu Hariharan, Partner at Y Combinator, echoes Rajan, saying that while valuation has to be parameter in decision-making, it is extremely important to select an investor that is likely to stand by you during the toughest phases. 'In entrepreneurship, you're going to get punched in the gut a few times. You want investors who really understand that, not the ones who just say that they do,' she says.

She says that especially at the Series A and Series B stages, founders should look to build relationships with potential investors before deciding to go with them. 'You have to have relationships with five or six people, you should know them deeply before you pick,' she says. She offers the example of Josh Reeves, founder and CEO of Gusto, a cloud-based HR platform. 'Josh at Gusto is amazing at building relationships,' she says. 'He would keep meeting with four or five key people that he likes and who he thinks understand Gusto really well for almost six to nine months. He would even go on hikes and long walks with them. That way you actually get to know the core of a person really well. And he has a fantastic board, a

---

[13]   Marc Andreessen, co-founder and general partner of Silicon Valley venture capital firm Andreessen Horowitz, uses the analogy of marriage. 'If your company is successful, we are talking about a fifteen- or twenty-year journey. These years, you may notice, are longer than the average American marriage. This is significant. The choice of key investors—who are going to be on the board of a company—is just as important as whom you get married to. These are people you are going to be living with, partnering with, relying on, and dealing with in positions, in conditions of great stress and anxiety for a long period of time.'

board that works very well, that has been supportive through thick and thin, and that's not by accident. That's by deliberate effort. He has never raised money from a single person that he has not known for at least six months.'

To understand whether an investor is likely to be a real partner in your success, Rajan advises speaking with other entrepreneurs who have worked with the investor in the past, to get feedback on the working relationship, and the levels of support and engagement that an investor typically provides'. 'Make sure that you talk to other portfolio companies of that firm, just to make sure what is their feedback,' he says. Before committing to an investment, a VC firm will carry out reference checks on the startup, and the founding team, often speaking to a wide array of individuals. Rajan advocates that the entrepreneur should take the same approach in dealing with VCs. 'Just like just like the VC will do reference checks on you and your company—they will do a lot of reference checks—you should do reference checks.'

One of the things that Anu Hariharan, Partner at Y Combinator, has seen founders do is call up other founders and specifically ask which of their investors really stood by them during their toughest period. 'So when you're doing reference checks, call other founders and ask them to describe the time that was toughest for them, and ask them who they thought were the investors who really worked with them during that period. Try to understand what they mean when they say that an investor stood by them,' she says. 'In addition, ask them who were the investors who did not stand by them,'. While most founders do not ask this question, it is often revelatory, and therefore critical to find out, she says.

Girish ended up choosing not the investor offering the highest valuation, but the one that he believed would be the

best for the company in the long run. 'We did not choose
the investor who gave us the highest financial valuation. We
chose the one who we thought had the best track record, with
whom we felt the most comfortable, who was smart and could
challenge us to perform better,' he says. 'There are so many
other things beyond just financial valuation. Pay attention to
all those details.'

Financial prudence is underrated

According to Naukri founder Sanjeev Bikhchandani, good
entrepreneurs are extremely risk-averse. It is a myth that
entrepreneurs are risk-takers, he says. 'I completely disagree. A
sensible entrepreneur, just like any other sensible person, will
always take the lowest risk path to his goal,' he says.

The ability to remain cautious perhaps becomes most readily
evident when it comes to managing downturns. 'So, one thing I
have always believed,' Naukri's founder Sanjeev Bikhchandani
says, 'is that the difference between a successful entrepreneur
and a not-so-successful one is how they manage downturns.
When the market is booming, the economy is booming and
money is coming in, funding is not a problem. Everything looks
good. But you are not really tested.' Market and economic
downturns test startups in a truer sense.

He offers his own example. 'In the year 2000,' he says, 'we
got lucky. We raised money, our first VC Series A investment,
fifteen days before the meltdown. The market corrected, and
because we had bootstrapped the company for ten years, and
we really knew the value of money, we simply took the money
and put it in a fixed deposit in the bank. We tore up the business
plan we had submitted to get the money.'

The going wasn't easy. For the first six months they did not entirely believe that they were in the middle of a meltdown, holding that it was only a temporary correction. Their investors too, pressed them to invest the money to grow rapidly Regardless, the founders decided to remain frugal and cautious. They might never get an investment again, they reasoned; they must use the investment judiciously. It so happened that they eventually ended up spending only 1.2 million dollars of the 1.7 million dollars they had raised. It was also the only instant that they had to raise money until their IPO. 'So, the lesson is, successful entrepreneurs and successful companies are capital-efficient,' Sanjeev says.

Deep Kalra echoes Sanjeev when he says MakeMyTrip survived because they were extremely prudent with how they managed their funds right from the beginning. 'One of the reasons we survived,' he says, 'was because of belief and faith. But the non-creative side of your brain—that has to be all about numbers.'

When raising money, Deep advises taking into a consideration a period of up to one year as cushion in terms of the runway that the amount will allow. 'There's a crazy amount of money coming in from various places; there are new business models evolving that could disrupt yours; you've got to take all these into account.'

Once you have raised money, you have to be equally careful in managing it. 'You have to be very clear on when you are going to be able to break even, when you have no cash; you have to know in your sleep how many months you will have to burn, for it to get over,' he says. 'And then you have to keep a buffer of six months.'

Summary

- **Bootstrapping vs raising money?** The decision to bootstrap or to raise money would depend on the nature of the business—whether it could continue to operate without needing a large amount of capital—and whether the founders need to raise money, and are willing to subject themselves to the additional scrutiny from investors that will come with it.

- **Raising money is likely to catalyse growth.** Raising money allows a startup to grow more rapidly by allowing it to invest in customer acquisition, hiring, and capability expansion. Investors can also provide access to a wide array of resources, and advice on running the company, including on matters such as hiring, developing strategy, and managing finances.

- **Raising money comes with attendant downsides.** Fundraising can be an arduous process, distracting founders from running the company. Once investors come in, there is additional scrutiny thrust upon the founders. Investors would sit on the company board and influence decision-making, potentially diluting founder's control over the company. Upfront and constant alignment is essential to ensure a healthy relationship between investors and founders.

- **When it comes to an investor-investee relationship, complementarity is key.** In looking for investors, prioritize firms on the basis of their sectoral focus, and the stage of the company that they typically invest in. In choosing to go with an investor, ensure compatibility for the relationship is likely to last over a significant period of the company›s existence.

- **Market, team, product, and business model are the four key dimensions investors examine to determine suitability for investment.** The market that a startup is trying to serve offers an indication of how large the company could grow to be. The team, the product, and the business model are likely to determine the extent to which it can capture the potential in the market. The relative importance of these four dimensions evolves based on the stage of the company. While a large market, and a strong team are more important in for an early-stage company, the product and the business model become more important in later stages. However, this is not a checklist. VCs look for extreme outliers and often invest in startups that might show a clear strength along a particular dimension versus any lack of weaknesses.

- **Financial prudence is underrated.** Great entrepreneurs are cautious when it comes to managing capital. Financial prudence serves a company well, especially in managing downturns when new investments might not be forthcoming.

7

Scaling Up

ACHIEVING SCALE IS A fundamental pursuit in the journey of a startup. With scale comes wider market validation, the financial and organizational wherewithal to chase larger problems and a bigger prize. With scale comes a sense of permanence to the company.

Scaling up implies transitioning from a small core team of employees, a limited customer base and constrained operations to a large setup and running operations at scale. It implies a startup growing wings and taking flight.

Knowing when to scale

Before a startup scales, it needs to be ready for it. Premature scaling is one of the primary reasons why startups fail. As part of the Startup Genome Project, a group of researchers at Stanford University and University of California, Berkeley, analysed more than 3,200 startups to identify why startups fail.

According to their analysis, 74 per cent of high-growth internet startups fail due to premature scaling.[1]

According to the Startup Genome Project, premature scaling happens when entrepreneurs start 'focusing on one dimension of the business and advancing it out of sync with the rest of the operation'.[2] It is a function of incorrect sequencing, brought about when founders prioritize an eventual step over an intermediate step. This could mean acquiring a large customer base, or hiring a large team, for example, before the product is ready.

INSEAD professor Nathan Furr, author of *Nail It Then Scale It*,[3] argues that the reason premature scaling kills startups is primarily two-fold. First, it uses up precious cash more quickly, leaving less runway to readjust after a misstep. This gives you fewer chances to achieve the product-market fit. Second, premature scaling makes you less agile, less able to quickly undergo a change in approach. Once you have hired a team and invested in your product, you become organizationally and mentally committed to your chosen approach, obligating yourself to a particular product or strategy. There is a tendency to fall into the sunk cost trap, persisting with a flawed approach, rather than abandoning it, once you have invested in it.

---

[1]   Max Marmer, Bjoern Lasse Herrmann, Ertan Dogrultan and Ron Berman. *Startup Genome Report Extra on Premature Scaling*, 29 August 2011, p. 14

[2]   Max Marmer, Bjoern Lasse Herrmann, Ertan Dogrultan and Ron Berman. *Startup Genome Report Extra on Premature Scaling*, 29 August 2011, p. 51

[3]   Nathan Furr, '#1 Cause of Startup Death? Premature Scaling', *Forbes*, 2 September 2011, forbes.com/sites/nathanfurr/2011/09/02/1-cause-of-startup-death-premature-scaling/?sh=30f601131fc9

So how does an organization know whether it is ready to scale or not? Former Google CEO Eric Schmidt believes that an organization must scale only when the product is ready for it. In its absence, scaling the organization is folly. He says it is tempting to believe you have a product that works before it works. Often the non-technical people listen to the technical people in the organization who say it works and start to scale the organization before the product is working. But no product can really scale before it works.[4]

In June 2010, Raghu and Aprameya launched the TaxiForSure website. They believed at that point that they only needed to put the product out in the market, and surely orders would start coming in. They got little traction initially. Nevertheless, they decided to expand their footprint aggressively. 'We had quit our jobs, and we were bored,' Raghu says. 'We did not want to sit idle, we wanted to do something.'

They would expand operations to new cities anchored only by expressions of interest from acquaintances, with little prior due diligence. 'My friends in Delhi would ask me how it was going, and I would tell them it was not going that well.' His friends would then tell him that if they started operations in Delhi, they would book their service. And that would become enough of a reason to expand to Delhi. When their friends in Mumbai would ask after them next, that would be all they would need to expand to Mumbai. Very soon they were in eight cities.

Not only did they expand their operations, they also expanded their product offerings. Even before they had perfected their operations under one product vertical, or in one city, they were

---

[4]   Chris McCann, 'Scaling Google with Eric Schmidt—Class 8 Notes of Stanford University's CS183C,' *www.linkedin.com*, https://www.linkedin.com/pulse/scaling-google-eric-schmidt-class-8-notes-stanford-cs183c-mccann/

operating across multiple product verticals, across multiple cities. 'We had airport transfers,' Raghu says, 'we offered point-to-point service, we had half-day and full-day packages, we had outstation packages, self-drive offerings, drivers-for-hire. We had everything.'

They were trying to scale their way to adoption. It was the perfect recipe for disaster. They were too preoccupied with trying to manage their operations to focus on what their customers truly needed. Product-market fit remained elusive. And because they had spread themselves so thin, their operations too were in disarray; they had spent little time in thinking through how they should structure their operations.

'We should have focused on one city and one product,' says Raghu. 'We should have been thinking surgically, identifying problems, identifying challenges and solving them one by one instead of spreading ourselves thin everywhere. A business has to be built with deeper focus.'

Former Google CEO, Eric Schmidt, offers a useful analogy for the process of getting the product right first. He recommends thinking of it in terms of a very long and tight funnel.[5] It takes a long time to get the product right. However, once you get the product right, you can scale up the team quickly and then embrace an expansion strategy.

An organization that scales before the product is working properly or has achieved a proper product-market fit is only setting itself up for failure. The more desirable alternative is to spend time in getting the product right, achieving product-market fit and then expanding outwards to drive adoption in a wider audience.

---

[5]   Chris McCann, 'Scaling Google with Eric Schmidt: Class 8 Notes of Stanford University's CS183C.' www.linkedin.com. 2015-10-19. https://www.linkedin.com/pulse/scaling-google-eric-schmidt-class-8-notes-stanford-cs183c-mccann/

Barriers to scale

As a startup grows, it comes across barriers to scale along the way; some of these might be external, others internal. As an organization expands, what might have served it well in earlier stages might no longer be of value.

According to Delhivery CEO Sahil Barua, there are five principal barriers to scale. Irrespective of the nature of the business, these five come up repeatedly. 'Whether you're doing hotels, e-commerce, logistics, biomedicine, whatever it is, you will hit the same five barriers,' he says.

The very first barrier that a startup comes up against is in terms of successfully expanding the customer base. An organization's destiny ultimately hinges upon how many customers it can serve, how widely its product or service is valued. In the absence of successful customer acquisition, a startup cannot grow, and scale would remain elusive. This is the primary reason why early-stage startups often invest heavily in marketing campaigns.

Once a startup has a critical mass of customers, it needs to be able to successfully serve these customers. There is a sudden shift in operational requirements. At this stage, then, the primary barrier is being able to successfully transition from being, as Sahil says, 'three guys and a dog in a garage' to a serious company.

In order to build operational muscle, the first challenge will be to expand the number of employees on the company's rolls. 'Three people will be doing the work of forty-five people,' Sahil says. 'You're flying by the seat of your pants. Things break down all the time; customers get upset. Your teams are upset because the three guys who are there doing the work of forty-five are pissed off because they are working 140 hours a week.'

The second barrier to scale, then, is building a team that can successfully manage the demands of serving a larger client base.

The third barrier comes up when you try to solve for the second. It is one that almost every startup gets to without fail, Sahil says. As startups try to expand your team, there is a tendency to hire more people than might be required. Moreover, given that the startup is growing rapidly, there is little opportunity to integrate efficient teaming mechanisms. As a consequence, there is now a large team that is pulling in different directions.

'You overcompensate and hire a lot of people, and they come in, and now they're all there,' Sahil points out. 'And you're trying to solve this customer problem. But now everybody is trying to solve it in a different way. Because you're a startup at this point in time, you have no processes, you have no guidelines on how these problems will be solved. Everybody is just trying to do whatever is fastest, and in the best interest of the latest problem. And so you live for every day.' The lack of processes and internal organization becomes the third barrier to scale.

Sahil offers an illustration. You might be successful at sales, but have not set up a process to carry out collections. So, after a point, you will run out of cash because you did not set up a process to ensure working capital availability, he says. Or, alternatively, you might have sold at a 10 per cent discount to one client, and at a 70 per cent discount to another. 'And now you don't know what to do. Do you go to the 70 per cent price or do you lose the 70 per cent customer?' In the absence of standard processes and operating procedures, and with a large number of new hires, the organization will struggle to run its operations efficiently.

Once you start to standardize processes, you get better, Sahil says. At some point, however, you will inevitably start hitting declining incremental growth. As your base grows, at some point it becomes increasingly challenging to add enough new customers to maintain a very high growth rate.

'You're starting to reach a stage where incremental growth is no longer 200 per cent a year. It is perhaps 50 per cent year-on-year, which is fantastic. If you went to Hindustan Unilever or Procter & Gamble and said you have 50 per cent growth a year they would bite your arm off. But for a startup, it can seem like coming off a cocaine high. You're suddenly wondering, "Where did my 200 per cent growth go?" This can take a toll on organizational psyche. Weakening growth can be deflating for organizational morale. It might seem that despite pushing for growth as hard as the team ever has, growth only seems to be plateauing.'

The fourth barrier then is to keep organizational morale high, ensure that the team remains motivated even in the wake of slower growth. Learning to keep your team motivated becomes important at this stage. Not only do you need to manage to grow sustainably, you also have to reset the mindset of the organization towards growth at this point. You will need to build processes that will have to be designed not for the exponential rate at which you might have historically grown, but the rate at which you are actually growing. This would entail revamping organizational processes to come to terms with this new reality.

Then comes the final barrier to scale. This would typically come late in the life cycle of the company, when it is perhaps reasonably large. According to Sahil, this is the ultimate and most dangerous barrier because it can drive the company to its end. 'The most dangerous and persistent barrier to scale is how you innovate internally, because now your processes have become barriers,' he says. The company's processes, the size of your team, your geographical distribution, the number of clients that you have, all of these things will have started becoming barriers, he says, limiting further growth.

The last barrier to scale, therefore, is your ability to reinvent, he says. 'How can you go back and rebuild all of the things that you took for granted? You will wonder why a certain process works in a certain way, and you will be told that it is because that is how it has been for three or four years. What happens is that some of your weakest processes will propagate for quite some time. Then you have to go back, actually fix them, and go and change them entirely. These will rarely be the operational processes because you will keep improving them. It will be the smaller support processes that you won't even realize exist that will have created problems over time.'

For Delhivery, it used to be their biannual reviews. 'It used to be a huge mess, a massive, massive, massive mess. We used to spend months and months and months, carrying out completely valueless activities, all of which we could have done once. We never changed it until it got to a point where we suddenly realized that 10,000 people were spending two months a year doing the review and that it had a cost!'

There is an additional barrier to scale, but it is not necessarily internal to the company. This is having access to funding. 'It is a huge barrier to scale, given two companies are doing the same thing,' Sahil says. 'If one company has a hundred dollars and the other company has a million dollars, the company with a million dollars could do a better job than the company with a hundred dollars.'

Building a playbook

Scaling up often involves expanding a core set of processes to a wider customer base, across a larger geography. As a startup seeks to scale, modularity and repetition become important elements. Modularity is the degree to which a system's components may be separated and recombined, creating both flexibility and variety in use. Modular systems are easier to replicate, and therefore, easier to scale.

To build modular systems, one must first break each problem down to its component parts. Once this has been achieved, each component can be solved in isolation, then put back together to form the larger solution.

Take each component of the problem you are solving, and closely examine if you are able to address it in the optimal manner. Keep tinkering until you believe there is nothing more that you could possibly do. Over time, you would see that your overall solution would gain in efficiency, and that you would arrive at faster, cheaper, more robust processes. There is, however, a point beyond which further iterations would only generate diminishing returns. If you continue to iterate, you might well be draining your returns without receiving commensurate returns.

Once you have identified the optimal approach, you must meticulously document it, down to its tiniest details. In doing this, you create a framework, or a playbook as it is called, for your startup. Once you have a playbook, you can apply it over and over as you look to expand. A playbook ensures that your learnings along the way are preserved, and you do not have to reinvent the wheel each time you replicate a unit of your business. This is vital to scaling up aggressively. This is exactly the approach OYO Rooms and Delhivery adopted.

After finding the product-market fit in Gurugram by 2014, OYO wanted to expand to other cities. They saw strategic value in expanding nationally. There was a fixed number of rooms in budget hotels in the country at the time, around forty-five lakhs by the team's reckoning. They reasoned that if they could list 1 lakh rooms on to their platform quickly, it would allow them to build a critical mass of rooms associated with their brand. Customers would start choosing them over competitors. Once customers started choosing their brand, other property owners would look to list their rooms with them, creating a virtuous cycle. 'We wanted to get these 1 lakh rooms, come what may,' Ritesh says.

In order to achieve this, they relied on a playbook they had painstakingly created. Ritesh shares, 'We knew which locations to go to based on demand. We knew what price to sign hotels at, we knew what kind of owners to partner with.' For instance, in certain cities they would look to partner with property owners directly, while in others they would look to partner with those who had rented properties. Property owners were more willing to offer rooms at lower prices. Renters will not be willing to list at low prices but will spend time operating their property. So in cities where OYO could already offer a stronger customer experience, they would go with property owners while in cities where they needed stronger operational support, they would go with renters. All of this was meticulously codified. 'Which means the next time a supply personnel had to sign up a property, he just had to take this playbook. This entire process made it easy to scale up,' Ritesh explains.

OYO Rooms did not stop at developing a playbook for signing up properties. They also created a playbook for hiring people as well as one for running operations, going to the extent of preparing a standardized list of items needed to redecorate a room. Building out these playbooks was critical in allowing the company to expand rapidly when it set out to do so. Every time it looked to expand to a new city, it could equip its personnel with well-tested and established ways of setting up and running operations instead of having them start from scratch.

Delhivery has a similar story. When Delhivery started in 2011, it had a single fulfilment centre, serving only in Gurugram. Within a decade, it has built a nation-wide presence, servicing more than 17,000 pin codes. While its growth may seem explosive, it did not progress beyond its first delivery centre for almost a year. After the first centre in June 2011, another did not start until April the following year. What the team kept doing in the interim was relentless iteration to arrive at the most efficient means to build a delivery centre. They kept perfecting their operations, day after day. They started out with thirty-five orders per day, and twelve months later, they were doing 300 orders per day. But while it took them almost twelve months to build their second centre, it took them only two to build their third centre. Ten years later, it takes them between less than forty-eight hours to build a new centre.

The secret to their tremendous speed is that their approach is fully codified. They understand what a centre's floor layout must be, where the operator should be stationed, the localities around it, the number of riders needed, the routes they must take, how the cash comes in, and what must be done with it. Every part of their operation is system-driven and codified, making their approach fully replicable and easily scalable. In fact, they have their operations codified to the extent that they know where every table, every switchboard must be, and what must be the power backup, each optimized to deliver maximum efficiency. While they started very small, and remained very small for a long time, the fact that they codified their operations allowed them to scale up exponentially when they were ready.

The secret of successful standardization at scale is rigorous attention to detail. As Ritesh says, 'playbookization' ultimately means making small innovations and making them idiot-proof.

Great companies take innovation and build it into a process, into a machine that keeps churning things out. It is this relentless repeatability that makes it possible to scale rapidly.

Balancing growth and profitability

Chasing growth versus profitability is a conundrum many founders face while scaling up. The choice is between pursuing growth at whatever cost it might come, or limiting cash burn early on in favour of most sustainable growth.

It stems from the fact that in the early stages of their existence, many companies allow massive capital outlays in the pursuit of traction, capability building and winning against competition. Marketing and outreach activities especially can involve expensive promotions.

There are two schools of thought on this. Proponents of growth suggest that unless a company achieves enough momentum, it will crumble under its own weight. If a startup grows too slowly, it runs the risk of not being able to take a significant share of its chosen market, and losing out to more enterprising competition. Those that favour profitability claim that rapid growth that is not sustainable over time is of limited use; a company cannot survive if it runs out of capital to fund its operations.

In at least two cases, growth is perhaps more desirable than profitability: when it is a winner-takes-all market, and when there are clear network effects that can be tapped into.

In a winner-takes-all market, it is far more crucial to rapidly gain market share than to be profitable at the outset. In such a market, one player typically establishes a monopoly while the remaining players contest for much smaller market shares. By 2020 in the US, Amazon held a market share of almost 44 per cent, while its closest competitor, Walmart, held a market share of about 7 per cent.[6]

Given the dynamic of e-commerce markets, it was justifiable for Flipkart to pursue growth, even at the expense of profitability. If monopolistic control of the market could be obtained, then profits would follow eventually. Even in 2016, almost a decade after its founding, when Flipkart founder Sachin Bansal was asked on choosing between growth and profitability, he emphasized that it was still growth that they were looking for. 'The market is big, and we'll continue to grow the business. It still requires more investment. That's what we're focusing on right now. We're not so worried about profitability.[7] While Sachin had a 'growth at any cost' approach for Flipkart, he had a different approach for his next startup, Navi, a financial services company. Financial services is not a winner-takes-all business, he contends. While they would aim to grow fast, they would also seek early profitability.[8]

For a business that is likely to benefit from network effects, it is vital to increase the size of the network as quickly as possible, even if it comes at the expense of early profitability. Consider the example of Facebook. The company heavily relied on the

---

[6]   Wayne Duggan, 'Latest E-Commerce Market Share Numbers Highlight Amazon's Dominance,' *Yahoo! Finance*, 5 February 2020, finance.yahoo.com/news/latest-e-commerce-market-share-185120510.html

[7]   Saikat Pyne, 'Exclusive: Sachin Bansal—"Growth over Profits"', *Business Insider*, 31 January 2016, businessinsider.in/exclusive-sachin-bansal-growth-over-profits/articleshow/50792841.cms

[8]   Madhav Chanchani and Digbijay Mishra, 'Sachin Bansal Bets Flipkart Fortune on Banking Services', *The Times of India*, 26 January 2020, timesofindia.indiatimes.com/companies/sachin-bansal-bets-flipkart-fortune-on-banking-services/articleshow/73626692.cms

network effects to kick in. The more the number of friends join, the greater the value to a single user. And the greater a user gets value, the greater the value to the company. For such network effects to kick in, Facebook had to acquire customers even if it meant not being able to monetize the customer base. While the company was founded in 2004,[9] Facebook finally became cash flow positive five years after founding in 2009, by then having amassed 300 million customers.[10]

In the case of Delhivery, the choice between pursuing growth at all costs versus prioritizing profitability was entirely straightforward. As a logistics player, it's a business model that does benefit through scale. However, these are capped beyond a certain limit. Logistics is also not a winner-takes-all market. The company resolved the predicament but choosing to pursue 'growth in the service of profitability', as Sahil describes.

While the company was not profitable in the first four years of its existence, the founders ensured that their actions would be guided by the objective of becoming profitable at a pre-determined point in time. They had a clear view of how and when they would become profitable. 'We knew exactly how the margins were going to rack up over time,' Sahil says.

Delhivery chose to meticulously model their business from the very outset. Early in the life of the company, they detailed out the investments that they would be required to make, and how their operations would be required to scale so that they

---

9   Sarah Phillips, 'A Brief History of Facebook', *The Gaurdian*, 25 July 2007, theguardian.com/technology/2007/jul/25/media. newmedia

10   CBC News, 'Facebook "Cash Flow Positive", Signs 300M Users', 16 September 2009, cbc.ca/news/technology/facebook-cash-flow-positive-signs-300m-users-1.826223

could generate returns. Even when they were not profitable, they understood how and when they would become so.

Understanding the financial state of your company is central to understanding where your business is headed. Sahil advises entrepreneurs to never to miss these details. He further advises that in case understanding and running finance is a blind spot, delegate it to someone who is part of your core team. 'I do believe that whether an entrepreneur himself has an accounting and finance background or not, it is very important for somebody who does have a grounding in finance to be part of the team.'

Sahil's basic premise is that a business has to make money. Entrepreneurs should not get caught in the fantasy that even if it is not profitable at present, it will be at some distant point in the future, unless a lot of thinking and rigorous financial modelling is there to give weightage to such claims. In the long run, growth and profitability, rather than being conflicting objectives, actually converge and go hand-in-hand.

Taking a dominant market share

According to Marc Andreessen, there are three things that a startup must do once it has achieved product-market fit.[11]

1. **Take a dominant share of the market.** Once the product has been refined, the company must look to expand beyond the initial base of customers to take a dominant share of the market.

---

[11]   Mark Andreessen and Elad Gil, 'Where to Go after Product-Market Fit: An Interview with Marc Andreessen' *Andreessen Horowitz*, 15 April 2019, a16z.com/2018/07/20/after-product-market-fit-marc-andreessen-elad-gil

2. **Look to build the next product.** This is especially true for tech businesses. According to Andreessen, every product in tech becomes obsolete quickly. Eventually, if a startup does not keep innovating, its product will be replaced by a better one.

3. **Build functions and processes around its core proposition.** This means building the finance, HR, legal, marketing, investor relations and recruiting functions.

If market competition is a spectrum, perfect competition and monopolized play lie at the opposite extremes. Perfect competition takes place in the absence of a dominant player in the market. Substitutability between sellers is high. Price is therefore dictated by market demand. In the case of a monopoly on the other hand, a single dominant seller controls the supply, and hence controls the price of the product. In a monopoly, most of the market is controlled by one company, which, in turn, captures the greatest share of value created in that segment.

According to Peter Thiel,[12] eventually every market converges to one end of the spectrum; there is very little that lies between the two ends of the spectrum. The behemoths of today—Google, Microsoft, Apple and Amazon—are monopolies in their respective markets of play.

Thiel's advice for startups is to seek to build monopolies: start with a really small market, take over the whole market and then, over time, find ways to expand that market in concentric circles. Thiel argues that there are four factors that allow for the creation of monopolies. These also allow for enduring retention

---

[12]   Sam Altman, 'Lecture 2: Ideas, Products, Teams and Execution Part II', *How to Start a Startup*, startupclass.samaltman.com/courses/lec02

of a dominant market share through the creation of defensive moats in the face of competition.

- **Proprietary technology**: Proprietary technology allows for a significant improvement on a key dimension. Thiel suggests that as a rule of thumb, it is best to aspire to proprietary technology that's an order of magnitude better than the next-best thing. For instance, sending money through PayPal was more than ten times faster than sending cheques over eBay, which would take seven to ten days to clear. If the technology allows for the accomplishment of entirely new things, it is an infinite improvement: when the iPhone came along, it unleashed a smartphone revolution.

- **Network effects**: Network effects lead to the value of a product or increasing with an increase in the number of users. The classic example of network effects is the telephone, where a more significant number of users increases the possibility of connecting to more people, thereby increasing the value for each user. Social media platforms are, of course, the perfect modern example. Network effects can create a bandwagon effect as the network becomes more valuable and more people join, resulting in a positive feedback loop.

- **Economies of scale**: Economies of scale imply that the marginal cost of scaling the solution across consumers and across geographies reduces with volume. Through unlocking economies of scale, the company can achieve a lower cost of production and distribution which, in turn, can translated into a lower price for the customer.

- **Branding:** A strong brand position is an intangible asset. However, it can translate into real gains for the company. It generates customer loyalty, and creates an ability to charge a premium. It is what compels people to line up for hours outside Apple stores every time a new iPhone release takes place.

In operating a marketplace for service providers and customers, Urban Company benefits from positive network effects. As the number of service providers on its platform increases, the ease of delivery to customers increases. As more customers are drawn through the assurance of high-quality service delivery, more and more service providers sign up to cater to the growing pool.

In order to ensure that the positive network effects continue and strengthen, however, Urban Company needs to avoid disintermediation of its platform. This can take place when after an initial transaction through the marketplace the customer chooses to go directly to the service provider for subsequent transactions. In effect what it would mean is Urban Company might have spent humongous sums of money to acquire a customer and have them serviced by a partner, but after that first interaction the customer leaves the platform. This would severely limit the lifetime value from a user for the company.

In order to avoid this, the platform has to add value in subsequent transactions, Urban Company CEO Abhiraj Bhal shares. 'If the value add is just of introduction, then you will get disintermediated in subsequent transactions,' he says. 'However, if the marketplace is adding value subsequently, and the value charged is lower than the value added, then people will stick to the platform.'

There do exist categories where they might get disintermediated. However, in the categories where they have chosen to focus and build deep capabilities, it is difficult to do so. They achieve this through leveraging economies of scale, and proprietary mechanisms that improve the value proposition of the platform for both service providers and customers. 'For categories such as beauty, we never get disintermediated,' Abhiraj says.

First, the company uses its scale to pass on procurement benefits to the service providers. The beauticians on the platform purchase cosmetics directly from Urban Company in the form of a standardized kit. With a large service provider base, the company can procure directly from manufacturers at favourable prices. They can save on commissions charged across the traditional distribution chain, from manufacturer to wholesaler to retailer. This can then be passed on to the service providers. 'All beauticians buy cosmetics from us,' Abhiraj explains. 'The value we add in the procurement of cosmetics is far more than the commission taken from service.'

Second, the company builds standardization of service packages and pricing. Such proprietary intervention ensures that customers are guaranteed a high quality of service at a standard price. If a customer were to go directly to a service provider, such standardization might not be guaranteed. 'When they disintermediate, everything is up for grabs—pricing is up for renegotiation.' Using the platform offers reduced friction and higher service assurance.

Third, service providers benefit through association with the Urban Company brand. Customers are provided insurance against service quality concerns. There is very strong customer support. Most importantly, by offering high-quality training to its providers, Urban Company ensures that the customer experience is consistent every single time. 'We give you the option to repeat professionals, but only 45 per cent of people do that; 55 per cent don't care because there is hospitality-like experience,' Abhiraj notes. 'The training is so deep that it doesn't matter who comes to service, the job will be done.'

Associating with the brand also generates direct benefits for service providers while allowing them to become a part of the Urban Company community. 'We provide health and accidental insurance to service providers. There is a sense of identity and belonging when they go as an Urban Company professional.' Given this, there is little incentive to circumvent the platform.

Network effects and economies of scale can often reinforce each other, as in the Urban Company example. It is important, therefore, to carefully examine how these could best be achieved.

The next product

Developing a winning product and capturing a large share of the market, however, is not enough for a company to continue to thrive in the long run. As Mark Andreessen notes, if all you do is take your current product to market and win the market without doing anything else, eventually your product will go stale.[13] Once this happens, a competitor with a better product could displace you. Building the next product, therefore, is important. It could either further strengthen product-market fit for the company, or it could help it expand to a larger base of customers. In either case, it will allow the company to continue growing.

---

[13] Mark Andreessen and Elad Gil, 'Where to Go after Product-Market Fit: An Interview with Marc Andreessen' *Andreessen Horowitz*, 15 April 2019, a16z.com/2018/07/20/after-product-market-fit-marc-andreessen-elad-gil

Andreessen admits that building the second product is not easy. 'It was hard enough to get to the first one. To come up with the second one is often even harder,' he notes. He outlines two approaches that companies typically adopt. When a company has been successful with their first product, it could look to invest heavily in R&D. This will allow it to expand its product portfolio through in-house development. Alternatively, it could look to use M&A (merger and acquisition) as a means to expanding its portfolio. With adequate resources, it could acquire a company with an adjacent or a superior product which could then be branded as its second product.

As technology has matured, driving innovation, has become lot easier, especially for internet businesses. Deep Kalra explains it thus: 'The beauty of the internet is that you can iterate, and you can experiment very, very quickly. Gone are the days when fast moving consumer goods companies—the likes of Hindustan Lever and Colgate—would launch a new product in selected cities like Kakinada, Chandigarh, Pune and maybe Vizag. Over the course of many months post this, they would gather feedback and analyse it. It would, then, take almost a year to launch, officially.'

On the internet, however, an entrepreneur can experiment and iterate rapidly. Companies can use A-B frameworks—incorporating a single change in a product while keeping other elements constant—to rapidly gain understanding of how users might react to a development. 'Keeping everything constant, you can expose 1 per cent of your traffic to a change you make in pricing, in user experience, or even in fundamentally different ways of buying,' Deep explains.

In building a new product, therefore, a company can test a proposed solution rapidly by exposing it to different cohorts of potential customers. A small team can develop, test, and deploy a new innovation far more rapidly than was historically possible. 'I can't tell you what a boon it is to business,' Deep says.

Summary

- **Knowing when to scale is vital.** Before a startup scales, it needs to be ready for it. Premature scaling is one of the primary reasons why startups fail. Achieving product-market fit is essential before a startup looks to scale.
- **Build a playbook to grow rapidly.** As a startup seeks to scale, modularity and repetition become important elements. Look to build modular systems and codify processes into a playbook that can offer a template for rapidly replicating solutions to known problems.
- **It is not essential to sacrifice profitability at the altar of growth.** Whether a company should prioritize growth at the expense of profitability early on depends on whether it can benefit from scale effects through growing faster. It is ideal to drive growth in the service of achieving profitability.
- **After achieving product-market fit, aim to take a dominant share of the market, while building defensibility against competitors.** Successful companies are often monopolies in their market. Having achieved product-market fit, look to expand outwards from the company's core area of focus. Ensure that you continue to be dominant over time by building defensive moats.
- **Build the next product.** If a company does not keep innovating, its existing product will become stale, and a better product could replace it in the market.

8
Setting Up for Success

A S A COMPANY GROWS, its internal processes and structures must evolve too, allowing for a strong foundation upon which the edifice of a large company may be built. While core operational processes must perforce hold firm as the company expands, these must be supported and enabled by a wide array of internal structures and processes.

An inability to handle expanding operations through weak supporting structures, and a shortage of human resources is a key barrier to scale. Overcoming this barrier allows a company to continue to expand. Building a robust set of supporting structures, hiring the right set of employees, and ensuring internal alignment, therefore, are vital for a company to endure over a long period of time.

Building a supporting structure

While business support processes, including financial and accounting, HR, and legal, exist to serve core operations, poor design and set up of these can create fault lines for the business as a whole.

In the first three years of Delhivery, CEO Sahil Barua and his co-founder Ajith retained almost complete control of the company's financial processes. 'We would not allow anybody to touch finance at all,' Sahil says. 'Every penny that was going in and out of the business, nobody else knew what was happening, who was spending it, where were they spending it.' That is not a process, he says. 'That's actually exactly the opposite. It's a complete absence of process.'

While the company had not faced any concerns thus far, they knew that it could simply be a matter of time. If their processes did break down, it could have catastrophic consequences for the company. '99.9 per cent of the time, your financial processes, even if they're weak, will not break down,' Sahil says. 'The 0.1 per cent of the time that they will break down, you will be absolutely in a mess.'

Eventually, they arrived at a solution through instituting two remarkably radical steps for a relatively young company.

First, Delhivery placed massive audit burdens on themselves. They got Ernst & Young, their appointed auditor, to push them to carry out quarterly instead of annual audits. They also brought in KPMG to do independent audits. These were counterintuitive moves; higher audit burdens implied inflicting massive overhead costs on the business. The benefits, however, made themselves evident quickly enough.

The audits inculcated rigour and discipline in the organization, setting a high bar for accounting. Being external to the company, the auditors did not shy away from telling the management the areas where their financial processes were opaque, and where they were just not experienced enough to be able to see that they were weak. In doing so, they allowed the management to address core issues in how they had historically been approaching these very processes.

Second, Delhivery put together an independent board of directors. Their reasoning was straightforward. 'Independent directors are the custodians of shareholder value,' Sahil contends. 'It is their responsibility to make sure that management is acting in the best interest of creating shareholder value. Apart from that, an independent director's job is also to make sure the company is following all the relevant governance standards.' Setting up an independent board of directors created an internal obligation upon the founders to institute robust processes.

Together, instituting rigorous auditing processes and bringing in independent directors forced the company to rebuild their financial reporting processes, their accounting processes. It vastly reduced the operational risk for the company. However, the company also benefited in unforeseen ways.

What happened as a result of overhauling their financial reporting processes was that they became far more attuned to which were the right metrics to track and report. 'Where we had a hundred metrics earlier, we suddenly came down to the ones that really mattered. We were talking about ten metrics, twelve metrics and so then all our processes got designed around those metrics,' Sahil says.

Once they knew which metrics to track, they created radical transparency around these. 'We created dramatic visibility of underlying economics. We shared it with the whole team,' Sahil says. 'These are the costs, this is how it was spent.' This helped create greater awareness with regard to the financial state of the company, and drove a sense of ownership. 'Wherever you go, you will see our personnel will not hire an extra vehicle if they don't need to, they will not hire an extra person if they don't need to. That sense of frugality has got into everyone's head.'

Delhivery's is a stunning example of how instituting strong processes can help strengthen the organization. However, supporting processes are unlikely to drive differentiation for the company on their own. Delhivery succeeded because they already had already developed a unique value proposition for their customers, and sustainable competitive advantages in their core operations.

Tarun Mehta, co-founder of Ather Energy, cautions that unless financial accounting is what differentiates you from your competitors, you should first spend time on developing your core capabilities. 'There are very few companies which would claim to be better than their competition because of superior accounting processes', he says. 'So, unless accounting is really core to what differentiates you from others, don't spend too much time on it.' He recommends that entrepreneurs understand the accounting process, but suggests that there is limited upside in focusing on it at the expense of other elements of the business. Instead, he recommends getting the services of a good auditing company which would manage the process.

On the other hand, he says, how you carry out budget allocation is critical. While accounting involves recording, summarizing, and interpreting past transactions, the budgeting process is forward-looking. In carrying out budgeting, a company must look at potential sources of income, and where they might be best allocated. 'Budgeting is the actual mathematical process of deciding what you're really good at,' Tarun says. Budgeting is closely linked to how a startup is seeking to differentiate itself, and build competitive advantages. 'You need to really figure out what you're really going to be good at, and make sure the bulk of the capital goes there,' he says.

Tarun offers an example. 'Let's say you say that you're Swiggy, and what you're going to be extremely good at is operations,' he says. 'You're not going to have leakage, your orders will hit 99 per cent on time. Your systems will be up all the time. So operationally, you'd be the most efficient startup.' Then in this case, the budgeting process should ensure that the bulk of the capital is allocated to ensuring operational efficiency rather than improving other elements of the business. 'You want to make sure that's exactly where your money's going to be. If you realize that the bulk of your money is going into iteration on the product side, and that keeps slowing you down, you want to pull money out of it. You don't want that to be your focus.' While better product design or better features might improve the customer experience, it is not the core focus of the business. What is not at the core of the business can be improved later, but it is critical to get the critical elements right first.

According to Tarun, not only does budgeting include which element of the business gets allocated how much capital, it also flows through to determining how many people you need to hire in which part of the company, the calibre of the people you need to hire, and operational spends. 'Budgeting cuts really deep,' he says.

For a growing company, a human resources function is vital. In fact, Sahil believes that a company must set up an HR function right at the start. 'The right time to set up is when you start the company,' he says. 'If you have a company which is over the size of fifteen people, you should be thinking about HR on day one because it affects everything.'

While a company might start off with the nucleus of perhaps two or three founders, soon you will need to bring in the first set of hires into the fold. As you do, you will need to think about how you are going to pay them, how you are going to compensate them for the risk they took in joining a startup, Sahil says. As the company expands, this issue will compound; you will have to think about you will pay the next set of people, and then the one after that. You will need to determine hierarchy within the company: how do employees interact with each other, and who reports to whom. You will also have to think about how those who join later will be compensated compared to earlier employees. Having an HR organization in place allows for all these decisions to be taken in a systematic manner.

Sahil notes that ultimately there are two core principles that are important in determining whether an organization is able to function smoothly, and retain employees over time: a) that the manner in which every individual is treated is fair, and is perceived to be fair, and b) the work that they do is valued. Well-designed HR processes allow for both these principles to be observed.

Sahil notes that he did not know the importance of having robust HR processes in place when he first started the company. 'I spent my entire two years at IIM Bangalore doing hardcore advanced corporate finance, financial derivatives, and statistics, and I just assumed that HR was some touchy-feely nonsense.' Only when he started a company did he realize that it was actually the harder part of the job. 'The easier part of the job is building the Excel models, and going out and executing, but the harder part is suddenly waking up and leading a team of 10,000 people,' he says. 'You have to figure out how to keep them motivated, how much to pay them, how to talk to them, how to promote them, and whom to promote, and these become very difficult decisions.'

In the initial days of the company, in his naivete, he did not fully understand the need for having HR policies in place. What am I going to do with a leave policy, he would question, for instance. 'But then you realize that while you may not want to do anything with the leave policy, the reality is thousands of other people will want to know how they can take leaves,' he says. 'At the same time, my approach doesn't work, which is to say whenever you want to, you take leaves, and it's an honour system, because then everybody will just be off at random times. And so these small things come back and bite you. And then you realize that there is a value to these processes, there's a value to this entire function.'

'So when should you start thinking about HR? Day 1,' Sahil says. 'When do most people start thinking about HR? Too late, in our experience. Most people just are not thinking about it enough. We didn't. So now, we really spend a lot of our time thinking about it.'

In the case of Urban Company, supporting structures were put in place relatively early in the life of the firm. 'The first person in HR was hired reasonably early, some three, or four months after starting the company,' founder Abhiraj Bhal says. While they did not have an internal team in place for finance, they hired a firm to help out initially. Around the one-year mark, they started building an internal finance team.

According to Abhiraj, if your organization is getting to scale, and building fast, 'one year is probably the ceiling' in terms of putting structures in places. By the end of the first year, Urban Company had almost three hundred people in it, and supporting structures were needed. 'If you are getting on the growth trajectory, then you had better plan to have them in place,' Abhiraj says.

Nevertheless, he cautions against investing in large support teams before having hit product-market fit. 'The most important thing for you to focus on when you don't have product-market fit is to nail the product, and get to product-market fit. After that, all of these things can come.'

Hiring

A company is, after all, a collection of individuals. Most individuals will be brought into the company through hiring.

Hiring goes hand in hand with growth. As the team expands, it allows you to build additional features into your product, deliver greater value to your customers, and execute more effectively. How well you are able to hire determines the immediate future of the company.

However, the importance of hiring well extends beyond just the immediate future. As Eric Schmidt notes, the people you hire define the organization's culture, whether you like it or not.[1] Organizational culture lies at the heart of a company; a company with a dysfunctional culture is unlikely to succeed in the long run. Hiring, therefore, determines the organization's destiny both in the short term, as well as in the long term.

Putting in place a hiring mechanism

Every year more than 2 million individuals apply to work at Google, and only 1 in 400 gets through. Lazlo Bock designed the modern hiring process at Google. In *Work Rules*, the book

---

[1]   'Scaling Google with Eric Schmidt—Class 8 Notes of Stanford University's CS183C', www.linkedin.com, 19 October 2015, https://www.linkedin.com/pulse/scaling-google-eric-schmidt-class-8-notes-stanford-cs183c-mccann/

he wrote on the subject, he offers the following broad guidelines on hiring:[2]

1. Set a high bar for quality. Before you start recruiting, decide what attributes you are looking for, and what 'great' looks like.
2. Find your own candidates through leveraging online platforms, alumni databases, and professional associations, instead of relying on recruiting firms.
3. Assess candidates objectively. Overcome biases by including subordinates and peers in interviews. Have an unbiased group of people, for instance, potentially from a different function than the one for which the candidates is to be hired, make the actual hiring decision. Ensure that interviewers make good notes, and compare them to how the new employee is doing, to refine your assessment capability.
4. Give candidates a reason to join. Explain why the work you are doing matters. Let the candidate experience the extraordinary set of people they will get to work with.

Within these broad guidelines, building a hiring mechanism tailored to your company's needs is ideal.

By the end of 2014, OYO was the largest player in the hospitality segment in Gurugram. They were determined to expand throughout the country. They had a simple hiring philosophy: Bring in people ready to stick their necks out for the mission of the company. OYO founder Ritesh Aggarwal says, 'For us, the very simple task was that anyone who comes

---

[2]   Laszlo Bock, 'Here's Google's Secret to Hiring the Best People', *Wired*, 7 April 2015, https://www.wired.com/2015/04/hire-like-google/

and joins us must be willing to do anything for the mission that we are all aligned with.'

Over the next six months, they decided to do two things. First, they built out a forward-looking hiring roadmap to ensure that when they needed to scale up rapidly, they would have the human resources in place to help them execute. Second, they established a rigorous, step-by-step mechanism for hiring.

They started out by tapping into the networks of their early employees. Ritesh explains, 'The way we built our team was to sit with the first five–six leaders we had hired, and asked them to give a list of the twenty smartest people they had ever known in their life, worked with and so on, and recommend them to us. The first sixty people that we hired subsequently were all hired based on those recommendations.' As they started to expand, they focused on standardizing their hiring process into a system that could be replicated over and over again.

OYO's early focus on having the right people and teams in place served them tremendously well, eventually, allowing them to out-execute their competition over and over again.

In developing a hiring policy for Freshdesk, CEO Girish Mathrubootham was influenced by the book *First, Break all the Rules* by Marcus Buckingham and Curt Coffman. Based on interviews with more than 80,000 managers at all levels, the authors offer examples of how the best managers handle employees. The most important learning for Girish was the importance of matching the natural strengths of a person to the role that she was assigned to. The book distinguished between skills, knowledge, and talent. 'Skills can be developed through training. Knowledge, too, can be imbibed, either through being taught, or through developing experience in a certain area. But talent is innate; it comes from within,' Girish explains. 'It may be defined by recurring patterns of thoughts, feelings, and behaviours. There are some who are born with a creative bent of mind, or are very articulate. There are some who are very logical and organized. If you could spot the inherent talent in an individual and then map it to the role that they would play in an organization, you could unlock her true potential. This early realization played a vital role in Freshworks' early hiring.

When Freshworks started, they neither had the pull of a large brand, nor the money to be able to recruit at the top colleges in the country. Instead of being guided by educational accomplishments, Girish decided to focus on identifying individuals that were the best suited to working with them. They would seek individuals with a genuine interest in, or ability for, a certain role, who had not quite received the right opportunities previously. Often, this meant departing from traditional forms of hiring.

They would go to colleges and find computer science graduates who had landed jobs in computer programming, but were not interested in pursuing programming in the first place. 'These kids would actually put up their hands and say we don't want to do programming, we want to work in marketing, or we want to work in customer support,' Girish says. Guided by the skills-knowledge-talent philosophy, as part of their interviewing mechanism they would test for natural talents. Did a person have innate creative writing skills, and can be moulded into a great marketer? Does she have a sense of empathy that would be suited to customer support? Does she have the articulation and the energy in their speaking that would be suited to a sales role? And based on their assessments, they would fill roles in the company. 'We built this company on these young graduates, some of whom, in fact, were very, very young sometime. This is how we used to always play to people's strengths,' Girish explains. 'We tried to focus not on their credentials but on what specific talent that they had, the interest that they had, and tried to match their potential to their role. That worked beautifully for us. It was our secret sauce in hiring people.'

Determining fit

In making hiring decisions, it is crucial to consider the organizational fit of the individual in question. Policybazaar CEO Yashish Dahiya says that he would count some poor hiring decisions made early in the life of the firm to be amongst the most significant mistakes that he might have made in building the company. Most of these stemmed from hiring people who would seem to pass through objective filters of background and capabilities, but not necessarily for organizational fit, a far more subjective filter. Yashish says that almost always such hires would leave the organization within two to three years.

If the person hired is not compatible with the rest of the organization, it only fosters dysfunction within. Such a person will not be at their best within the organization, and the others will not necessarily work well with them. Such decisions are therefore best to be avoided.

Having faced the consequences of poor hiring decisions early on, Policybazaar now ensure that they take into account the question of fit seriously. According to Yashish, this is not very difficult to do. If you are a perceptive person, you will pick it up in everything that a person does, he says. The way they send you a mail, the way they make a phone call, even the way they write their CV. If there is a hint that a person might not be a good fit, it is probably best to not hire them.

One of the primary traits that Yashish looks for is 'a lack of selfishness'. According to Yashish, if a person is constantly wondering where their career is headed, and what might a company do for them as opposed to how they could contribute, they will not necessarily be a very good hire, especially in a startup. 'Because there will be ups and downs,' he says. Every time the company is not doing well, they will wonder what is in it for them. Such a person 'will not have the ability to stick for the long run'.

One of the ways Yashish tests for it is by looking at how doggedly a person negotiates their salary. 'Now, is that a good thing or a bad thing, I don't know,' Yashish says. 'But for me it is a sign. This person comes to you and he talks all these grand things about what he wants to achieve with his life. But if the salary becomes the most important discussion point, then the person has just revealed himself.'

When Delhivery started hiring, they too looked for personal attributes that they believed would make a person a good fit in the organization. In the beginning, when they were a virtually unknown entity, there were not a lot of people willing to come and work with them, So, in the case of those who did join, they were looking for people who would stay in the company for a long time. 'We couldn't afford to be in a situation where we could just have a revolving door and have people coming in and going out all the time,' Sahil says. It was very important for the team to hire people who would like working on the problems they were working on, and with that particular team. They wanted to ensure that they shared a core set of values.

The first thing that they would look for is intellectual curiosity. 'This is a difficult business,' Sahil says. 'You have to have the ability to appreciate the scale and complexity of the problem that we are trying to solve.' Delhivery's business is one that is built around more than 10 million square feet of real estate in terms of its warehouses, and more than forty thousand delivery riders, with vehicles driving on every highway in the country. Being able to appreciate the level of complexity that the business generates is important.

The second thing would be courage of conviction. The idea, Sahil explains, is to ensure that once you have decided to go down a certain path, you move down the path and try to reach the point that you intended to in the first place. To offer an example, Sahil points out that when the company is making large-scale tactical changes, including changes in its facilities, you can not lose heart halfway through. You can not decide to automate a facility, develop the design, and then 30 per cent into implementation, develop cold feet because it's too complicated to execute.

'If you've done the math, if your intellectual curiosity has led you to a point where we should make a certain set of investments or decisions, then we go and make the decisions,' Sahil says. Before arriving at a decision, you look at the data available, and evaluate risks that might apply. But once a decision has been reached, you stick to it. 'We may be slow to make the decision. But once we make it, we will give it the respect that it deserves, which is to stick with it. Unless of course, the data again changes and are proven completely wrong,' he says, explaining Delhivery's value system. To have the courage of conviction to see things through is perhaps rarer than intellectual curiosity, Sahil says. 'A lot of teams are very bright, but they are not necessarily fighters on the ground.'

The third thing that remains critical to Delhivery is a certain sense of fortitude in their recruits. In a business that is so dependent on effective execution, operational fortitude is critical. What they look for, therefore, is a willingness to get things done. 'There's a hub which has got ten times the volume that you projected? Too bad, get it done! It rained all night last night and trucks are not showing up on time? Too bad, get it done! We just have to get it done,' Sahil says.

In screening for fortitude, they would look for a certain wry sense of humour that might allow an individual to carry on in the face of unforeseen challenges. In fact, they demand for it, Sahil says. Working in operations can be extremely frustrating. There is a wide gamut of occurrences that could throw a spanner in a company's operations; it could be a disgruntled policeman who decides to shut down operations in one part of the country, a highway closed off due to protests by a set of villagers in another. There is likely to be much that will lie beyond an individual's ambit of control. Because so much can become uncontrollable, they look for individuals who have a certain connect to the reality of running a business in India. A lot of people in the company come from backgrounds that would have allowed them to understand the market they are operating in really well. They understand that at times, things don't work as they should. 'And they have a sense of humour about it, and a sense of patience about it'.

In some ways, what they then look for is an underlying interest in understanding the complexity of running a business in India, and of the problems inherent to the country itself. 'We harp about this a lot when we are grabbing a bottle of whiskey. But our joke is always that *hamara dhool mitti ka kaam hai* (ours is a rough-and-ready business). We are trucks on the ground and warehouses in unattractive areas,' Sahil says. In Delhivery's early days, the founders would actually ask people where they were from in the interview, and what did they understand of the world. '*Kaunse gaon se ho?* (Which village are you from?) What do you know about what's around you? What do you know about how retail outlets get fulfilled? Have you ever been to a local retailer? Do you drive a bike, do you even know how to drive a bike? So we asked all these kinds of questions that helped us understand the kind of person we were hiring.'

The last thing that they would look for was a sense of personal integrity. They needed to be certain that the person they were working with could be trusted to do the right thing, even when left to their own devices. That they would not steal from the company, that they would not lie to their co-workers. One could sometimes be in a position that might allow them to act to the detriment of the company. Delhivery wanted to make sure that those who might be tempted to do, or likely, to do so were not absorbed into the company.

Over time, these set of values have served Delhivery well and have been codified into the values of the organization. These remain the set of values that they screen for in determining who would be a good fit in the company.

In addition to looking for alignment of individual and organizational values, they also consciously look for diversity in backgrounds. 'Diversity in backgrounds is exceptionally important,' Sahil says. According to Sahil, it is crucial to understand what diversity of backgrounds really means. He says it does not necessarily stand for diversity of educational backgrounds. Three people with different educational background might end up thinking in the same manner.

Instead, diversity of thought is important. That might be a consequence of educational background, but also upbringing, and the kind of person an individual is, Sahil points out. While Delhivery might have a large number of people from an engineering background, that does not make them less diverse. 'The way that people think is not the same,' Sahil says.

Be wary of the industry insider

Once a company starts attaining a certain size, there is a temptation to bring in senior personnel with experience in the industry. The hope is that, having seen how things worked in a larger organization, they would be able to bring in their knowledge and experience to bear to help the startup overcome challenges stemming from its increasing size.

However, it does not always work out well for the startup. In some cases, experienced hires might come in well set in their ways, with preconceived notions as to how certain problems needed to be solved. In others, they might not fit in well within a smaller, more nimble organization whose way of working might be very different from what they might be used to. Often, such hiring decisions culminate in a drawn-out divorce.

TaxiForSure founder Raghu holds that one of the biggest mistakes the founders made in the early days of the company was hiring people from the taxi industry to be executives in the startup.

They had hired individuals with previous experience at a large, incumbent tax-booking company, imagining that their familiarity with the industry would help scale TFS more rapidly. However, the founders soon realized that almost invariably these hires would show little willingness to imagine a way of solving a certain problem that was different from the way it had been solved at their previous company. Their thinking was rooted in the prevailing norms of the industry; they seemed incapable of going beyond.

Raghu offers one particular episode in lieu of illustration. During those days, TFS had a call centre to handle booking requests. During peak hours in the evening, they would have limited bandwidth; some customers therefore could not be serviced. Typically, 10 per cent of calls could not be received.

TFS was, therefore, potentially missing out on additional bookings. A sizable number of the calls would come from repeat customers, that is, customers requiring a booking from the same location every day. These would be office workers looking to book a ride to get home.

When this was brought up for discussion in a company meeting, instead of acknowledging the problem and trying to solve it, one of the experienced hires contested that this should not even be a concern. After all, in his previous company they would miss 40 per cent of the calls during evening hours, he pointed out.

The solution was very obvious, Raghu says. They needed to integrate an automated Interactive Voice Response system for repeat customers. If a person called from a number that was known to book a ride from the same location day after day, they could simply be asked to confirm their location through the IVR by pressing a certain number on their phone. If the location was different, they could be routed to the call centre. This would reduce the burden on the call centre, and diminish the number of missed bookings. However, because TFS already seemed to be doing better than their previous organization, the experienced hires did not even consider missed bookings to be a concern.

Delhivery started hiring senior professionals into its ranks three years into their existence, and scaled up their efforts in 2015 when they were four-and-a-half years old. Founder and CEO Sahil Barua says that they felt they needed to do so because they were facing challenges in terms of continuing to scale. They hoped that hiring senior professionals would help solve some of their problems.

However, they soon realized that simply hiring senior people was not the answer. In fact, at times, such hires ended up creating more concerns than they resolved.

Sahil offers the example of a very senior person that they had hired to oversee operations. Shortly into his stint in the company, the founders realized that his approach to managing the division was entirely at odds with the Delhivery way at the time.

For instance, at Delhivery, the founders have always taken pride in being hands-on; if there is a glitch in operations, they would look to work closely with the operations team to address it. However, when the senior hire came in, he would actively discourage such interventions. He believed it did not support capability building within the team. While he might have been right, at the time, the founders believed that it was more important for the company to build trust with customers, and demonstrate to the operations team that they were all in this together. It helped to address glitches swiftly, and to do it with the founders working alongside the team. However, because there seemed to be two leadership centres with opposing perspectives, it was not clear to the team who they should listen to. This only ended up sowing confusion, and discord. 'Teams would not talk to each other,' Sahil says. 'It just was a nightmare overall!'

In another instance, they hired a senior person to oversee the development of a warehouse management system. He had come from a large, highly reputed company. Initially, they were convinced that given his experience, he would build the system in less than no time. Four or five months later, they realized that he was effectively trying to recreate the system put out by his former company. That was exactly the system that they had been trying to replace at Delhivery simply because it did not meet their requirements; they needed to build differently. 'No matter how many times we sat down, and said, you really need to change the way you're thinking and you really need to understand how we're thinking about this, it did not work,' Sahil says. 'He was a very senior guy. He had his ways of thinking.'

They had looked to hire experienced processionals because they had believed that they did not fully understand how to successfully navigate to the next level of scale. They had imagined they could solve their problems by hiring those with experience at other organizations. They soon realized that they were trying to bring in systems and processes that did not necessarily fit in their organization.

In retrospect, Sahil admits that they should not have imagined in the first place that they could solve their problems simply by hiring from other organizations. They had to learn to find their own solutions, instead of hoping to plug in one that might have been built for a different type of organization.

Designing compensation structures

Compensation is typically made up of three components: salary, benefits, and equity in the company. Early in the life of a company, the equity component might form the most significant part of compensation. Given that an early-stage startup is unlikely to be able to offer market-leading salary or benefits, offering a share in ownership allows prospective employees to benefit from the company's eventual growth through an increase in the value of the equity they would hold. As the company grows, the equity share granted to new employees is likely to reduce, even as the salary offered achieves greater parity with larger companies.

Sahil holds that compensation should be designed taking into account the long-term, while ensuring that it can meet short-term objectives for a prospective employee. What this implies is that while the salary and other benefits offered must meet an employee's more immediate financial objectives, the equity share awarded should be based on its potential value in the long term.

In terms of the salary offered, Delhivery's philosophy is to typically be in the 60th to 70th percentile with regard to the market for functions that might not be core to Delhivery's business. They seek to lead the market in terms of the salary offered for their operations function, given its central role in Delhivery's business. However, as a principle, they would avoid potentially irrational and unsustainable contests with competitors in terms of the salary offered.

Delhivery first introduced salary bands four years into their existence when there was a significant expansion in their team size. Having salary bands in place ensures that at the same level within the organization, differentiation in salary between individuals is avoided. Early in their existence, such differentiation had become a major concern. They had been willing to negotiate salary with prospective employees at the time of hiring. So, often, at the same level, there would be different salaries being offered to different individuals, and there was no way to bring in parity. Now, as part of their recruiting process, they no longer engage in such negotiations. Having been offered a role, if someone comes back claiming to have a better counter-offer, and asks for better terms, Delhivery would typically not pursue the engagement further. 'We warmly encourage people to take whatever offers they have that are better than ours,' Sahil says.

In terms of offering equity to employees, they have sought to design their compensation structures to be market-leading. They offer stock options at every level of the company, down to the field agents. They also supplement the stock options offered when an employee joins with additional periodic grants. This creates a sense of ownership within the company, and ensures that employees remain committed.

In heavily indexing compensation to equity in the company, Delhivery's intent has been to create the maximum possible financial value for employees who play a direct role in the company's growth. According to Sahil, the value of equity in the early stages of a company increases faster than any annual salary increment that the company could offer. For instance, an annual salary increment of 15 per cent would lead to the salary of an employee becoming four times at the end of ten years. In the same period, the value of equity in a successful startup, especially if awarded early in the life of the company, is likely to increase by a lot more. 'The math of compounding simply doesn't work in the case of salary,' Sahil explains. 'The only way to create maximum financial value is by making sure that employees share the benefits of equity compounding, not salary compounding.'

Ensuring that employees are beneficiaries of growth is also why Delhivery is committed to additional periodic equity grants. 'At the rate at which we are growing, value is getting created every year. I have to find a way of compensating for the enterprise value getting created. The logic of equity compensation is that I take a proportion of the value created, and allocate that,' Sahil emphasizes.

Delhivery's emphasis on equity distribution sends a message to prospective employees that it is a company that values growth, and is willing to share that with employees. Additional equity allocations remind employees that in contributing to value creation, they also get to accumulate additional value.

Equity allocations are especially valuable if there is liquidity in a company's stock options pool, allowing employees to trade options prior to the company's public listing. While a lot of startups issue stock options, often these are not necessarily valuable because of limited liquidity. At Delhivery, building liquidity in the options pool has been a key priority from the beginning. Instituting a company stock purchase programme has been a key measure, amongst others, towards this end. As the company has grown, and inched closer to becoming a public listed company, interest from external investors has further increased liquidity.

Policybazaar also embraces a compensation structure that is highly indexed to equity. Founder Yashish Dahiya explains that their objective has been to ensure that for anybody who stayed at the company for a period of more than four years, the equity allocated to them would become the primary driver of value in their compensation, instead of salary. The salary, in fact, should ideally become comparatively inconsequential once a person has worked at the company for long enough.

Policybazaar also ensured that stock options in the company were liquid from the very beginning. In making stock options trade-able, Policybazaar ensured that employees realized that these could be exchanged for money, and therefore held real value. 'We opened up trading in stock options for this very reason,' Yashish says. 'We wanted people to know that the value of these options was real.'

Measuring performance

Aligning individual performance with organizational objectives is key to ensuring that such objectives are achieved. Management by objectives, popularized by Peter Drucker in his 1954 book *The Practice of Management*, is one of the most widely employed methods for managing performance. This involves translating organization objectives to individual objectives that are agreed to by both management and employees.

Delhivery carries out goal setting for the entire company at the start of the financial year. It starts with the CEO, and then cascades down the hierarchy. It is a deliberate process that the company engages in, and would typically take two months to complete. Teams and individuals are expected to lay out in detail what they are going to do over the year, and how they are going to create value. 'We do a lot of our thinking in this period, about how we're going to do things,' founder Sahil Barua says.

For the operations team, goal setting is based on performance metrics that are linked with the company's business such as, for instance, organization performance in terms of service levels and cost. There are specific threshold targets that are decided upon, based on organizational needs. Once determined, these are translated into objectives for individuals in the team.

Performance measurability is very high in the case of operations as team and individual objectives are linked to organizational performance which is tracked through key organizational metrics. In the case of operations therefore, performance monitoring and measurement is carried out in real-time. Every Delhivery rider would, for instance, get a performance score and a rank within the team based on the day's performance; as long as the minimum expected thresholds are being met, the rank is of little consequence. Because performance measurement is system-driven, it is highly objective and transparent.

For other functions, goal setting is carried out based on criteria that may be specific to each function. Performance evaluation is carried out using a ratings system in some teams, with individuals being evaluated in terms of whether they meet expectations, perform above expectations, or perform below expectations. Alternatively, performance measurement is carried out using a continuous feedback mechanism whereby where an employee receives feedback on the job, and is guided in a systematic manner by openly discussing their strengths and weaknesses. Such feedback is collected using a tool, and discussed in an annual performance review.

In the case of Policybazaar, there are certain core organizational metrics that are measured for each business unit (BU) within the company, and form a basis for measuring performance. These would typically include, for instance, number of transaction, policy premium, revenue contribution, and profitability. Their importance might vary based on the BU.

For instance, Policybazaar founder Yashish Dahiya explains, a higher value of transactions is more important for motor insurance, whereas a higher premium is more important for life insurance. This differentiation is important in setting targets. If the number of transactions were made the key metric for life insurance, employees would try to split a policy with a higher premium into two different policies for the buyer, so that they could a higher number of transactions. Therefore, performance indicators must be linked to business reality.

Beyond these core metrics, there might be additional objectives set at the BU level. Typically, these would be determined by the BU, and not necessarily centrally handed down.

Building organization culture

Organizational culture encompasses the set of values, beliefs and behaviours that determine the internal environment in a firm. Culture has a profound and immeasurable impact on every aspect of an organization's existence. It has a direct impact on the kind of individuals that a firm attracts, and by extension, shapes decision-making at every level.

In building organizational culture, Delhivery's approach is to subtly emphasize the importance of organization values, without necessarily making overt efforts to disseminate these. In fact, Sahil says that it is important to demonstrate adherence to certain values in building an organizational culture, not necessarily importance to disseminate them. 'Demonstration is the fastest form of dissemination in these matters,' he says.

What that means is if intellectual curiosity is a core value around which the company would like to build their culture, then they seek to encourage behaviour that reflects the presence of this trait. For instance, Sahil says, if there are three people in a room, and two of them are afraid of asking a certain question, but the third does, and is positively recognized for doing so, that would encourage intellectual curiosity amongst the other two as well.

Bringing in mentors and independent advisors

Mentors and advisors often play a crucial role in the life of a startup. They can be a sounding board for founders, helping to think through strategies and decide upon the right direction for the company. They can help stay focused on the path. They can offer a shoulder when things are not going according to plan. A well-connected advisor could also open doors for the company, facilitating access to potential investors, team members, and customers. Besides, having a reputed advisor being associated with a company can help generate credibility that might be hard to build for a small company.

Naukri founder Sanjeev Bikhchandani has been associated with MakeMyTrip since the early days of the company. Both Deep and Sanjeev had been educated at St. Stephen's and IIM Ahmedabad, and had come to be acquainted with each other. When Deep was looking to plunge into entrepreneurship, he had looked to Sanjeev for advice. His encouragement has been a key factor in Deep going ahead with the decision. Sanjeev also served on MakeMyTrip's board from 2005 to 2010.[3]

Deep Kalra says that he has been able to reach out to Sanjeev whenever he has needed advice and has received wise counsel. Sanjeev has been a very successful entrepreneur himself, and understands what it takes to build an internet business. As an advisor that is essentially external to the firm, he is also able to offer unbiased advice. 'It is strange, but sometimes, even if you are the founder of the company, what is right for you might not be the same as what's right for the company. It's very weird; there are times when you'll have personal biases will come in,' Deep says. Sanjeev succeeds in rising above the fray. 'He'll say, "Hey listen, remove yourself from the situation, and I am not your friend when I am giving you this advice, I am the friend of the company, and this is what's right for the company."' Especially when there are potential conflicts at play, Sanjeev's role as an impartial counsellor becomes particularly valuable.[4]

---

[3]   Varsha Bansal, 'My Mentor's Value System Helped Me Make My Own Trip: Deep Kalra', *The Economic Times*, 25 July 2017, economictimes.indiatimes.com/small-biz/entrepreneurship/my-mentors-value-system-helped-me-make-my-own-trip-deep-kalra/articleshow/59749661.cms?from=mdr

[4]   Varsha Bansal, 'My Mentor's Value System Helped Me Make My Own Trip: Deep Kalra', *The Economic Times*, 25 July 2017, economictimes.indiatimes.com/small-biz/entrepreneurship/my-mentors-value-system-helped-me-make-my-own-trip-deep-kalra/articleshow/59749661.cms?from=mdr

Instituting a board of directors with independent advisors also allows a company to tap into impartial counsel. This is what Delhivery did. Delhivery set up a board with independent directors four years into their existence, unusual for a startup of that age. Delhivery's independent board signalled credibility to investors. Sahil says, 'The idea was to also tell our investors that when we say we are doing the right thing, don't take only our word for it. Here's a bunch of independent directors you can go and talk to, and they should be able to give an accurate opinion.'

Summary

- **Start building supporting structures early on.** Start thinking of building supporting structures such as HR, and accounting early in the life of the company. Having enabling structures in place aids rapid and sustainable growth.
- **When hiring, look for 'fit' in the organization.** While skills are essential, ensuring fit in the organization, and unity of an individual's values with that of the organization will serve well in the long run.
- **Get skin in the game.** Incentivize employees to become interested stakeholders in the company's growth by incorporating generous ESOP elements into compensation structures. This is likely to ensure that the objectives of the firm and employees are aligned.
- **Set goals for teams and individuals, and build processes to measure performance against these.** Setting goals in a systematic manner will ensure alignment between organizational objectives with individual or team efforts. Tracking team and individual performance will ensure visibility on whether organizational objectives are being

realized. It will also offer a means to reward strong performance.

- **Build organization culture.** Culture encompasses the set of values, beliefs and behaviours that determine the internal environment in a firm. It has a profound and immeasurable impact on every aspect of an organization's existence. Seek to build culture by continuously reinforcing and encouraging behaviours that align with organizational values.
- **Seek external help when needed.** Mentors and advisors can play a pivotal role in setting the right direction for the company, and offering impartial advice. Seek out mentors and advisors when in doubt.

9

Building a Behemoth

IF A STARTUP SURVIVES and is successful, it might eventually come to resemble a large, traditional organization. With that might come inefficiencies that often plague such organizations. What determines successful navigation through this phase is both the startup's ability to manage governance and complexity, as well as retain the nimbleness required to continue innovating.

Evolving structure and team

As a company grows, it would hire more people. As the number of people in the organisation increases, coordination becomes increasingly tricky. While it might have eschewed hierarchy and formal processes when it was smaller, these take on more importance.

In the 1990s, British anthropologist and evolutionary psychologist Robin Dunbar found a correlation between primate brain size and average social group size. He suggested that there was a limit to the number of people with whom one could maintain stable social relationships. Within this limit, an individual in a group knows who each person is and how they relate to every other person. Using the average human brain size and extrapolating from the results of primates, he proposed that humans could comfortably maintain only about 150 stable relationships.[1] In the case of organisations, the Dunbar number, as it has come to be known, stands for an organisation's size beyond which it becomes essential to lay down structures and processes to function effectively.

When Policybazaar started in 2008, it had only fourteen people in the organisation. Within a decade, it had grown to have more than two thousand. What Policybazaar has done to continue to be nimble as it has grown is to carve the organisation into a set of small BUs, each working largely independently. Policybazaar founder and group CEO Yashish Dahiya shares that each unit would typically have not more than 100 to 150 people. It would be led by people who would have spent enough time with the organisation to understand its ethos, and are able to work independently. Each unit would be empowered to have internal functional teams, for instance, to manage technology, or supply chain relations, if required.

Yashish explains that they decided to break the organisation down into smaller parts when they realised that they were being less effective in driving impact as a large organisation. The BU structure allows people to take responsibility, and do whatever is needed to win in their specific segment, Yashish explains.

---

[1] 'Dunbar's Number: Why We Can Only Maintain 150 Relationships', *www.bbc.com*, 1 October 2019, https://www.bbc.com/future/article/20191001-dunbars-number-why-we-can-only-maintain-150-relationships

Policybazaar first started implementing the BU structure almost seven years into the firm's existence. At the time, their growth was slowing down, coming to hover around the 30 per cent YoY mark; inefficiencies were setting in. Once they broke the company down into smaller units, they witnessed dramatically faster growth. They have consistently grown at more than 100 per cent YoY over the following four years after rolling out the BU structure.

So effective has this intervention been that the company has started carving each BU into even smaller micro-BUs. For instance, Yashish explains, if health insurance is a specific BU, within it, it would have three micro-BUs, one focusing on pre-approved health insurance, one on old-age health insurance, and the third on pre-existing diseases. In terms of the organisational structure, below the group CEO, there are two brands, Policybazaar and Paisabazaar. Below the brands are the BUs, and within each BU, there are micro-BUs.

The driving force behind carving out micro-BUs is the fact that each target segment has its own unique characteristics when it comes to purchasing insurance policies. These would be a function of both the target population demographics, as well as product category. Building micro-BUs allows for greater customisation in approach, in line with the specific characteristics of each segment. 'The kind of focus that you require to handle people who are seventy years of age is very different from the focus that you require for people who are twenty-five years old,' Yashish says. Older people will have a higher incidence of medical issues. However, they might also have mobility issues, so you cannot expect them to visit the hospital every time. They will need more home visits. In identifying the right insurance for this segment, the sales team would need to account for these characteristics. Similarly, selling health insurance and life insurance involve entirely different user journeys. 'In health insurance, for example, you do not need income documents. Whereas in life insurance, you do,' Yashish explains. In order to increase penetration in a particular segment, you need to account for the specific characteristics of the segment. 'The fact is that it takes a lot of detail to win,' Yashish says. Given this reality, centralised control will be counter-effective. 'It is really left to the micro BU head as to what they need to do in their area,' Yashish says.

Splitting the business into smaller units allows for higher growth by allowing for much higher focus on each segment. For instance, health insurance as a BU might achieve a certain level of growth, but its growth will also be constrained by non-specificity in addressing customer problems. When broken down into micro-BUs, it is possible to be far more focused, and better address customer problems. For instance, Yashish explains, in selling health insurance to the seventy years old and above population, the micro-BU head can drive the development of more specific marketing campaigns, identify more suitable sales agents, and engage more deeply with customers. Even the technological infrastructure available might be different. For instance, the sales team might have a higher-quality microphone for telephone calls, given older people might find it hard to hear. 'In a micro-BU, you can have very deep focus.' As each micro-BU grows rapidly, it will translate into faster growth for the company.

In developing micro-BUs, Policybazaar looks to make them mutually exclusive, so that there is no overlap between target segments, but collectively exhaustive, so that each possible segment is addressed. He admits that this does throw up a challenge in not allowing for effective cross-selling of products as each micro-BU remains focused on a single product. But given that the market is still growing, driving deeper penetration is more important than increasing the purchase size for each customer.

Since Policybazaar operates with a very high degree of specialisation, it becomes increasingly difficult for rival players to compete on the same footing. Across the group and the two brands, Policybazaar and Paisabazaar, there are likely to be close to fifty micro-BUs. 'For a competitor to actually compete, they have to focus on fifty different things,' Yashish says. 'That is exactly where competitors struggle.' The typical competitor is likely to focus on insurance as a whole, not on a micro-segment, split by demographic and product category. In fact, Yashish says that many companies might not even reach the level of complexity the overall level that a micro-BU might be operating at.

While the BU and the micro-BU structure might seem to add more complexity to the organisation, Yashish says that in fact, these have allowed for de-layering of the organisation to take place. The micro-BUs have direct access to the Yashish, the group CEO, and are responsible for running their own unit. Had the company opted to have a traditional matrix organisation, central functions would have become more powerful, and bureaucracy would have set in. By creating a micro-BU structure, and allowing micro-BUs direct access to the CEO, Policybazaar has ensured that it does not become too hierarchical. 'So you stay ready for growth,' Yashish says. The structure also makes it easier to isolate and address issues. For instance, if one large, unified sales team was handling multiple processes, a glitch in the system might be challenging to isolate. However, given the structure's modularity, a specific issue with a certain process is likely to only affect a certain micro-BU, and may be addressed much more rapidly.

'The BU and micro-BU structure comes from the frustrations of a growing organization,' Yashish notes. 'You start getting frustrated at some point with the speed of things.' In cutting down on the size of each unit, and driving more specialized segment focus, Policybazaar has been successful in staying nimble.

Organizational challenges in a large organization may stem not just from the structure of the organization, but also the individuals within. As an organization expands, it sometimes so happens that some individuals are not able to adapt to their evolving role. 'Many individuals who might have driven the business with tremendous energy and enthusiasm when it was relatively smaller, might struggle when it scales up by an order of magnitude or more,' Yashish explains. They might not be able to manage an increase in the size of the team. 'Suddenly, instead of working with other individuals, they have to work with multiple teams or might have to work under managers,' Yashish says. Alternatively, while being a generalist might have helped them really well in managing a diverse range of tasks when the company was small, they might not possess specialized skills, or might not be able to work well with those that do, once the organization is larger.

In such situations, organizational management might need to transition certain individuals out of the organization. It is a particularly difficult choice. Yashish admits that he does not like to let go of people who have been with the organization through its period of struggle. Many of them might not find the same kind of opportunity outside Policybazaar, and he feels he owes it to them to retain them in the organization. But when certain individuals might not be stepping up in terms of their performance, or in terms of their managerial ability, it adversely impacts the organization, and needs to be addressed.

MakeMyTrip founder Deep Kalra echoes Yashish's concerns. 'As companies mature, a very painful reality becomes apparent—not every manager, not every leader grows apace with the company,' he says. It is often painful because on occasion you might need to supersede individuals who might have been with the organization for a very long period with laterally hired talent. 'It is not only painful for the person who got superseded, but it is painful to do, especially if the person has been with you through thick and thin,' Deep says. He says circa 2008 they had to replace a very senior person in the organization who was not performing up to expectations with a specialist hired from outside the organization. Deep resisted making the call, and dithered for the longest time. However, eventually, he reached out to Sanjeev Bikhchandani, who was on MakeMyTrip's board, for advice. Sanjeev convinced him that it was the right decision for the company. When they did go ahead with the decision, it had a major positive impact on the company. 'It turned around our P&L,' he says. 'We turned profitable.'

The CEO's role

The role of a CEO evolves dramatically as the company scales. According to Anu Hariharan, Partner at Y Combinator Continuity Fund, the role of the CEO goes through three key phases, linked to the stage of the company. For an early-stage company, the primary role of the CEO is to build a product that users love. Once a company achieves product-market fit, the CEO must work towards maximizing the opportunity that the product has surfaced. As the company scales, the CEO must focus on determining the medium- to long-term direction of the company, while looking to invest in transformative new ideas.

In the early stages, when there are no more than thirty or forty people in the company, the CEO is the 'doer-in-chief,' Anu notes. An early-stage CEO is the primary instigator in the running of the company. They would typically oversee a core function, but often need to extend their focus to matters beyond. They would be deeply embedded in the company's day-to-day operations, directly participating in solving any problems that might come up.

As a startup scales, the CEO must transition from being the 'doer-in-chief' to the 'company-builder-in-chief.' According to Anu, the role of a growth-stage as well as a late-stage CEO boils down to three things: hiring a leadership team and making sure they work well together, creating purpose and alignment, and nurturing company culture.

'The most important thing to become 'company-builder-in-chief' is to hire a leadership team,' Anu says. A young founder will often not know how to run core functions in a growing company. It is therefore critical to hire a strong executive team. The CEO must be humble enough to recognize that they will need to hire people who are more experienced than them, and even better than them in certain ways. They must also learn to recognize what great executive talent looks like, especially in terms of the skills, experiences and personality traits that the company needs. 'You have to be really good at hiring really good leaders,' Anu says.

As you go about building a leadership team, you also need to ensure that there is what Anu describes as 'mission-to-metrics' alignment. It is the CEO's role to define the mission of the company, the strategic direction that the company should take, and metrics that need to be tracked to measure company pace and performance.

When founders are unwilling to bring in experienced professionals, it is often because they are unwilling to listen to counsel, convinced of their own infallibility. MakeMyTrip founder and CEO Deep Kalra has a term for such behaviour; he calls it founderitis. 'It's a disease when founders start to believe they are the last ones and are the elixir for all ideas in the company, they are the gospel truth and will always decide what's right and wrong,' he says. He says that companies where such behaviour exists are unlikely to scale beyond a certain level. The key-man risk is too high in such companies, he says; far too much is contingent on one person getting every decision right. 'No one person can always be right all the time,' he points out. 'You've got to have the culture where people can challenge each other and refine decisions. The moment you start believing in your own infallibility as a founder, it's the beginning of the end for your company.'

Delhivery founder and CEO Sahil Barua observes that the most fundamental way in which his role has changed is that his focus has shifted from the short term to the long term. 'My horizon has changed from the short-term to the medium term to the long-term to the really long-term,' he says. For instance, rather than apportioning a significant portion of his time to thinking about the financial returns for the year as he was wont to do earlier, he now devotes far more time thinking about how the company would survive over a very long period of time, and how they could best make use of investments in the company.

In addition, his role has shifted from overseeing execution, to ensuring skilful delegation. While earlier he would spend a lot more time 'managing problems', as the organization has grown, he spends a lot more time 'managing people'. He invests far more time now determining who in the organization should be doing what. He also devotes far more time to managing external stakeholders, especially investors in the company, many of whom would have representatives on the board. 'I want to make sure that our investors understand what we're doing, they buy into the long-term story, they're well informed about the company, and they support the company,' he says.

Making the transition from early-stage CEO to a late-stage CEO is a hugely challenging process, says Sahil. One of the most difficult elements is to learn to relinquish control. First, it requires being able to trust the wider team to execute properly, even when not being closely monitored; it takes time to develop such trust. What makes it doubly difficult is that it requires you to admit to yourself that you might not always be needed to ensure proper execution. 'You have to ask an important question to yourself which is "Am I needed?", and with a shock, you realize that you're not very often. It is a great jolt to the ego to realize that you're not necessary any longer,' he says. 'If anybody asks me what they should do as a manager, I say "make yourself redundant". And then I realize exactly how hard it is to make yourself redundant. Because you don't want to. It is very hard. To not be there every day on the front line makes you feel like you are not creating value, and learning how to deal with that is extremely difficult.'

Difficult as that might be, Sahil contends that learning to broaden your horizon and being disciplined about it is perhaps even harder. 'You keep switching between what is important in the long term what is important in the short term, and being able to resist the urge to take that schizophrenia to the rest of the organization is not easy,' he says. He admits that even after having spent years learning to maintain his focus primarily on the long term, he does tend to lose perspective occasionally.

Speaking amidst the COVID-induced lockdown, with Delhivery's operations either shut down, or constrained across most locations, he says that a crisis like that is when the CEO's role becomes really important. Under ordinary circumstances, the CEO should get out of the way, and let people do what they're doing. But when things go awry, they must lead from the front.

The CEO's role, ultimately, is to make the least bad decision when all that are available are bad decisions, he says. 'When you have good choices in front of you, anybody can make the right decision. Anybody can sail a boat in fair waters,' he says. 'The role of the CEO is to make the best decision when all you have is bad choices.'

Hiring an outsider CEO

For a company to continue to grow, it must continue to innovate. According to Ben Horowitz, founding CEOs possess three key attributes that equip them to propel a company to continue innovating:

- Comprehensive knowledge: Founding CEOs have an exhaustive understanding of the technology required in building a product, and the likely competitors, and the market itself
- Moral authority: Innovation often requires modifying the foundational assumptions of the company; the founding CEO typically wields greater authority in this regard, having perhaps helped to put these together
- Total commitment to the long term: Founding CEO's take a long view of their companies, their goal from the start being to build something significant

Sometimes, however, founding CEOs might not have the skills required to manage the company as it grows larger. According to Anu Hariharan, when a company is growing rapidly, the CEO must learn how to build a company at the same pace. It implies rapidly learning to hire the right set of executives, driving accountability, and steering a large company in the right direction. If the CEO is unable to learn how to play the role, it is likely to hurt the company. Alternatively, the founding CEO might decide that they no longer want to continue in the role. They might have grown the company to a certain stage, and might want to pass on the baton. At this stage, the company might decide to hire an outsider CEO who might possess relevant experience. 'The founder sort of realizes that while they thought they could do the job, but they are holding the company back,' Anu says. 'In this case the founder often says, "I am actually slowing the company down, I want to bring in an outsider CEO."'[2]

In bringing in a CEO from outside the organization, one of the most important considerations has to be that the CEO's values must match with those of the organization, as well as the founders. They must be able to carry the company forward in a spirit of collaboration.

When Policybazaar were looking for a new CEO, an alignment in values was more important than any specific capabilities or experience that they might bring in. In February 2020, Sarbvir Singh was appointed CEO of Policybazaar, with Yashish transitioning to chairman of the Policybazaar group. Singh had no prior experience in insurance or operations However, Yashish could trust him to be a good fit

---

[2]   Noam Wasserman, 'The Founder's Dilemma', *Harvard Business Review*, 11 August 2014, hbr.org/2008/02/the-founders-dilemma

in the organization, and take the organization forward in a collaborative manner.

Sarbvir was a senior of Yashish's at IIT Delhi. They've known each other for twenty-six years. Recalling his interactions with Sarbvir at IIT, Yashish says, 'He was the sports secretary while I was involved in running and swimming. He used to come to me before every event and ask me about my plan for the event. I, on the other hand, would never have a plan. But, because a senior had asked, I had to make up something. I would say something like, "Since this is a 1500-metre race, I will run at a certain pace for the first 700 metres and then speed up. Everybody expects me to speed up at 1100, but I will speed up earlier to build up my lead and eventually win." He always appreciated my plan, not once did he question it. Further, he would always stand at the 700-metre mark to ensure I didn't miss it. At the 700-metre mark, he would clap once, "Okay, Yashish!" And every time he stood there, I never lost.'

Bringing in a CEO from outside is a difficult decision to make. In arriving at the decision, it is imperative to ensure that the individual brought in is aligned with the ethos and culture of the organization, and that the founders are able to repose their trust in the person.

Innovating in a large company

As companies grow, they find it harder to continuously innovate. However, a company that is unable to innovate is unlikely to survive over the long term.

According to Sahil Barua, just like people, organizations too can tend to get comfortable with where they are. 'Organizations age, just like people age,' he says. He believes that the first step towards being an organization that continues to innovate is fostering a culture that encourages people to have an interest in developments around the world, to have a point of view on everything, and to question the status quo.

At Delhivery, intellectual curiosity is a core value. By extension, an interest in understanding developments across a wide range of subjects is deeply valued; a habit of reading widely, for instance, is encouraged. 'We are aware of what's going on across markets. We have an understanding of technology, of how the world is changing, where there are problems,' he says. According to Sahil, this allows the team to come up with new perspectives while solving problems. Similarly, the company encourages a culture of asking questions: 'When somebody agrees to do something a certain way, there has to be one guy who puts his hands up and say, "Well, what if the exact opposite happened?"' Sahil says that as companies grow, most of them are unable to preserve a culture that is dynamic, and encourages people to question the traditional way of doing things.

Second, they seek to foster a culture that values direct observation. As companies get larger, the layers within the company increase too much, Sahil notes. Senior management can tend to become a step removed from the workings of the company on the ground. At Delhivery, they avoid this by ensuring that even senior management in the company get directly involved with operations. 'We spend a lot of time on the ground. Because we spend a lot of time on the ground we can see what's happening,' he says. Their understanding of operations on the ground allows them to propose solutions that are far more likely to work, as opposed to solutions that might have been developed in a vacuum. This philosophy applies not just to finding solutions for operational issues, but also in arriving at strategic decisions. For instance, in determining whether they should enter the Bangladesh market or not, a Delhivery team actually spent time in Dhaka researching the market, instead of arriving at the decision from a distance.

Third, they encourage people to take risks. What this means is they encourage teams and individuals to come up with ideas, and if these seem marketable, they are willing to put the organization's muscle behind them. Not every idea would receive support. Before implementation, they would force people to put together a proper rationale for why they would want they organization to take certain risks, and how these risks would pay off. Once the decision has been made to go forward though, the organization would stick with it. When you put the organization's muscle behind an idea, the person who came up with it has the pleasure of seeing it being implemented, Sahil says. For others, it is a message that the organization is willing to support new ideas, even audacious ones, and that encourages more people to come up with their own ideas.

Fourth, Delhivery continuously evolves its organizational structure. Sahil says that since their founding, they have not had a stable organizational structure except in some parts of their operations function. 'The organization must evolve in response to its environment. The way an organization evolves is by restructuring itself,' he says. 'So we change our structure, we change where resources are allocated, which teams people belong to, we move them around. That gives us the ability to respond very, very quickly.'

For instance, in 2019, Delhivery created a network team by integrating elements of the operations, engineering, and data science teams. What this team does is design the architecture of the company's logistics network, take key decisions including where should the delivery hubs be, how large should these be, how should traffic route across these hubs. Historically, this role had belonged to the operations and the engineering teams, supported by the data science team. However, the company realized that the network had become far too complex and it was unlikely that their existing decision-making methods were the most optimal. So they carved out a new team, integrated new, more modern tools into the decision-making process.

The first three months were a struggle, Sahil says. The mandate for the new team was not entirely clear, and there was a concern that teams might step on each other's turf. The move paid off though. As the team began to optimize the network, delivery times improved. While earlier Delhivery would deliver 75 per cent of orders in two days, and 100 per cent in three, once the network team started functioning, the company started delivering more than 95 per cent of orders within one-and-a-half days.

Similarly, when Delhivery was looking to build an international business, management realized that there did not exist a good freight exchange platform that they could leverage, and so, they decided to build one in-house. Sahil says that they put together a new team in two weeks by pulling out resources from existing teams, and with that set out to build a new business. This flexibility in terms of organizational structure allows the company to continuously innovate.

Expanding beyond national boundaries

International expansion can be a crucial element in driving continued growth for a company. If a product is likely to demonstrate high product-market fit beyond the domestic market, then international expansion offers a path to expanding the size of the targeted market. International expansion can also be a means to accelerate growth, especially if incremental penetration in the domestic market is slowing down. In some cases, international expansion can also be a means to better serve the domestic market.

Before expanding internationally, founders should ask themselves if they have a sound business model. In its absence, international expansion might only serve to complicate operations, and might be best avoided. Founders must determine what they seek to achieve through international expansion, and how it might fit in their overall strategy. Based on this, market selection must be carried out with great deliberation; expanding to a market that might not necessarily fit into the company's overall strategy is only likely to stretch resources for limited or no gains.

Once a market is selected, the company must explore whether it would be best to enter a certain market independently, or as part of a partnership. This decision should be taken on the basis of local market features, regulation, and implications for the company in the medium to long term. In entering a new market, the company might either encounter local players offering a similar product or service, or encourage the growth of new players with a similar proposition. Having in place a clear differentiation strategy is essential. Finally, international expansion is likely to demand investments upfront. The company might need to set up a local office, for instance, and build local operations. This must be taken into account in developing the expansion strategy.

International expansion for Urban Company was borne out of a necessity to find the next set of customers. Urban Company's offering of on-demand home services sees traction primarily in major urban centres. While founder Abhiraj Bhal believes that the company has so far only tapped into 0.5 per cent of the potential market in India, he admits that it might take time for wide adoption across the country. 'India is a very large market, but it is also a slow-moving market,' he says. In expanding to international markets, Urban Company is looking to tap into demand in more mature markets, as part of driving its next phase of growth.

The tipping point for the decision to expand internationally came when Abhiraj saw a presentation in which a local player in UAE was claiming to be the Urban Company of UAE. Given that this indicated that there was already an existing demand in the market, they decided to expand to the country. UAE is a relatively small market, with a large Indian diaspora; Urban Company was likely to encounter a demographic that was in some ways similar to the one they served at home. 'UAE was a less risky market, a calculated sort of international bet,' Abhiraj says. They hoped to use the country as a testing bed for future international expansion. Once the company saw adoption in UAE, and started to grow, it gave them the confidence to expand to more markets.

In looking to identify additional markets for expansion, the company studied the homes services landscape worldwide, seeking to find pockets of similarity with segments of the domestic market where they had been successful, and a market that was large enough that an upfront investment would yield meaningful returns later on. This is how they honed in on Singapore and Australia.

In Australia's case, it also helped that a trusted former employee had moved to the country. In expanding to a new market, being able to tap into institutional knowledge is essential. Urban Company could build their team around this individual who was willing to start operations for the company in Australia. 'He was a very valued team member. He was willing to start Australia for us. That became the reason for us to start,' Abhiraj says. In making decisions, it is essential to have strategic coherence, but on occasion, certain calls might be based on gut feel, and on the comfort that the team feels in going ahead with these, Abhiraj admits.

In the case of Delhivery, international expansion is an important not as a means to serve customers in international markets, but to serve their domestic customers better. 'Our international business is rooted in our India business,' Founder Sahil Barua says.

Delhivery is one of the largest enterprise logistics companies in India, controlling one of largest freight and warehousing networks in the country. They are able to offer cross-border freight services. Given this capability, they can intensify their operations in other countries along international routes. 'India is a large part of the world. We are a large net importer of goods and services. So, we are using India as a base to build operations in other countries,' Sahil says. 'On the China-to-India line for instance, in express parcels, we are the largest player and we are able to get that volume because we have a large India operation.'

Sahil says that they do not necessarily look at international expansion in terms of building their own assets and operations in every country that they would like to be present in. There are logistics assets in other countries, set up by local players. They want to figure out how to digitally integrate them. Historically, many global logistics players had focused on physical integration, building their own assets, setting up operations, and hiring local teams across countries. Delhivery does not seek to follow that path; it would instead look to partner with local players. Delhivery does not need to have its own infrastructure in place in Shanghai or in Hong Kong, Sahil says. Local players in these markets would have assets, and Delhivery would acquire transaction rights to use them.

However, in some parts of the world, this might not necessarily hold; there might a paucity of local assets. Sahil points to countries in India's neighbourhood. Bangladesh, Nepal, and Sri Lanka do not have strong local players. In these countries, instead of partnering with local players, Delhivery's approach is to provide their technology platform for local players to scale up their operations. 'We are building local champions,' Sahil says. Their intent is to help a local player in these countries build their operations. In doing so, they would ensure that local players would understand Delhivery's processes, they will already use their technology platform, and can be seamlessly integrated into their network. This would help Delhivery serve their domestic market better. 'India has 1.4 billion people, it's a large enough market. Our entire international strategy is grounded in our India strategy,' Sahil says.

Acquiring a company

When a company starts out, it looks to grow organically. It would direct its efforts towards such measures as building a better product, strengthening sales and marketing efforts, and strengthening internal processes. Once the company has grown large, the opportunity to expand inorganically exists.

A merger or acquisition allows a company to accomplish one or more of the following:

- Increase market share, and strengthen position in the market by joining with a rival operating in the same segment
- Expand its product portfolio through assimilating the target's product offering
- Integrate capabilities that might hitherto be missing, either in the segment that it operates in, or in an adjacent segment

- Prevent the acquisition of the target by a major rival, thus also preventing the target from acquiring critical capabilities
- Absorb talent that might be part of the management at the target company, and which might not be willing to join directly

A merger or acquisition taking place within the same market segment typically leads to the formation of a stronger organization. Not only are their synergistic benefits that can be taken advantage of, it often leads to the setting aside of a rivalry that might be both bruising and expensive.

When MakeMyTrip acquired Ibibo in 2016, not only did it strengthen its presence in the online travel segment, it was also to put an end to the challenge that Ibibo had mounted. After acquiring India's largest bus ticketing service redBus in 2013, Ibibo had ramped up its marketing efforts to position itself as a clear challenger to MakeMyTrip. Ibibo had rapidly gained market share, and in the process, had forced MakeMyTrip to ratchet up its own spend on marketing. MakeMyTrip had to almost triple its marketing spend from the previous year to keep pace. Eventually, to end the unviable situation, the two companies decided to call a truce, entering into an agreement to form a combined $1.8 billion entity that would be the dominant player in the market. [3]

An acquisition can be a means to expand a company's product portfolio. Ibibo's acquisition of redBus, in fact, is a case in point. While Ibibo had grown to be a major player within the air travel booking segment, redBus had emerged as the

---

[3] Rohin Dharmakumar, 'Ibibo High Stakes Poker', *The Ken*, 23 November 2016, the-ken.com/story/ibibo-high-stakes-poker

dominant player in online bus ticketing segment. Through the acquisition, Ibibo could also play in the bus ticketing segment.[4]

An acquisition can also be a means to integrate specific capabilities. Before acquiring Myntra in 2014, Flipkart had sought to grow its presence in the profitable apparel segment with limited success. Myntra had an apparel-only focus, and with the acquisition, Flipkart could gain from Myntra's dominant position in the segment. Besides, through combining operations, it could achieve economies of scale, and lower its operational expenditure. The acquisition also went beyond enabling Flipkart to strengthen its operations in the apparel category. It allowed Flipkart to consolidate its presence in the e-commerce sector in the face of Amazon's expansion in the country.[5]

When an acquisition is carried out with an eye on talent, it is characterized as an 'acquihire'. In such an acquisition there is a greater emphasis on the skills and expertise of the founders and employees of the target. It is particularly advantageous when the acquiring company is looking to assimilate specific capabilities that might not be available with in-house talent. Such a move might be especially useful when the company is looking to set up a new vertical, or expand in a new country. In expanding to a new country, a company must account for a cultural, market, and regulatory environment that it might not understand fully. Expanding through an acquihire might be easier.

---

4   Utkarsh, 'Redbus to Be Acquired by ibibo Group for $138 Million', *Inc42 Media*, 15 June 2013, inc42.com/buzz/redbus-to-be-acquired-by-ibibo-group-for-over-100-million

5   Pranbihanga Borpuzari, 'Flipkart Acquires Myntra: Here Is Why It Makes Sense', *The Economic Times*, 22 May 2014, https://economictimes.indiatimes.com/tech/internet/flipkart-acquires-myntra-here-is-why-it-makes-sense/articleshow/35471764.cms

When Urban Company entered Australia, it acquired on-demand beauty service provider Glamazon. The company's business assets in Australia strengthened Urban Company's position in the market, no doubt, but the move was also driven by an aspiration to assimilate the company's founder. 'We really admired and liked the co-founder Lauren Silvers, particularly her understanding of the Australian market, of the services landscape, and the consumer,' says Abhiraj Bhal, founder and CEO of Urban Company. 'She was great at marketing, and some of the softer skills important in that geography. She now leads all our marketing efforts in Australia.'

Mergers and acquisitions allow a company to expand inorganically, as well as strengthen its position in the market. Understanding the risks and benefits involved, and carefully executing a post-merger integration plan ensures that the move is effective and advantageous.

Summary

- **As a company expands, team structures and individual responsibilities will have to evolve.** The organizational structure that might have served the company well at an earlier stage in its lifecycle might no longer serve it well, and will need to evolve. Similarly, individual roles and responsibilities will have to evolve too. On occasion, when an individual is no longer fit for a certain role, the company might need to find a replacement to ensure the organization's well-being.
- **The CEO's role will evolve too as the company grows.** When the company was small, the CEO might have overseen every single aspect of the company. In later stages, effective delegation and planning for the long term become

more important. To successfully manage a large company, the CEO might also need to hire people who are more experienced and better skilled in certain ways. He or she should not feel threatened at this prospect.

- **On occasion, bringing in an outsider CEO might be what is best for the company.** A seasoned CEO hired from outside might be better equipped through past experience to manage a large company. In bringing in an outsider CEO, an outsider that the individual is not only a superb executor but can also drive product development. In addition, it is critical that their values match with those of the founding CEO if they are to work together productively.

- **Keep the innovation engine running.** It becomes harder to innovate in a large organization, but the company may not survive in its absence. Innovation must be emphasized, and the organization must build in appropriate organizational structures and incentives to ensure continued innovation.

10

The Exit

THE VAST MAJORITY OF startups fail and are shut down. However, on occasion, a startup may survive and grow large enough for it to become an attractive target for acquisition. In the rarest instances, a startup continues growing long enough for it to go public. This is often where the greatest prize lies.

The decision to sell or to go public is one of enormous consequence not only for the future of the company, but also for everybody involved in the journey—the founders, the employees and the investors. The question is inevitable, however, if a startup succeeds. There will come a time when this decision would need to be made.

Going public

Going public implies selling a stake in your company to public market investors through shares. As these shares are bought and sold in the public market, their price reflects the market's estimate of the company's value. Companies with a dominant market position and a sustained growth trajectory are rewarded by public markets.

Listing a company on public markets is attractive and advantageous on multiple fronts. In fact, when Sahil Barua and his co-founders started Delhivery, it was with the express intent of taking it public eventually. Even as they were looking to grow Delhivery, they always viewed it as a public company, and built accordingly.

According to Sahil, the greatest advantage that going public offers is access to a very large and inexhaustible pool of capital. 'For a company, it takes away one of the most important external constraints that any business could have,' Sahil explains. While going public does subject a company to the vagaries of the market, it is often easier to raise money from a large pool of public market investors than it is from a select group of private investors.

Perhaps a little paradoxically, public listing also allows the company to raise capital more easily from private entities. According to Sahil, in India if you're not a public company, being able to raise debt is not particularly easy. Private lenders place greater faith in listed companies. It becomes more difficult to raise financing from private investors as the company starts getting larger,' says Sahil. 'Therefore, the only way is to go public. At this point, lenders are more comfortable lending because your financials are out in the open, and your stock price indicates how you're doing.'

Third, public listing also creates diversity of ownership, freeing the company from being controlled by a small clique of investors. Public market investors span a wide range in terms of investment size and sensibilities. Distributed ownership protects the company from a shift in the position taken by any single investor. 'I think diversity in shareholders is usually a good thing. Since you work for a large set of shareholders, it ensures that you are not held to ransom by a small set of people,' Sahil says.

Fourth, public listing is a powerful signalling mechanism, not only in the eyes of investors but also for potential B2B customers. It communicates that the company is well-run, and that its operations are above-board. And thus, it deepens the trust of customers. For instance, Sahil points out, India has historically not had a lot of well-run companies, especially in niche segments such as logistics in which Delhivery operates. A relatively new company may easily be seen as untrustworthy.

Going public allows a company to create credibility in the eyes of customers. It allows a company to be seen in the same light as other, more established companies which might have been around for longer. Moreover, as Sahil points out, the regulatory processes in place ensure that there is external oversight, creating greater assurance. 'You are being governed by a board, you are reporting to shareholders, you are generating financial returns that are publicly available, your books are audited and the Securities and Exchange Board of India is constantly checking the quality of your trading. These are all good things because it gives the customer confidence in your dealings,' he says. 'For example, if you're Walmart or Amazon, it matters to you that your suppliers are of high quality, and you would like that to be the case. Thus, running a well-governed company is a competitive advantage.' Regulatory processes drive transparency, deepening customer confidence and thereby strengthening the company's market position.

Fifth, public listing creates value for employees. 'Stock options have to have value for employees, they have to be able to predict even more value in the future which is easier in the case of a listed company,' Sahil says. 'I want to have the best talent, and the only way to have the best talent is to make sure that their value-creation opportunities are unlimited. And the only way to ensure that is to go public.' Public listing creates wealth for early employees who might have joined the company in its early days and awarded with stock options. It creates validation for the company's fundamental soundness. And the prospect of stock price appreciation makes the company attractive for prospective employees. In terms of value creation for employees, public listing is a powerful measure. This, in turn, allows the company to keep attracting great talent.

Finally, public listing allows for ease in mergers and acquisitions. 'As a public company, I can just issue stock and the other party can simply buy it,' Sahil says. 'Sure, there are far more processes involved too, but the fact of the matter is, raising capital in a private round to do an M&A is far more complicated than issuing stock, public markets.'

This, however, is not to say that an IPO is the best exit strategy for a startup. There are many downsides to IPOs too, and often many companies choose to forgo the route.

Functioning as a public company comes at a cost. Operating in the public gaze means there is heightened scrutiny of short-term performance. Public markets are ruthless and can often turn on a dime. To thrive in a public market, a company needs to constantly meet, and exceed, investor expectations. Besides, public markets demand rigorous transparency in reporting. This is not always easily achieved; regulatory compliance must be achieved through additional effort, which, of course, drives up costs. The cost and difficulty in adhering to compliance requirements become a major reason why many are sceptical of going public, Sahil contends.

An additional reason that companies avoid going to public markets is the general notion that private markets give you a higher valuation. While Sahil acknowledges that there might be some truth to it, he also offers a qualification. 'My view is that it's true only for bubble stocks, and not for good stocks,' he says. 'The world's largest and most valuable companies are held publicly. Being publicly held, however, does not stop them from being the world's most innovative companies and taking massive risks to build incredible businesses. Amazon, Apple, Facebook and Google, put together, are probably larger than the rest of the entire index. So, the math doesn't bear out that you'll get higher valuations if you're privately held.'

Preparing for the ascent

Preparing for an IPO is a mammoth task, one that requires months of preparation. It requires adherence to provisions of the Indian Companies Act, as well as those of the stock exchanges in India, the National Stock Exchange (NSE) complying with the NSE or the BSE, a company has to have a minimum paid-up capital of ₹10 crore. In addition, the market capitalization post the issue should not be less than ₹25 crore. Amongst other requirements, there has to be at least a three-year track record of either the applicant seeking listing, or the promoters/promoting company.[1]

'It' s a very clear and standardized checklist,' Sahil explains. 'You start with drafting your documents and you file. You have to begin by recasting all your accounts in the quarterly format for the past twelve quarters, at least, complying with

---

[1]   NSE, 'Eligibility', www1.nseindia.com/getting_listed/content/eligibility_criteria.htm

the NDS (Negotiated Dealing System) or IFRS (International Financial Reporting Standards) standards. Restating your financial accounts takes a good amount of time, post which you have to make sure that your provisioning is compliant with being a public company. According to the Companies Act, you need to constitute a board wherein at least one third is made up of independent directors and appoint at least one woman director. The total number of directors, too, must comply with the Companies Act: minimum three, maximum fifteen.'

Once the board is constituted, you start preparing the issue. 'First, you get bankers on board, two to five, as per the discretion of the founders. Out of those, you choose one who will lead the issue.' These merchant bankers carry out the IPO process on behalf of the company, acting as intermediaries between the company and the investors. They are responsible for preparing the registration statement and draft prospectus. They also act as underwriters against under-subscription of the shares.

'Next, you decide the size of the issue—the number of shares and their price,' Sahil continues. 'Then you've got the procedural steps of filing with the Securities and Exchange Board of India (SEBI). You disclose your shareholding structures, the offer, the Draft Red Herring Prospectus (DRHP) and the documentation with the SEBI who will scrutinize everything.' The DRHP details the initial share offer, and financial information and risks associated with the business. SEBI verifies the facts disclosed by the company; it looks for errors, omissions and discrepancies. Once SEBI approves the application, a date is set for the IPO. At this point, the company must file an application with the stock exchange where it plans to float the issue.

The next step is to market the company to large institutional investors, as part of what is called the 'roadshow'. 'As part of the roadshow, you go and meet some hundreds to thousands of investors across conferences all over the world. On the first day you're sitting in Mumbai, the next day in Delhi, the third day sitting somewhere else, the fourth day of it somewhere else; you're just flying around the world for about a month and doing it so you finish off those hours.'

After SEBI's approval, the company also starts preparing for the IPO internally. Once the roadshow is over, there is a period of silence of two to three weeks. 'This is the period when you prepare to pull the trigger. You need to prepare the finance and accounting team. The large part of it is getting your systems in shape to report. And then, you need to get the auditors and lawyers to certify it all and make sure you're ready to go public. Once that is done, you list and go public.' Sahil says that it often takes a veritable army to prepare for an IPO: multiple banks, lawyers, audit firms, and specialized service providers must come together for a company to go public.

Once the shares are issued to the shareholders in the primary market, they are listed in the secondary market. Once that happens, trading in these shares can be carried out.

An IPO is a transformative process. Going public is one of the most significant milestones in a company's journey, one that very few achieve. Once a company's shares start trading, its owners stretch far beyond simply its founders, investors and employees. They can come from all walks of life and across geographies; a Canadian pension fund with headquarters in Ontario, an experienced middle-aged trader sitting in Kolkata, or a young woman at a university in Ahmedabad, teaching herself how to invest in stocks.

In the end, though, even an IPO is simply a step in the journey of a company. When Deep Kalra started MakeMyTrip, he was not really thinking of an IPO. However, when the opportunity presented itself to either sell the company or go for an IPO, he was certain what he wanted to do. 'We never dreamed of an IPO till two board members said that we should start thinking about listing,' Deep reveals. 'And someone asked me, "Do you want to list or do you want to sell?" I said "Why would we ever sell? We want to build something, we have only started!"' They decided to go public so that they could continue building the company.

'When you go public, it is only the base camp of Everest,' Deep says. 'It is just a stage. When you reach that stage, you can take a little bit of money off the table. But the last guy holding the can is the entrepreneur. Investors can get out. But entrepreneurs don't. You take the company forward. You have public funds, you have a currency with which you can trade, you can buy and sell companies overseas, you can do a lot of stuff when you are public. The biggest thing you can do is you can issue stock and you can issue stock to everyone. The coolest story, the nicest story we have had is when our runner boy, Arif Khan from Bulandshahr, whom we had given some stock long ago, bought a house with his stock units. That was just awesome.'

Bringing down the curtains

Not every company becomes a listed company though. In many cases, founders choose to sell their company. In fact, many founders look to build a company with the express intention of eventually selling it. 'Some entrepreneurs build a company convinced that they don't want to sell it. There are others who look to build so that they can sell it and unlock value,' says Raghu, the TFS founder.

'If you are an entrepreneur who is trying to build something to sell, then your approach to the whole journey has to be different,' Raghu notes. 'You will always have to be looking at exit opportunities. You must look at the value you will release for your acquirer. Is it an ancillary activity or a core activity for a specific company that you're trying to build for? Are you going to give them a significant speed to market? Then you hire good people because you are trying to sell. You interact with potential buyers and keep them warm.'

While Raghu contends that there is nothing inherently wrong in starting a company with the express intent of selling it, MakeMyTrip founder Deep Kalra does offer a warning in this regard. 'I do believe the more you focus on the exit, the further away it will go,' Deep says. 'I know enough people who've built their companies to sell it. And they never got sold for anything decent. Never. Because you start focusing on the wrong thing. You start focusing on company packaging and valuation, not on the company's reason for being. The raison d'être for any company is not to make money; that's a by-product. The real raison d'etre is to solve a customer pain point, to solve a customer problem, and hopefully to delight customers.'

He offers the example of Amazon and Apple as companies that consistently delight customers. 'I think these are great companies who do it fairly consistently. If you do it consistently, you will realize the real flywheel, the real virtuous cycle getting built in.' It is far easier for a company that focuses on consistently delighting customers to get a great exit than one that has been expressly built with that aim, Deep contends.

If a founder did not start their company with the express intent of selling it, then arriving at the decision to sell can be a particularly difficult one. Andreessen Horowitz founder Ben Horowitz writes in his book *The Hard Thing about Hard Things* that determining whether selling the company will be better than remaining standalone in the long term involves a large number of factors, most of which are speculative or unknown. However, what makes it especially difficult is that there are also emotions involved: 'The task would be far simpler if there were no emotion involved. But selling your company is always emotional and deeply personal.'[2]

Horowitz offers a basic rule of thumb. A company should remain independent if it meets two criteria: (1) it is early-on in a very large market, that is, the market is an order of magnitude bigger than has been exploited to date, and (2) it has a good chance of being number one in that market. If the answer to either of these is no, Horowitz suggests that you should consider selling it. Underlying this simplistic framework is the caveat that you also have to answer what the market really is, and who the real competitors are.

For instance, when Google launched, they received multiple acquisition offers. Many of these were considered very rich offers at the time. However, given the ultimate size of the search market, and the fact that Google had built a nearly invincible product lead that would enable them to be number one, it made sense that Google did not sell. However, it only made sense because Google was in the search market and not in the portal market where Yahoo was a formidable opponent. Horowitz suggests that had Google been in the portal market as well, it would have made sense to sell.

Horowitz admits that the emotional elements of the decision can be especially difficult to negotiate, and suggests that it would be best to try to mute them. This, he suggests, can be achieved by (a) ensuring that the CEO gets paid a market salary once the company becomes a viable business, and is an acquisition

---

2   Ben Horowitz, *The Hard Thing About Hard Things* (Harper Business, 2014), p. 257.

target. This would ensure that the decision would not hinge on the CEO's personal financial situation. And (b) by ensuring transparency with employees as to whether the company might be sold. According to Horowitz, the easiest way to ensure such transparency is to make it clear that if the company achieves product-market fit in a very large market and has an excellent chance to be number one, then the company will likely remain independent.

When Raghu and Aprameya started TFS in 2011, exits were still a rarity, especially in the form of a sale. 'We started at a time when there were no exits in the ecosystem,' Raghu says. 'There were no major exits. The first exit was RedBus, the second was Freecharge, the third was us and the fourth was Myntra. So there were no exits in the ecosystem then. The thought wasn't really to build to sell.' However, TFS did eventually sell to their primary rival Ola Cabs in 2015.

Standing in the middle of 2014, this would not have seemed particularly likely to happen. In fact, until the middle of 2014, TFS seemed to be inching ahead of Ola, their primary home-grown rival in the Indian market. They had raised money recently, having closed a $10 million Series B round in May.[3] They planned to use this investment to expand in fifteen new cities, especially in Tier II and Tier III cities where increasing disposable income, and construction of new infrastructure and airports was likely to drive up demand for a cab aggregator platform. They were also eliciting interest from more investors, especially from the likes of large hedge funds in the US and Hong Kong.

---

[3]   Jai Vardhan, 'Taxiforsure Raises $10 Mn Series B Led by Bessemer Venture Partners', *YourStory.com*, 1 May 2014, https://yourstory. com/2014/05/taxiforsure-funding-series-b/amp

Ola would need to expand aggressively, and perhaps raise money, to continue to compete. In July, Ola too raised money, receiving $40 million in a Series C round of investment.[4] Soon after, it embarked upon a massive cycle of expansion, burning cash to gain more customers. In late August, it slashed its prices by almost 20 per cent, in a bid to drive up demand.[5] It also ratcheted up available incentives for drivers. Most drivers worked with both Ola and TFS. With stronger incentives, more drivers would shift to booking rides on Ola's platform at the expense of TFS. Soon, it was surging past TFS, with many more rides booked per day on its platform.

In offering discounts and better incentives, Ola was burning through cash rapidly. TFS was convinced it would not be sustainable. Eventually, Ola would need to cease, or risk running out of money. Once it went back to offering their usual rates and incentives, both the customers and the drivers they had gained recently were unlikely to stick around. After all, there was likely to be little loyalty to the platform amongst those who had been lured in simply by a better rate, or a better incentive scheme. TFS decided to sit it out.

And then the ground beneath their feet shifted. In September 2014, Chinese e-commerce giant Alibaba underwent an IPO. Japanese conglomerate Softbank owned a 34 per cent stake in Alibaba. Alibaba's IPO generated a massive windfall for

4   Josh Horwitz, 'Uber's Got Competition in India—Bangalore-Based Olacabs Nets Another Massive Funding Round', *www.techinasia.com*, 10 July 2014, https://www.techinasia.com/ubers-got-competition-in-india-bangalore-based-olacab-nets-another-massive-funding-round-40-million-bangalore

5   Ashish K. Mishra, 'Behind TaxiForSure's Sellout', *www.livemint.com*, 20 March 2015, https://www.livemint.com/Companies/t7TozTlZCAmvtSxog3OQ7L/Behind-TaxiForSures-sellout.html

Softbank, netting it more than $50 billion.[6] Founder Masayoshi
Son and his second-in-command Nikesh Arora now had their
eyes set on India.

Flush with funds, Softbank invested $210 million into
Ola in October 2014. At the time, this was one of the largest
rounds of capital raised by an Indian company, second only to
SoftBank's $627 million infusion into Snapdeal.[7] This is when
things changed. With this humongous investment, Ola could
continue to dole out incentives indefinitely. TFS had no choice
but to enter the fray.

In early November, TFS too slashed its rates, and strengthened
its incentives. It immediately saw a massive surge in the rides
booked per day. Within two weeks, the number of rides booked
per day doubled. By the end of the month, the number of rides
getting booked on the platform was six times the number at
the start. It had taken them three years to grow to a respectable
size, and a month to grow by six times that.

However, deep discounts and generous incentive schemes
meant the company was bleeding money; it was entirely
unsustainable. While they still had capital available from their
previous funding round, they realized they would have to raise
more money. Following their previous round of fundraising,
many other investors had expressed interest in the company.
Raghu and Aprameya had kept in touch, keeping the connections

---

[6]   Eric Pfanner, 'SoftBank's Alibaba Alchemy: How to Turn $20
      Million into $50 Billion', *Wall Street Journal*, 19 September 2014,
      https:// www.wsj.com/articles/BL-DGB-37805

[7]   Malavika Velayanikal, 'Snapdeal Bags $627M Funding, Ola Nets
      $210M, as SoftBank Ploughs $10B into India', *www.techinasia.
      com*, 28 October 2014, https://www.techinasia.com/softbank-
      to-invest-10-billion-in-india-snapdeal-gets-627-million-ola-210-
      million

warm. When they embarked upon their expansion drive in November, they decided to reach out to potential investors, and be completely transparent with regard to their plans as well as how successful they were being with regard to execution.

This meant describing the situation as it stood at the start of the month, and then offering weekly updates. Every week, they would outline the steps that they would take going forward. The following week they would report on what had worked, and what had not.

As TFS continued its explosive growth over the course of the month, investor interest in the company burgeoned. For its size, TFS's growth had been nothing short of astounding. That the founders were willing to be extremely transparent inspired confidence; they seemed to understand the mistakes that they had made, and how to solve the problems that they were experiencing. Raghu was invited to the US to pitch for a new round of investment.

Raghu was scheduled to land in the US on 8 December on a Monday morning. He had lined up meetings with more than twenty different investors. The due diligence required before an investment had already been carried out. Only two steps remained: face-to-face meetings in which Raghu was to present the case for investment to the senior management at each firm, and the final nod for investment. Raghu was hoping to raise between $200 to 250 million, enough for TFS to hold its own against Ola.

On 6 December, in a case that immediately grabbed national attention, a woman passenger in an Uber in Delhi was assaulted by the driver. The rising number of crimes against women, especially in the national capital, was already an incendiary issue. The government had to act quickly. In this instance, it seemed that Uber had not carried out adequate due diligence in recruiting its drivers. Moreover, there were no emergency mechanisms built in to safeguard passengers. Government regulators in Delhi decided to impose a ban on Uber.[8] There was a fierce backlash against taxi aggregator firms who were seen as ducking safety obligations. The air was rife with rumours that other firms, including TFS, would be banned as well, not only in the national capital, but even other states, such as Karnataka and Maharashtra.

Raghu landed in San Francisco on Monday, and made his way to a partners' meeting at a large VC firm. He had expected that there would be some discussion with regard to the still-developing situation around Uber. However, he had not expected it to take up most of the meeting.

'At the partnership meeting on Monday morning, out of forty-five minutes, thirty minutes were spent on what would happen to Uber,' Raghu says. The pattern repeated itself in firm after investing firm. The senior management at each firm was concerned that the company would get banned. They wanted additional regulatory clarity before committing to what would be a large round of investment.

TFS had not received any formal notification from government regulators. In any case, Raghu was convinced that any ban on cab-hailing services would eventually be rolled back. They offered an essential service after all.' However, the investors that TFS was in discussions with were very apprehensive. If they chose to invest in the company only to have TFS banned subsequently, they would be placed in a tricky

---

8   Malavika Velayanikal, 'Banning Is Easy: Now the Question Is, How Can Uber Be Regulated?', *www.techinasia.com*, 12 December 2014, https://www.techinasia.com/how-can-uber-be-regulated

situation. The still developing situation in India had made TFS a very risky investment.

Raghu flew back to India, in disbelief at the turn of events. 'We had some money in the bank. Whatever incentives and price cuts we had running, these could continue for some time, at least another two to three months. However, we knew that no new money was going to come in because of the lack of regulatory clarity during that period.'

This was a major life lesson for Raghu. He suggests that founders need to have more outside-in perspective than inside-out. 'We were so ingrained in our own business that we never focused on what was out there. You need to keep tabs on what's happening around you because those things can really change the ecosystem. TaxiForSure had simply fallen prey to an unanticipated and unforeseeable series of occurrences, to events outside their ambit of control. 'Looking back,' Raghu says, 'we found ourselves in a situation where the Alibaba IPO happened. Then SoftBank invested large sums of money in Ola. And then the Delhi Uber assault case happened. If any of these had not happened or if the timing had been different, we would have been in a better place.'

Given that they were unlikely to be able to raise money in the near future, and with capital from earlier investments running out, the choice was becoming clearer for TFS: 'Either we run out of money and sell the company for peanuts or we get to the negotiating table when we still have some money left.'

As founders, Raghu and Aprameya did not want to sell the company. However, there was one consideration that was paramount in their minds. They had to do right by their stakeholders. This meant doing the right thing not just by their investors, but also the employees and the cab drivers who had chosen to work with TFS. 'At that time, we were 2,500 people strong and had loyal drivers. We could have run down the company and made these people lose their livelihood. But it didn't particularly seem the right thing for us to do.' While they did not like the idea of selling the company that they had so painstakingly built, they still went ahead with it, because it seemed like the right thing to do when they considered their stakeholders.

TFS decided to enter into negotiations for an acquisition with both Uber and Ola, their primary competitors. Raghu wanted to have a conversation with all potential acquirers. 'If we didn't have either Uber or Ola at the negotiating table, we would not have received the kind of deal that we did,' Raghu says. 'If you're talking to only one company, you can't negotiate because if you only have one buyer, then it becomes a buyer's market, not a seller's market. The only way to do this is to have multiple people on the table because then it becomes a seller's market.'

TFS would be a valuable acquisition for both Uber and Ola for, through it, they could get access to its supply of drivers. TFS had built a large supply of drivers; whichever company would acquire them would also receive access to their supply. 'In this market, consumers have no loyalty,' Raghu explains. 'The largest supplier takes everything. The only way you can get control over the businesses is by having access to a dedicated supply.' Access to a larger pool of drivers implied access to a larger network of service providers. This would directly translate into more ride bookings, and a better topline. This was the primary reason every rideshare operator in India was investing in driver incentives. The one that controlled the supply would control the market.

In entering negotiations, while the founders were looking for a valuation that was commensurate with the large strategic importance of the acquisition to TFS's rivals, they also wanted to ensure that their employees would benefit from the move. They believed that TFS's employees too deserved to be rewarded for their efforts in growing the company, not just the founders. And therefore, they brought three conditions to the negotiation table: that the acquiring company retain the employees at least for a period of one year, that the issuance of equity stock options for all employees be accelerated so that everybody received the equity due to them within one year, and that everybody was awarded a bonus equivalent to two months' salary.

While Uber was offering a very attractive valuation, they did not seem to fully understand TFS's business, or the market in India. A case in point was the fact that they were unwilling to shift to a model that accepted cash payments, a cornerstone of TFS's model in India. 'Since their model had been working elsewhere, they wanted to force the same model in India,' Raghu says. 'But we knew that India was different. So, one would need to build for India and not replicate what was working elsewhere.'

Far more crucially for the founders, Uber was unwilling to agree to their conditions with regard to TFS's employees. Not only were they unwilling to agree to ESOP acceleration, and two months' bonus for the team, they did not even want to absorb TFS's staff onto its rolls globally. At the time, Uber had a little less than 850 people on its rolls globally whereas TFS in India was a lot bigger; absorbing the entire staff was not something they were willing to consider.

'They only wanted our supply of drivers, Raghu says. 'They didn't want our product team, they didn't want our marketing team, they didn't want to have our call centre team. They just wanted our supply and to fire 90 per cent of the people.' This was unacceptable to Raghu and Aprameya.

Ola, on the other hand, was willing to honour TFS's conditions. Not only were they willing to retain TFS's staff for a period of at least one year—enough time for anybody looking to leave to find alternative employment—they also agreed to ESOP acceleration as well as two months' salary bonus for all employees. They promised that TFS' brand would continue to exist for at least one year. In addition, Ola understood TFS's business, and meant to integrate their key innovations into its own model.

Their conditions met, the founders accepted the offer. Ola bought TaxiForSure for $200 million.[9] At the time, it was one of the biggest acquisitions in India's nascent startup ecosystem.

The second innings

While the sale of a company can mark a significant success for an entrepreneur, the reality of selling a venture often represents a loss of identity and community. It involves coming to terms with the realization that the founder's identity is no longer as intimately linked to that of the company as it perhaps was earlier. If the founder no longer continues with the company after the acquisition, it implies a parting from the team, and the extended community linked to the company. It often involves letting go of a routine that might have been honed over several years.

Transitioning out of a company can also be a period for tying up loose ends. Following Ola's acquisition of TaxiForSure's, Raghu had to shoulder the responsibility of ensuring a smooth

---

9   Alok Soni, 'It's Official. Ola Acquires TaxiForSure for $200 Million in a Cash and Equity Deal', *YourStory.com*, 2 March 2015, yourstory.com/2015/03/ola-acquires-taxiforsure

transition. The operations of the two companies need to run smoothly after their merger. In addition, it also involved looking after the interests of TaxiForSure's employees and the drivers who had worked with the company. As founders, Raghu and Aprameya felt they had an obligation towards their employees and partners. Not only did they seek to find the right roles within the merged entity for their employees, they also looked to identify opportunities outside the firm. In this process, Raghu also found his second calling.

According to the terms of the acquisition, each employee was to receive two months' salary as bonus, and had their ESOPs accelerated. Access to capital, combined with experience of having worked at a successful startup led many employees to start their own companies. Many of them sought out Raghu as a mentor, would ask him to join the board of their company. While he started out as a mentor, eventually Raghu started investing in companies. 'A lot of startups were getting established and if I liked something, I wanted to put my money where my mouth was,' he says.

Raghu says working as an investor has helped him develop a deeper understanding of perspectives that he had not fully considered, or appreciated as an entrepreneur. 'As an investor, I understood what really happens on the other side of the table, and it made me realize all the things that we had missed out on while working on TaxiForSure,' he says. He has a much better understanding of what an investor must prioritize. He is also able to better understand what happens in the background when a startup is looking to raise funds.

Having been an entrepreneur himself, Raghu believes that he is able to connect more deeply with entrepreneurs. 'While you might sit on the other side of the table as an investor, you still feel a connection with entrepreneurs due to your shared experiences,' he says. An entrepreneur-turned-investor is highly sought after for this very reason. 'Entrepreneurs who turn investors add immense value to a startup as a mentor or board member, making founders eager to extract an investment from them.'

Sanjeev Bikhchandani, founder of Naukri, is also a major investor in India's internet economy through Info Edge, Naukri's holding company, which has been a prolific investor in the startup ecosystem in India, investing in a large number of companies including insurance aggregator Policybazaar, and restaurant aggregator, Zomato. He too sees value in successful entrepreneurs becoming investors. 'I think entrepreneurs understand entrepreneurs slightly better,' he says.

After selling FreeCharge to Snapdeal, Kunal Shah too became an investor for a short while. He worked with Y Combinator and Sequoia Capital to identify promising businesses, as well as operated as an angel investor. However, he eventually turned to entrepreneurship again, founding CRED. 'If you have built and created all your life, the idea of not creating is never a good idea,' he says.

Sachin Bansal left Flipkart in 2018, but returned to entrepreneurship within the year, starting Navi Technologies, a technology-based financial services company. As did Aprameya who started Koo, a social media company, and Raghu who started Zolve, a neobank, both starting their new companies in 2020.

Entrepreneurship often offers a long and tortuous path, with the end uncertain, and out of sight. Not all who start on the path might end up where they wished to go. Others, having reached the end, might realize that it is, but, the start of a path anew.

It is the journey itself however that is important. It is the journey that offers both learning, and meaning. And where one ends, another might begin.

> *Still round the corner there may wait*
> *A new road or a secret gate,*
> *And though I oft have passed them by,*
> *A day will come at last when I*
> *Shall take the hidden paths that run*
> *West of the Moon, East of the Sun.*

—J.R.R. Tolkien

Summary

- **Going public allows a company to tap into a very large and inexhaustible pool of capital.** As a company starts getting larger, its need for capital expands. It might easily extend beyond what might be possible through its operations, or through raising from private investors. Going public allows a large company to raise capital more easily, even if it might come at the expense of additional scrutiny, and making itself subject to the vagaries of the market.
- **Going public is a strong signalling mechanism.** It communicates that the company is well-run, and deepens the trust of customers.
- **Determining whether a company should continue standalone or get acquired is difficult.** A company should remain standalone if it meets two criteria: it is early on in a very large market, the market is an order of magnitude bigger than has been exploited to date; and if it has a good chance of being number one in that market.,

- **When negotiating a sale, it is ideal to engage with multiple potential acquirers.** Getting multiple interested parties to the negotiating table allows for stronger bargaining positions, and achieve a superior outcome.
- **An exit could lead to new beginnings.** When an entrepreneur's journey with a startup comes to an end, other voyages might beckon. Many entrepreneurs look to become investors, having gained first-hand experience in building a company. Others might look to start up again, wiser and better equipped to succeed.

Acknowledgements

WRITING A BOOK IS rarely an individual effort. This book, certainly, is not. We are grateful to everyone who has made it possible.

This book is an amalgamation of inputs from some of the most iconic individuals in the Indian startup ecosystem: Abhiraj Bhal, Anand Daniel, Anu Hariharan, Deep Kalra, Falguni Nayar, Girish Mathrubootham, Kunal Shah, Raghunandan G, Rajan Anandan, Ritesh Agarwal, Sachin Bansal, Sanjeev Bikhchandani, Sahil Barua, Tarun Mehta and Yashish Dahiya. We cannot thank them enough for their willingness to entrust us with their stories, for sharing their insights and experiences so generously with us.

Padma Vibhushan N.R. Narayana Murthy is an idol to legions of youngsters throughout the world. We sincerely thank him for sharing his personal learnings in the form of a foreword. As the CEO of Niti Aayog, Amitabh Kant has championed the cause of entrepreneurship in India and built an ecosystem conducive to sparking innovation. We are indebted for his support for the book.

The book is inspired by the series that started at IIM Ahmedabad. In early 2016, while thinking about their startup, Ujwal, Srejan Goyal, Samyak Daga and Harpreet Singh were plagued by questions on starting up, such as thinking of ideas, forming a team and taking the plunge. They realized that there was a wider audience that wanted to understand what entrepreneurship entailed. This led to the start of the How to Start a Startup (HTSAS) lecture series, with the hope that it would offer tangible learnings to those interested in starting and running a company.

Soon a set of enthusiasts joined in—Shobhit, Nalin Gupta, Sajal Jain, Nishad Shah, Anirudh Murali, Umang Shah, Garima Maheshwari, Rajesh Ranjan, Soumyo Madhab Mitra, Aditya Khanna, Gaurav Bagde and Mehul Verma. In making the lectures possible, they made this book possible too.

No other higher education institution in India perhaps promotes entrepreneurship in India as much as IIM Ahmedabad. No other institution, most certainly, could offer more support to its students. Prof. Ashish Nanda, former director of IIMA, was instrumental in HTSAS becoming possible, putting the institute's weight and resources behind the idea. Prof. Amit Karna, former Chair of CIIE.CO, was instrumental in the conceptualization of the series, from challenging the team to make it more meaningful and filled with tangible learnings at each step. CIIE.CO CEO Kunal Upadhyaya has been a mentor and guide. From first helping invite entrepreneurs for the series to later offering suggestions as we wrote the book, his support was a constant source of encouragement. CIIE.CO COO Priyanka Chopra was instrumental in not just getting stellar individuals to be a part of the book but also offering valuable guidance throughout the process of writing it.

Prof. Neharika Vohra, former Chair of CIIE.CO Initiatives, made a formal association of this book with CIIE.CO possible. We cannot thank her enough. Dr Supriya Sharma at CIIE.CO has been a true partner in making this book possible. From offering feedback on the first draft to working with us through every step of the editing process to coordinating outreach, her help, support and guidance has been invaluable.

Prof. Rakesh Basant, former Dean of Alumni and External Relations, was instrumental both in the starting of the lecture series and the book. The HTSAS series kicked off because of him, when he invited Sanjeev Bikhchandani to campus. We seriously started considering the idea to write the book only when we mentioned the concept to him, and he encouraged us to pursue it.

Prof. Errol D'Souza, Director of IIMA, was instrumental in having this book come out under IIM Ahmedabad's banner. His unrelenting support and patient ear have been an inspiration and personal learning for us. Prof. B.H. Jajoo, former Dean of IIM Ahmedabad, graciously reached out at short notice to N.R. Narayana Murthy for writing the book's foreword. Prof. Chinmay Tumbe first introduced us to our editor at HarperCollins India. He liked the book's idea and was perhaps far more convinced of its potential than the authors initially were; we owe him a huge debt of gratitude.

No writer could ask for a better editor than Swati Chopra at HarperCollins India. We cannot thank her enough for her input and patience in working with two first-time authors who often showed a scant understanding of the editorial process. This book would not have been possible without her.

We cannot thank Shreya Lall and Padmini Smetacek enough for their inputs over the book's multiple drafts; Saurav Das for the cover design. Outside of HarperCollins, Nandakumar K. went through the first draft of the book and returned with extremely valuable editorial inputs and feedback. Thank you.

Ayushi Srivastava, Devyani Arora, Roopal Dahiya and Shivay Dubey worked with us in researching the material and putting together an early draft. Your help and support has been instrumental. Abhishek Goyal and Neha Singh at Tracxn were incredibly supportive of the endeavour and offered extraordinary support at short notice in carrying out our research.

Aakash Upadhyaya, Abhay Mishra, Akshaya Prabhu, Archit Choudhary, Amit Kumar, Deepak Kumar Singh, Mehak Priya, Prabuddha Guha, Sailesh Balasubramanian, Sambhav Jain, Skand Mishra, Vineet Gupta read through the early drafts of the book. Their comments and inputs were of great assistance in making this book better.

Like most endeavours in life, this book would not have been possible without the support of our families. No expression of gratitude will be quite enough.

The idea of writing a book itself was first suggested by Ujwal's father, CA Arvind Kalra, who believed that understanding how a startup gets built would hold meaning and value for a wider audience. To him goes the credit of first putting us on this path. We sincerely thank him for sparking the fire and encouraging us. Darshan Kalra offered constant support even when it seemed we had encroached upon a task we were perhaps not equal to. Her endless motivation and support kept us going. Swati Kawatra and Aditya Kawatra provided constant feedback throughout the process; criticism could sting, but it helped us push towards a superior outcome.

This book would not have been possible without the constant support of Shobhit's parents, Satyajit Pradhan and Shampa Anupurba. Ritwika Rituparna read through multiple drafts of the books and offered invaluable feedback, taking great pains to point out specific changes that might make it a better read. Siddharth Das helped think through how one should approach the writing process itself. In lending an ear through the trying process of writing this book, he allowed sanity to prevail. Anupam Pratihary's extraordinarily thoughtful feedback and constant urging to aim for a book one could take satisfaction in having written contributed enormously to the final outcome. We are truly grateful.

About the Authors

Ujwal Kalra is a serial entrepreneur, currently serving as the co-founder and CEO of NAKAD, a supply chain startup that makes credit and commerce easily available to small and medium businesses. Earlier he worked at Boston Consulting Group where he was a founding member of Growth Tech India, a BCG initiative to work with startups. At IIM Ahmedabad, Ujwal co-founded and headed the 'How to Start a Startup' series on which this book is based. He was an Institute Merit scholar at IIMA, graduating in the top 5 per cent of his batch. An alumnus of IIT Guwahati and DPS Vasant Kunj, Ujwal has been awarded numerous awards in his young career, including The Economic Times Young Leader, O.P. Jindal Scholarship, Dun & Bradstreet Award and Dunia Scholarship, UAE. He also represented India at Kairos, a USA-based entrepreneurship society.

Shobhit Shubhankar is a consultant at Boston Consulting Group. He has worked across South-East Asia with project experience in private equity, technology, telecommunications, and industrial goods practice areas. He has also worked at B Capital Group, a multi-stage global investment firm investing in technology companies. He is an alumnus of IIM Ahmedabad where he was a founding member of the 'How to Start a Startup' series, and graduated in the top 5 per cent of his batch. He has a bachelor's degree in chemical engineering from IIT BHU Varanasi, and serves on the board of the IIT BHU Global Alumni Association.

About CIIE.CO, IIM Ahmedabad

CIIE.CO is the innovation continuum that backs fearless entrepreneurs building disruptive solutions. Founded at IIM Ahmedabad in 2002 as an academic centre, CIIE.CO has grown and pivoted to support ideas and entrepreneurs through offering incubation, investment, research-based support, and ground-breaking publications. During the course of its history, CIIE.CO has relentlessly aspired to fill the multiple, ever-evolving gaps in the Indian innovation and entrepreneurship space. Among many other initiatives, it has conceptualized and hosted India's first accelerator, created India's first, and so far only, cleantech-focused fund, supported over 1,000 entrepreneurs, invested in over 160 startups, and inspired over a million people with insightful publications, including the bestseller *Stay Hungry Stay Foolish*. One such initiative is the 'How to Start a Startup' lecture series, the germination bed for this book.